The Devil
in the Shape of a Woman

Also by Carol F. Karlsen

The Journal of Esther Edwards Burr, 1754–1757
(ed., with Laurie Crumpacker) (1984)

The Devil
in the Shape
of a Woman

WITCHCRAFT IN
COLONIAL NEW ENGLAND

CAROL F. KARLSEN

VINTAGE BOOKS
A Division of Random House, Inc.
New York

First Vintage Books Edition, May 1989

Library of Congress Cataloging-in-Publication Data
Karlsen, Carol F., 1940–
The devil in the shape of a woman.
Reprint. Originally published: New York: Norton, c1987.
Bibliography: p.
Includes index.
1. Witchcraft—New England. I. Title.
[BF1576.K37 1989]   133.4'0974   88-82395
ISBN 0-679-72184-3 (pbk.)

Manufactured in the United States of America
10 9 8 7 6 5 4 3 2

For Alice, Kate, and Tess
In memoriam

Contents

Tables

Preface

HISTORY OFFERS FEW subjects as endlessly fascinating or
as intellectually frustrating as witchcraft. The word itself evokes
images so diverse, ultimately so contradictory, as to defy definition. It is associated with old age, frightful ugliness, and
female wickedness on the one hand, with youth, beauty, and
female sexual power on the other. Most difficult to reconcile
is the complacent sense of witchcraft as something quaint and
faintly amusing, like the makeshift goblins who come to our
doors on Halloween night, and the horror of its all too real
violence, the implacable encroachment on human life that
characterized much of its history.

The fascination with witchcraft is perhaps especially pronounced in the United States, where its most dramatic episode took place too late, and among too educated a populace,
for us to dismiss it as mere "superstition." Since the moment
almost three hundred years ago when the Massachusetts community of Salem went into a paroxysm of accusation and
counter-accusation, confession, denial, and death, witchcraft
has compelled the attention and challenged the ingenuity of
a long and almost continuous line of American writers—

beginning with the Puritan minister Cotton Mather and proceeding through Thomas Hutchinson, Nathaniel Hawthorne, L. Frank Baum, Arthur Miller, and John Updike.[1] If popular impressions of the subject have been shaped more by fictional than factual accounts, there has hardly been a lack of scholarly interest. The last decade and a half alone has witnessed major reinterpretations of New England witchcraft by the historians Paul Boyer and Stephen Nissenbaum, and John Demos, as well as by the sociologist Richard Weisman.[2] To this list we must add works that reflect the growing feminist awareness of the place of witchcraft in women's history, which has brought writers as diverse as Mary Daly, Erica Jong, and Starhawk to the witchcraft discussion, though not specifically to its colonial American setting.[3] These and scores of other interpreters have understood witchcraft in their own way, finding in it their own truths, and their own lessons for their own time.

The story of witchcraft is primarily the story of women, and this I suspect accounts for much of the fascination and the elusiveness attending the subject. Especially in its Western incarnation, witchcraft confronts us with ideas about women, with fears about women, with the place of women in society, and with women themselves. It confronts us too with systematic violence against women. Though some men were executed as witches during the period of massive witch hunting, mainly in the sixteenth and seventeenth centuries, witches were generally thought of as women and most of those who died in the name of witchcraft were women.

This violence creates an additional obstacle to understanding witchcraft. No one knows exactly how many people died in Europe and America during the witch-hunting years—estimates range from tens of thousands into the millions—and few authors attempt to calculate the proportion of women to men among them. Four-fifths is a conservative estimate.[4] Even when they note that witches were usually women, most works pass over the fact quickly or conclude that witches were scapegoats for hostilities and tensions that had little to do with sex or gender.[5] Those few historians who have seriously addressed the question of women and witchcraft either briefly discuss the misogyny of the period and the difficulty particular women may have presented to their neighbors, or rely for explanations on modern psychological theory. These latter studies offer valuable insights into the many dimensions of witch fear, but they leave readers with the impression that sustained historical investigation of the realities of women's position in their communities is either impossible or unnecessary.[6]

This is not simply to call for recognition of the sheer numbers of women who have suffered in the name of witchcraft. That acknowledgment must be made to counter the trivializing and glossing of both witchcraft and women's history. Only by understanding that the history of witchcraft is primarily a history of women, however, can we confront the deeply embedded feelings about women—and the intricate patterns of interest underlying those feelings—among our witch-ridden ancestors.

Had those feelings evaporated over the centuries, we might see more clearly, but we still live with witches in our culture, however much their shape may have changed over time. The diverse images the subject elicits in some of our most respected writers, not to mention Hollywood and the advertising industry, attest to the continuing power of woman-as-witch in our collective imagination. Our fascination with the historical witch has, I think, allowed us both to feel and dismiss this power, both to recognize and deny those deeply embedded emotions that women continue to evoke, in men and women alike.

This book explores some of the sources of this power by focusing on witchcraft in seventeenth-century New England. Like many of my predecessors, I am also concerned with the meaning of witchcraft for New England's first settlers. But my more pressing concern is why most witches in early American society were women. By confronting the definition of the witch in its historical setting, by understanding the ideological and social sources of New Englanders' preoccupation with women-as-witches, we can better understand why the witch still lives in our imagination today.

Some words about the book's organization. Both the meaning of witchcraft in colonial New England and the reasons why women were so tenaciously associated with it emerge only after careful examination of several distinct but related parts of the witchcraft story. Individual chapters bring these parts into sharp focus, but not until all the chapters are in place does the full picture come into view.

The first chapter immerses us in the world of New England witchcraft. The words of seventeenth-century settlers show that witchcraft was, first and foremost, a set of dynamic religious beliefs. Though not all men and women held the same beliefs, by confirming or denying individual accusations, the colonists illuminated the process by which witchcraft took shape in early New England communities.

The next three chapters examine witchcraft cases more closely, focusing on the characteristics of the accused. The patterns that emerge reveal which colonists were more likely to be accused of witchcraft, and which were more likely to be prosecuted, convicted, and executed as witches. These chapters make clear why a focus on women-as-witches is justified for colonial New England. We see that whatever else New Englanders said witchcraft was, they shared many unspoken assumptions about women and witchcraft that must be incorporated into their definition and ours.

The final three chapters interpret the characteristics of witches within New England's gender system. Chapter 5 explores Puritan beliefs about women in general and finds an ideology of womanhood designed to serve the world Puritans were attempting to create in both England and New England. We see the connections between Puritan ideas about women and New England's ideas about witches. Chapter 6 shows the fit between New England's witchcraft beliefs and its social structure. We see how witchcraft played a critical role not only in shaping, maintaining, and describing that social structure, but in reconciling men's feelings about women with the demographic, economic, religious, and sexual changes of the time. Chapter 7 completes the picture by focusing on those women whom Puritans believed were "possessed" by witches. We see witchcraft, finally, as a deeply ambivalent but violent struggle *within* women as well as an equally ambivalent but violent struggle *against* women.

The book concludes with a brief comment on the demise of New England's witchcraft beliefs and prosecutions at the close of the century.

To allow the fullest expression of New Englanders' witchcraft beliefs and fears, I have preserved their erratic habits of spelling, punctuation, capitalization, and speech, modernizing only in those few cases where the meaning is unclear. Because the names of many of New England's accused witches recur throughout the book, I have included an Appendix listing those mentioned most frequently, with brief notes to spark recognition of their backgrounds and witchcraft experiences.

I would like to express my gratitude to the many individuals who helped make this a richer and more readable book than I could have written on my own. My adviser Edmund Morgan, as well as Nancy Cott and Kai Erikson, read and reread it as a dissertation; they provided models of scholarship and clarity, and the kind of advice and encouragement every graduate student should have. The women from several New Haven study groups and early feminist gatherings listened and criticized as the ideas took shape; in their support and their commitment to rediscovering women's history they were ever-present reminders of the importance of the work we were doing. The Danforth Foundation, the Mrs. Giles Whiting Foundation, and the Mary McEwen Schimke Scholarship gave me the time to research and write. Later, my colleagues at the University of Michigan gave me the time to revise.

Though I am not sure when I began to see the dissertation

as a book, friends, colleagues, and students helped immeasurably along the way. For sharing their perceptive questions, their extensive knowledge, and their time, I would like to thank Barbara Black, Jon Butler, John Demos, James Farrell, Thomas Green, David Hall, Grace Harris, Louise Lamphere, Anne Margolis, John Murrin, Stephen Nissenbaum, Marylynn Salmon, Kathryn Kish Sklar, Carroll Smith-Rosenberg, Maris Vinovskis, and the participants in several professional meetings and seminars, especially the members of the Philadelphia Center for Early American Studies. The staffs of countless research libraries, historical societies, and local record repositories kindly tracked down the manuscripts and legal documents I needed. Elaine Barber, Susan Buckholtz, Carlos Cariño, Rita DeSoto, Maud Kernowski, Ron Newbold, and Frances Ortiz cheerfully helped locate and check published sources. In their careful attention and enthusiasm, Elizabeth Calhoun, Carl Fassl, Terry Flemming, Meg Kruizenga, Amy Simon, and Stacy Spencer made proofreading and other final details pleasant rather than onerous.

John MacAloon, Mary Beth Norton, Conrad Russell, Christine Stansell, and Robert Wells read the entire manuscript and made invaluable suggestions for revision. James Davidson said he was offering his "two-cents worth," but gave instead a most generous and meticulous reading. Steven Forman did as much and more; he made me fully aware of what it means to an author to have a skilled and supportive editor.

To those who have lived more intimately with this book, I owe a special debt of gratitude. Some helped with parenting, some read, criticized, and proofread, all listened and encouraged. John Fout, Elizabeth Frank, William Hart, Kent Harvey, Ann Hendrickson, Tanya Sugarman MacAloon, Judith McGaw, Barbara Nagler, Sylvain Nagler, Beverly Perch, Theodore Perch, Nancy Pontoli, and Lauren Rowell have been as much extended family as friends, putting their own needs aside at times to meet mine. My immediate family has more often done the same. Kirsten Harvey, Todd Harvey, and Brooke Karlsen have been there from the beginning. They, and Manuel Ayala, Jeanne Boydston, Lori Ginzberg, and Joel Steiker, have made the years of researching and writing rich indeed. I especially thank them for their love and forbearance.

My deepest appreciation goes to Jeanne Boydston. Hardly an idea in this book has not been sharpened by her insightful questions and suggestions, hardly a paragraph has not been improved by her facility with language. She has given as freely of her time as she has her knowledge of women's history. Her most generous gifts have been her humor and good humor through it all.

Finally, I am grateful to the three women to whom this book is dedicated—my mother, my grandmother, and my aunt. Two of them never knew about this book, and the third never saw it completed. But without them, it could not have been written.

C. F. K.
June 1987

Handmaidens of the Lord should go
so as to distinguish themselves
from Handmaidens of the Devil

COTTON MATHER
*Ornaments for the
Daughters of Zion,* 1692

ONE

New England's Witchcraft Beliefs

ON 14 MAY 1656, Boston widow Ann Hibbens stood
before the magistrates and elected town representatives of the
Massachusetts General Court, the highest judicial and legisla-
tive body in the colony. She had recently been tried on charges
of witchcraft in the colony's Court of Assistants, and despite
her plea of innocence the jury had voted to convict her. The
magistrates, at least some of whom she knew well, had not
concurred with the jury's verdict, and for that reason the decision of the Court of Assistants had been deferred. Hibbens
now agreed to be retried by the whole General Court, but the
reprieve was to no avail.[1] After hearing the evidence presented against her, and her own response to the charges, the
court determined that she was guilty. Governor John Endicott
pronounced her sentence: "she was to goe from the barr to
the place from whence she came, and from thence to the place
of execution, and there to hang till she was dead." Five weeks
later, on June 19, Ann Hibbens was executed as a witch.[2]

In 1656, few New Englanders would have been surprised
to see a woman prosecuted—or even executed—for witchcraft. No fewer than sixteen trials had taken place within the

1

previous decade; at least eight and probably nine women, as well as one man, had already suffered Hibbens's fate.[3] In England, moreover, from which most of the colonists had emigrated, witchcraft trials and executions had been regular features of the social landscape since 1542, when Parliament first made witchcraft a capital crime. Just a few years before Hibbens's trial, between 1645 and 1647, several hundred people had been hanged in the wake of England's most serious witchcraft outbreak. More than 90 percent of these English witches were women.[4]

Ann Hibbens's trial stood out though for the social status of the accused. Her husband had been a merchant and magistrate before his death two years earlier, and she held a sizeable estate in her own hands. The court referred to her as Mrs. Hibbens, rather than by the more frequently heard "Goodwife." This and the considerable disagreement about the disposition of her case suggest that despite her reputation among many of her neighbors as a troublesome woman, she still maintained the social position she had held since she and her husband had arrived in Boston in the early 1630s.[5]

In England, witches had come primarily from the lower ranks of the social order.[6] In New England too, many of the witchcraft suspects prior to 1656 were poor women, but there were enough exceptions to indicate that a change was underway. The special conditions of life the colonists faced in their new communities led them gradually to alter some of their ideas on witchcraft. Most notably, they became less certain than their parents and grandparents had been that witchcraft was the special province of the female poor.

Yet New England witchcraft had its roots in the villages and towns of England. It was so much a part of the culture the settlers transported from the old world to the new that the continuities rather than the differences stand out. The colonists shared with their counterparts in England many assumptions about what kinds of people witches were, what kinds of practices they engaged in, and where and how they attained their supernatural power. They also knew how to detect witches and how to rid their communities of the threat witches posed. Indeed, belief in the existence and danger of witches was so widespread, at all levels of society, that disbelief was itself suspect.[7]

Perhaps the strongest link between witchcraft in England and in New England was the special association of this crime with women and womanhood. Although clear from the pattern and content of accusations, this association was never made explicit in New England culture. While authors of theological descriptions of witchcraft sometimes employed female pronouns when speaking generally about witches, more commonly they used the "generic" male. If in theory men and children could be witches as easily as could women, in fact even during outbreaks, when men and children were most vulnerable, their numbers among the suspected were proportionately small, and they were rarely the main targets of accusations.[8]

Puritans offered an explanation, if indirectly, for the presence of men and children among the accused. Witchcraft was not considered hereditary, but it was thought that witches passed their craft on to the people closest to them. On a late-seventeenth-century list of reasonable grounds for examining a witch, Connecticut officials included the following:

> If the party suspected be the son or daughter, the servant or familiar friend; neer Neighbor or old Companion of a Knowne or Convicted witch, this alsoe [is] a presumton, for witchcraft is an art that may be learned and Convayd from man to man and oft it falleth out that a witch dying leaveth som of the aforesaid heirs of her witchcraft.[9]

Husbands and daughters of witches were the most likely suspects, especially daughters and most especially after they became mature women themselves. Although much less often, sons and granddaughters were also accused, as were women and men who were associated with, defended, or questioned the proceedings against individual witches.

The New England settlers also carried with them a dual conception of witchcraft and the menace it posed. For most colonists, the critical concern was the harm witches inflicted on neighbors and on neighbors' property. Witches were criminals who worked in supernatural ways. This was the traditional concern in England, and there as in New England the main stimulus to witchcraft accusations. But the clergy and some members of their congregations considered the primary threat to be the relationship between the witch and the Devil. In the early seventeenth century, ministers and other Protestant thinkers in England had begun to argue that because witches entered into a contract, or covenant, with Satan—exchanging their natural subjection to God for a diabolical subjection to Satan—they were not merely threats to their neighbors' physical and economic well-being, but heretics. Witches were enemies not only of society, but of God. When confronted with witches in New England, ministers in particular worried about the Devil's success in recruiting people to help destroy Puritan churches.[10]

These two views often converged. Ministers and their supporters sometimes expressed personal fears about the dangers of witches' attacks on themselves and their families, and ministerial writings regularly discussed the harm witches caused others.[11] At the same time, people with little apparent commitment to Puritanism talked about the Devil's attempts to get people on his side.[12] The circumstances of a case, such as the influence of an accused witch's family, or the credibility of the accuser, or the time and place that the accusation was lodged, could decidedly affect which view magistrates and juries were willing to accept. The clergy, by virtue of the power of the pulpit and their access to both the press and the secular authorities, had more opportunities to insist on their view of witchcraft as Satan worship; as the seventeenth century wore on, some ministers did so more frequently, simultaneously generating support and opposition, both within their own ranks and among the population at large.

Ann Hibbens's case offers an unusually clear view of the two versions of witchcraft at work. Hibbens had been excommunicated from the Boston church sixteen years before her witchcraft trial, not for witchcraft *per se,* but (among other sins) for her obstinate challenge to religious, secular, and familial authority, and for her evil influence over other church members. To the then governor of the colony, the town's ministers, and some of the leading men of the church, she embodied the characteristics that distinguished Satan's supporters from other people.[13] Their opposition was serious—but not alone sufficient to brand her a witch. Not until she was *also* formally accused by her neighbors of supernatural activity and specific malevolent acts was she brought into court on witchcraft charges.[14]

Hibbens was executed because these two fears—that witches threatened their neighbors' well-being, and that they were Satan's minions—converged in her trial, creating together what one early historian called a "popular clamour . . . against her."[15] Her experience was not unusual in this respect. If the spiritual leaders of the community did not think an accused person had committed herself or himself to the Devil, or if there was no community consensus that someone had been specifically harmed, a witchcraft trial would most likely end in an acquittal, if indeed the case ever came to court. Without significant support for at least one of these views, accusations were rarely taken seriously at all by the authorities; the accusers in some of these cases themselves faced slander suits. When both views were operating, the accused was likely to be declared a witch: an enemy of both New England society and the Puritan faith. When both concerns were particularly widespread and intense, accusations could multiply, affecting the lives of not just one or two people but many: in the case of Salem in 1692, hundreds of New Englanders were charged with possessing the powers of the witch.

The New England witch was a human being with super-human powers.[16] Foremost among these was her ability to perform *maleficium*, that is, to cause harm to others by super-natural means. The motive most commonly ascribed was mal-ice, stimulated, ministers argued, by pride, discontent, greed, or envy. Although the witch's powers could bring harm to anyone, her victims tended to be her close neighbors or other people who knew her well enough to anger her. Witchcraft accusations often emerged out of the context of personal dis-putes, with one of the parties attributing some personal adversity to the diabolically supported malevolence of the other.

The nature of *maleficium* varied in kind and degree, but a witch was thought to specialize in certain kinds of harm. She was frequently suspected of causing illnesses or death, partic-ularly to spouses or infants and young children. Typically, an accuser would speak of a "thriveing Child" who suddenly "gave a great screech out as if it was greatly hurt," after which it did "pine away," continuing "in a sad Condition" until it "soe dyed."[17] The *maleficium* could also take a less serious form. One young man blamed a witch when he "fell downe flate upon [his] back" in the middle of a fight with her son. Another man testified that after passing the house of a witch, he became "bewildered and Lost his way and having wandered a while he cam bake againe to the same place."[18] Minor injuries or accidents, along with temporary blindness, memory loss, or clumsiness, were regularly laid at witches' doors.

The objects of a witch's malice could be domestic animals as well as people. She might "overlook" horses, cows, and other livestock, causing them to sicken and die, or simply bewitch them into wandering off.[19] Or her threats could lead to more unusual behavior in animals, as when one man's sow was "taken with strange fitts, Jumping up and knocking hir head against the fence," or when another man's cattle "would Come out of the woods with their tounges hanging out of their mouths in a strange and affrighting manner."[20] Storms, especially at sea, fires, and crop damage were also attributed to malefic witch-craft.

A witch was thought to interfere with nature in other ways as well. She was commonly accused of obstructing reproductive processes, either by preventing conceptions or by causing miscarriages, childbirth fatalities, or "monstrous" (deformed) births.[21] She was sometimes suspected of having "used means to destroy the fruit of her [own] body," either while pregnant or after the birth of her child.[22] If women and children were the chief victims of these injuries, men were the primary targets of another kind of harm. Witches were thought to enter men's bedchambers at night and prevent them from sleeping by beating, choking, biting, sitting or lying on, and smothering them. One man described this form of affliction as a "great oppression," which left him with "noe strenth or power in [his] hands to resist or help [himself]."[23] Although men occasionally testified that they had been seriously hurt in these nocturnal attacks, for the most part the injuries were limited to short-term paralyses or other temporary impairments.

Domestic processes were also the target of a witch's vengeance. She might spoil beer in the brewing or make it "jump out of the barrill" or disappear altogether.[24] She was believed capable of causing cows to stop giving milk and hens to lay fewer eggs. Cloth and clothing production were frequently hindered by witchcraft, as one woman found when she tried again and again to spin but "could make no work of it."[25]

The manner in which a witch performed *maleficium* varied. Sometimes the affliction came through a look or a touch; at other times the damage was attributed to a curse. A witch's grumbling words or thinly veiled threats following an argument were taken as evidence that she was either planning or actually initiating some harm. But it was not necessary to witness the curse to know that a witch was at work. Often the damage alone—a healthy woman suddenly taken with a fatal illness, or a tub of good butter inexplicably gone rancid—was enough to trigger a recollection of an unpleasant encounter with a reputed witch and to suggest the moment the spell was cast.

Animals were frequently the agents of malefic witchcraft. A witch was believed to have animal familiars, or imps, who nourished themselves on her body, performed evil acts at her command, and were themselves supernatural beings. Familiars assumed various forms to disguise their activities. Witnesses sometimes testified to seeing familiars so grotesque in shape as to suggest their demonic origins. More often, witnesses would talk about recognizable creatures: "a white Thing like a Cat," "sumething Like a Littell Doge," or "some small Creatures, like Mice or Ratts."[26] Since it was believed that familiars needed to return to their mistresses for feedings at least once a day, one of the ways of proving a woman a witch (called a "watching") was to isolate and secretly observe her until the creature came to her.[27]

A witch could also turn herself into an animal in order to carry out her evil deeds without being recognized. Or she could recruit real animals to do her bidding, or turn other people into animals if it suited her purposes. New Englanders sometimes found that their horses "head bin much abused by riding" the previous night, or complained that they themselves had been "hag-ridden" during their sleep.[28]

Witches were also suspected of causing injuries with the assistance of "Poppets," rag dolls, or other vehicles of image magic.[29] It was widely held that a witch could inflict harm by stroking, squeezing, prickling, or otherwise "tormenting" some devised image of her victim.[30] To discover such images among the possessions of an accused witch was another way of verifying accusations of *maleficium*, and witches' houses were searched—at times successfully, according to some colonists—for such evidence.

The capacity to injure in supernatural ways was the most common of the powers attributed to witches. Their other powers were most often exercised in connection with *malefi-*

cium, though some women were suspected of witchcraft without evidence of damage done to individuals or their property. The testimony against the accused suggests that many of them were thought to have access to preternatural knowledge or to perform feats beyond what was considered humanly possible. Some witches were accused of telling other people's fortunes or predicting "what should come to pass" in their own lives, by means of "a Venus glase [looking glass] and an Egg" and other magical aids.[31] Others were said to conjure, or summon evil spirits, "with Sieves, Keys, and Pease, and Nails, and Horseshoes."[32] Still others were charged with such varied crimes as having knowledge of private matters (for example, other people's thoughts or "secret speeches"), flying through the air (with or without the aid of "a stick or pole"), completing domestic tasks in exceptionally short order, or rendering themselves invisible.[33]

Since witches were thought to cause illnesses or thwart generative processes, it is at first surprising that a woman could also be known as a witch for curing illnesses or aiding childbirth procedures. Yet women who healed people or relieved symptoms which doctors had unsuccessfully treated could come under suspicion of using magic in their medical practice. Similarly, a woman who safely delivered infants that were not expected to survive might find herself accused of witchcraft. In these cases, it was not simply the effects of their actions that were at issue, but the means: the unexpected results were attributed to knowledge or skill that could only come from occult agencies.

All of the powers a witch possessed, including *maleficium,* were said to have derived from the covenant she had signed with the Devil. Satan gave her these powers, as well as his promise to satisfy her worldly desires (a promise many people believed he never kept), in return for her allegiance and support for his efforts to "over Come the Kingdome of Christ, and set up [his own] Kingdome" in New England.[34] The covenant was thus both a diabolical alliance and a mutual exchange of services. It was also evidence of witches' rebellion against God and worship of the Devil; to the clergy in particular, "to worship the Devil [was] Witchcraft."[35]

Most colonists were more worried about the effects of witches' powers than the manner in which they attained them; still, concern with the Puritan implications of witchcraft was not entirely limited to the clergy or even the godly few. Trial testimony frequently included evidence that the pact with the Devil had been made or the services rendered. Confessing witches acknowledged "signing the devils book," having sexual intercourse with him (a service apparently provided *to* them rather than *by* them), and allowing the Devil to perform their daily work for them.[36] Witches were also said to gather in congregations. Witch gatherings were generally described as festive occasions, with drinking, feasting, and reveling; but they usually involved far more serious rituals as well, such as initiation ceremonies in which new witches "Renounced [their] former baptisime" (and thus their loyalty to God) and were rebaptized as a sign of their new allegiance to Satan.[37] Many people supported the official view that "any action or work that inferreth a covenant with the Devil . . . sufficiently proved a witch."[38]

The concepts of *maleficium* and the satanic covenant converged in New England when witches actively recruited others to join Satan's cause. Acting as his instruments, witches were said to use both enticements and torture to seduce and coerce other people into signing a covenant with the Devil. Since most witches were women, it is not surprising that the people they chose to recruit were almost always other females, though usually much younger ones. Males were found among the recruits in even smaller proportions than they were among accused witches. Presumably, some of the potential converts went easily into the ranks of witches. Others, however, fought to maintain their allegiance to God. It was not an easy struggle, for the enticements were often appealing and the tortures merciless. Those caught in the throes of this particular form of demonic affliction were called "possessed."

Witches might at first encourage these women by offering them wealth, material possessions, security, husbands or marital felicity, or relief from daily chores—any of the things the Devil had promised them when they agreed to be his servants. If the enticements were insufficient to lure potential recruits, witches resorted to torture. The signs of possession now became clearly visible. Observers spoke of the possessed as "choaked," subjected to "Thousands of cruel pinches," "stuck [with] innumerable pins," and "cut with Knives, and struck with Blows that they could not bear."[39] The afflicted were also "visited with strange Fits," during which they were "sometimes weeping, sometimes laughing, sometimes roaring hideously," oftentimes "hurryed with Violence to and fro in the room."[40] At times their violent motions ceased, and they fell into trances; parts or all of their bodies were paralyzed and they were unable to see, hear, or speak, "and often, all this at once."[41] Their afflictions could continue for a day or two, never to return, or could alternate with calm periods (during which victims could not remember what had happened) lasting for weeks, even months. Their attacks were also characterized by an inability to hear or speak the word of God, and by an intense, if intermittent, hostility to clergymen.

A witch might be aided in these attacks by her animal familiar, or by the Devil himself. Occasionally the witch or Satan was thought to be physically present in the body of the possessed person, "confound[ing] her Language," holding dialogue with her, or speaking through her to other persons present.[42] Commonly, the younger woman would be under severe pressure to "set her Hand" to the Devil's book.[43] If she did so, however, she would remove herself from the status of "possessed" and take on the status of "witch." If, on the other hand, she persisted in her resistance, she might be "brought home unto the Lord" by a local clergyman, who saw the exorcizing of her demons as part of his ministerial role.[44] For both the possessed female and the ministers who carefully observed her behavior, possession was a battle between the witch (acting as Satan's agent) and the possessed for the latter's soul.

Reactions to possessed females were mixed. Most observers probably agreed with the clergy's explanation that the possessed were simply victims of both witches' malice and the Devil's desire for more handmaidens to serve him. For these people, the possessed were gifted with "spectral sight," the ability to identify their invisible adversaries. Encouraging the possessed to reveal the names of their tormentors, then, was one of the best ways of determining the identity of the witches in the community. But for other observers, the possessed were themselves a suspect group. How could one know if these females had not, in fact, already been seduced or coerced into signing the covenant with Satan? Or since many cases of possession occurred among servants, wasn't it possible that their "possession" was merely a clever device to avoid the tasks assigned them? If this last was the case, perhaps all they needed, as one man suggested, was to be "kept . . . close" to their spinning wheels and whipped to "thresh the Devil out of [them]."[45]

These skeptical interpretations of possession coexisted in New England society alongside the official Puritan view. Sometimes the possessed were not encouraged to name the witches responsible for their afflictions (not even by their own ministers); any names voluntarily offered by them were not taken seriously, and no one was formally accused. Other times, most notably during outbreaks, the possessed became important—if not the most important—sources of witch identifications. At all times, however, as we shall see, the possessed provided the most visible support for the clergy's argument that the greatest danger of witchcraft lay in the power of witches to enlist others in the Devil's cause.

A witch could also be identified by the presence of the "Devil's mark" or the "witches' teat" on her body. Theoretically at least, the two terms meant different things. Puritan doctrine had it that the mark was placed on the witch's body by the Devil at the signing of the covenant, to seal their bargain and allow him to recognize her as one of his followers. Traditional belief held that the teat was where animal familiars sucked on her body. In New England, these two beliefs converged, and the two terms became interchangeable. Although the mark or teat could be located anywhere, it was most often found on or around a woman's breasts or vagina. Any "Excresence of flesh," however, could be taken as a sign that someone was a witch.[46] "Juries of women" were impaneled by local authorities to search the bodies of the accused for this sign of a witch's familiarity with the Devil (or with lesser demons).[47]

Because of the use of supernatural powers in so many witchcraft practices, the identity of a witch was hard to prove in a court of law. Since self-condemnation was the surest evidence of guilt, and since witches were considered so dangerous, many thought the community (in the form of its officials) justified in resorting to extreme methods of extracting a confession. The magistrates insisted on "the voluntary confession of the party suspected," but they saw no contradiction in allowing the use of torture where there was "strong and great presumcon" of guilt.[48] Though it is unclear how often physical coercion was employed, it clearly was in some cases.

The accused were regularly subjected to psychological pressure, from family members and neighbors as well as from the authorities. Several women who incriminated themselves during the Salem outbreak, for instance, later retracted their statements, arguing that their confessions had followed upon "the unwearied sollicitations of those that privately discoursed them, both at home and at Salem."[49] Others specifically charged the religious and secular authorities with only listening to what they wanted to hear.[50]

Confessions were not always encouraged; nor was credence given to all accusations. However widespread and firmly held the witchcraft beliefs were, accusations were not always followed by trials and convictions. At the very least, prosecution required the concurrence of at least some of the accused witch's neighbors, who knew her on a daily basis and were willing publicly to testify against her. It also required the imprimatur of local courts, which initially heard the evidence and decided whether the case should be tried in one of New England's higher courts. Finally, magistrates and juries of the Court of Assistants, or the General Court, who alone could try witches, might refuse to hear the case or might prosecute it vigorously. At any stage in the process, the clergy might intervene to support or oppose the accusation.

The witchcraft beliefs of colonial New Englanders, then, drew on two religious traditions, one longstanding, the other relatively new. Both contributed to the complex and evolving identity of the witch. The case of Ann Hibbens hinted at that complexity—and the way witchcraft beliefs would develop in New England over the course of the seventeenth century.

1620–1646

In these early years the young colonies adopted their own legal codes, which included witchcraft among the crimes punishable by death. No one, however, was prosecuted under these laws—or under the English witchcraft statutes in force in the colonies—until 1647. Considering the prevalence of witchcraft beliefs and the frequency of witch trials in England during the early seventeenth century, it is at first surprising that no women were formally accused of witchcraft in New England during the first twenty-six years of settlement. In part this can be attributed to the colonies' initially small population—and to other demographic and economic conditions of early settlement which we will soon describe. But the distinctive views of witchcraft held by the first settlers are nonetheless pertinent.

During these early decades, *informal* witchcraft accusations were made against at least two Massachusetts women, Anne Hutchinson and Jane Hawkins, and insinuations made about a third, Mary Dyer.[51] Hutchinson and Hawkins were banished from the colony, and Dyer was eventually executed, but none of these women was officially tried as a witch. Witchcraft *per se* was never mentioned in any of the actions taken against them. Yet their stories, which are interrelated, reveal much about how some of the colony's early leaders viewed witchcraft.

Anne Hutchinson was one of the central figures in what has come to be known as the Antinomian controversy. The details of this conflict need not detain us.[52] At the heart of this controversy were different interpretations of Puritan doctrine, one embraced by most of New England's clergy, the other by Anne Hutchinson, her followers, and a minority of ministers. In the eyes of her adversaries, Hutchinson's views bordered on antinomianism, a belief that God's gift of grace relieved Christians of responsibility for obeying the moral law of the Old Testament.

Although Hutchinson disclaimed this charge, within a few years of her arrival in Boston her outspoken theological views and her personal assumption of religious leadership had aroused the hostility of many of the colony's leading men. The weekly meetings she held in her house attracted too many of Boston's citizens to go unnoticed, and she criticized the theological positions held by many of the clergy. Jane Hawkins and Mary Dyer were two of her staunchest supporters. By 1637, Hutchinson's opponents had decided that she posed too great a threat to the colony to tolerate; they brought her before the General Court, and later before the church itself, to defend her actions and her views. By 1638, she had been denounced as a heretic, excommunicated from the church, and ordered to leave the colony for good. The magistrates took action against Hawkins shortly after they had disposed of Hutchinson, and they executed Dyer, although not until many years later, when she had become a spiritual leader herself. Both of these women were also considered heretics by their adversaries.

The linking of heresy and witchcraft here is most apparent in the official response to Jane Hawkins, the only one of the three women who was not a church member and the one with the least status in the community. Hawkins had regularly attended Hutchinson's weekly meetings and, like Hutchinson, had persisted in defending her religious principles even after it had become clearly dangerous to do so. Also like Hutchinson, she was a midwife and lay physician. According to Massachusetts' governor, John Winthrop, Hawkins was known "to give young women oil of mandrakes and other stuff to cause conception," and "grew into great suspicion to be a witch, for it was credibly reported, that, when she gave any medicines . . . she would ask the party, if she did believe, she could help her, etc."[53] Winthrop did not say when this suspicion developed, or in whom, or what her beliefs were. Even though Hawkins seems not to have been charged with witchcraft, the authorities brought her into court to answer for both her medical practices and her religious beliefs. They did this only after they had decided to rid the colony of Hutchinson and others who persisted in their heretical opinions.[54]

The exact sequence of events is unclear, but Hawkins was first brought before the magistrates in March 1638, a month after Mary Dyer had delivered a malformed, stillborn infant. Hawkins was the acting midwife, and Hutchinson was also present at the delivery. Several Puritan writers later implied that diabolical forces were at work during the delivery.[55] At the time, however, the court did not mention the event. They simply ordered Hawkins "not to meddle in surgery, or phisick, drinks, plaisters, or oyles, nor to question matters of religion, except with the elders for satisfaction" and told her to leave the colony by May.[56] Whether she left the colony at this time is uncertain. If she did, as Winthrop implied, she must have returned, for the colony records do not show her officially banished until 1641.[57]

Anne Hutchinson's and Mary Dyer's witchcraft was first discussed publicly (if obliquely) by John Winthrop, in connection with what he called Dyer's "monstrous birth."[58] Winthrop insisted that he had not heard of this event until after Hutchinson had been cast out of the church, and after, we might add, Dyer had made public her continuing support of her friend by escorting her from the meetinghouse. When the news reached him, he said, he called for an immediate investigation, including an exhumation of the corpse. Although childbirth fatalities and deformed births were interpreted in a variety of ways in the seventeenth century, Winthrop saw this one, at least initially, as evidence of what he already believed—that Hutchinson and Dyer, like Hawkins, were instruments of Satan.[59] Describing the decaying corpse as a monster with horns, claws, and scales, Winthrop went on to suggest its demonic origins:

> When it died in the mother's body, (which was about two hours before the birth,) the bed whereon the mother lay did shake, and withal there was such a noisome savor, as most of the women were taken with extreme vomiting and purging, so as they were forced to depart; and others of them their children were taken with convulsions, (which they never had before nor after,) and so were sent for home, so as by these occasions it came to be concealed.[60]

The reference to the shaking bed implied that the fetus itself was a devil, since it was believed that Satan could impregnate a witch and that demon offspring struggled violently against their own demise. The noisome smell also evoked images of devils, thought to give off a noxious odor too powerful for human tolerance.[61] Without directly saying so, Winthrop insinuated that Hutchinson, Dyer, and Hawkins, in participating in this episode, all revealed themselves to be witches.

When Hutchinson's own last pregnancy ended in a spontaneous abortion a number of months later, Winthrop and several other men seized on the event as evidence of yet another monstrous offspring. As minister Thomas Weld later described it, "Mistris Hutchinson . . . brought forth not one . . . but . . . 30. monstrous births or thereabouts, at once; some of them bigger, some lesser, some of one shape, some of another; few of any perfect shape, none at all of them (as farre as I could ever learne) of humane shape." Weld seems to have felt on shaky ground, for he insisted that he had no intention "to delude the world with untruths." This time the women's personal misfortunes were attributed to God, not the Devil. Linking both Dyer's and Hutchinson's unsuccessful pregnancies to their "misshapen" religious beliefs, Weld wrote: "God himselfe was pleased to step in with his casting voice . . . in causing the two fomenting women in the time of the height of the[ir] Opinions to produce out of their wombs, as before they had out of their braines, such monstrous births as no Chronicle (I thinke) hardly ever recorded the like."[62] If not the Devil himself, then at least the Devil's influence was still palpably present.

On another occasion Governor Winthrop made explicit the link between Hutchinson's witchcraft and her assumption of spiritual leadership. Recording in his journal the story of two young men who had fallen under her spiritual influence in Rhode Island, Winthrop noted that Hutchinson (and her two female followers) "gave cause of suspicion of witchcraft" there simply because the men were so easily "taken with her heresies." It was for the same reason, he said, that she and her two followers had come under suspicion "when she dwelt in Boston" several years before.[63] Although Winthrop made no specific mention of Mary Dyer, the same passage does contain a further reference to Jane Hawkins's reputation as a witch.

It is important to note that Anne Hutchinson's interpretation of Puritan doctrine allowed women a vastly enlarged sphere of religious activity. Indeed the special vindictiveness with which she was treated stemmed from her appropriation—as a woman—of a central spiritual role in her community. During the course of her civil trial, her adversaries reminded her in a number of ways that her behavior was "not tolerable nor comely in the sight of God nor fitting for your sex."[64] Puritans argued that men and women were spiritual equals, but they did not mean to extend this equality to earthly relations, even that of women to the church. Equality of the sexes would threaten the very foundations of New England's

social hierarchy, and it was in the context of this perceived
threat that opponents of Hutchinson, Hawkins, and Dyer came
to view them as witches.

At the same time, there is no evidence of popular support
for witchcraft trials in these three cases. If John Winthrop and
the men who shared his beliefs understood the formidable
challenge Hutchinson and her two followers posed to the
Massachusetts theocracy *as witchcraft,* most New Englanders in
the 1630s did not. These men did share with their neighbors
the association of witchcraft with midwifery and deformed
births, and the assumption that women of low status were more
likely to be witches than women of high status. Through
repeated allusions to "monstrous births," and their focus on
Hawkins's role as Dyer's midwife and Hutchinson's devoted
friend and follower, Winthrop and his allies justified to themselves their response to these women. But no one actually
brought witchcraft charges against any of the three, which
suggests that efforts to have witchcraft defined as heresy were
at best only minimally successful.[65] In later years, Puritan
leaders would also accuse female Quakers of witchcraft, but
here too with little impact on popular belief. The idea of the
witch as a female challenger of the religious system never per-
meated colonial consciousness, and in itself never resulted in
witchcraft convictions.

1647–1663

By the late 1640s, the place of witchcraft in New England's
social world had shifted dramatically, setting off tremors of
suspicion: soon, accusations and trials began in earnest. The
first trial and execution for witchcraft was recorded almost
simultaneously in two private journals, that of John Winthrop
and that of Matthew Grant, the town clerk of Windsor, Connecticut. Both entries were brief. "One———of Windsor
arraigned and executed at Hartford for a witch," Winthrop

noted in late May of 1647.[66] Grant's entry was both more and less specific: "May 26. 47 Alse Young was hanged."[67] Little is known about this woman except that she was probably the wife of John Young, who bought a small parcel of land in Windsor in 1641, sold it in 1649, and then disappeared from the town records, and the mother of Alice Young Beamon, who would be accused of witchcraft in nearby Springfield, Massachusetts, some thirty years later.[68] No evidence of the charges against the first Alice Young has survived. As with so many women who would subsequently be convicted of witchcraft in New England, we know of her existence only through her reputation as a witch.

Between 1647 and 1663, New England experienced a period of intense witch fear. No fewer than seventy-nine persons were accused of witchcraft, thirteen of whom were named during the first outbreak in Hartford in 1662–63. Of these seventy-nine, thirty-three appear to have been tried as witches, and fifteen were found guilty and hanged. Sixty-one of the seventy-nine people accused were female, as were thirteen of the fifteen who were convicted and executed. Nine of the nineteen men accused, and both of the men who were hanged, were married to women who were witches. Several of the women, all Quakers, were banished without trials. Witchcraft accusations during this period were most common in Massachusetts, although Connecticut saw more convictions and executions. New Haven, still a separate colony, witnessed several trials but only a few convictions; only one trial took place in Plymouth, and none in Rhode Island.[69]

Massachusetts Bay executed its first witch in 1648. She was Margaret Jones, and like Jane Hawkins and Anne Hutchinson, she was a midwife and lay healer. Jones was accused of several different practices, only some of which had to do with her profession, but it is impossible to say which activities initiated the accusations against her.

Minister John Hale, who witnessed Jones's hanging in Boston when he was a boy, later said that she "was suspected partly because that after some angry words passing between her and her Neighbours, some mischief befel such Neighbours in their Creatures, or the like: [and] partly because some things supposed to be bewitched, or have a Charm upon them, being burned, she came to the fire and seemed concerned."[70] John Winthrop included neither of these charges in his list of the evidence presented against Jones, but suggested that the crimes had to do with her medical practice. She was accused of having a "malignant touch," Winthrop noted, and her medicines were said to have "extraordinary violent effects." When people refused to take her medical advice, he added, "their diseases and hurts continued, with relapse against the ordinary course, and beyond the apprehension of all physicians and surgeons." Winthrop also mentioned that Jones was believed to possess psychic powers: "some things which she foretold came to pass accordingly; other things she could tell of . . . she had no ordinary means to come to the knowledge of."[71]

John Hale's account brings to the surface some of the community's views of witchcraft. He pointed out that several of Jones's neighbors tried to get her to confess and repent. One of them, he said, "prayed her to consider if God did not bring this punishment upon her for some other crime, and asked, if she had not been guilty of stealing many years ago." Jones admitted the theft, but she refused to accept it as a reason for her conviction as a witch. Hale's writings, on the other hand, showed that stealing, and other crimes such as fornication and infanticide, were regularly associated with witchcraft, by both the clergy and the larger population.[72]

The other witch executed in 1648 was Mary Johnson, of Wethersfield, Connecticut. She had also been accused, in 1646, of stealing, but the theft was never directly mentioned in connection with her witchcraft.[73] Johnson's case differed in other ways as well from that of Margaret Jones. Under pressure from minister Samuel Stone to confess, Johnson fully described her crimes. She admitted that her "first Familiarity with the Devils came by Discontent" with her work as a servant. "A Devil was wont to do her many services," she said; when "her Master once blamed her for not carrying out the Ashes . . . a Devil did clear the Hearth for her afterwards" and when her master sent her "into the Field, to drive out the Hogs that used to break into it, a Devil would scowre them out, and make her laugh to see how he feazed 'em about." In Stone's account, Johnson's discontent was inextricably tied to her acceptance of Satan's services. She then confessed to Stone that "she was guilty of the Murder of a Child, and that she had been guilty of Uncleanness with Men and Devils."[74] On the basis of this confession, Mary Johnson was hanged as a witch.

In 1651, Mary Parsons of Springfield, Massachusetts, was imprisoned. She was charged with "being seduced by the divill" into "making a covenant with him," possessing the two daughters of the town's minister, George Moxon, and committing infanticide.[75] Apparently Parsons admitted at some point to at least some of the charges. According to John Hale, she confessed that

> she had lost a Child and was exceedingly dicontented at it and longed; *Oh that she might see her Child again!* And at last the Devil in likeness of her Child came to her bed side and talked with her, and asked to come into the bed to her, and she received it into the bed to her that night and several nights after, and so entered into covenant with Satan and became a Witch.

She also claimed responsibility for the death of one of her two deceased children, and implicated her husband in several witchcraft crimes, including infanticide. Though she later denied being a witch, she was bound over to the General Court for trial, where she was acquitted of witchcraft but convicted of murder. Either she was hanged, or she died in prison before she could be executed.[76]

Her husband, Hugh Parsons, was accused by other Springfield residents of killing his own child, bewitching the Moxon children, and inflicting numerous other injuries on his neighbors. Like most other male witches whose wives had witchcraft reputations, he was not executed; but unlike nearly all of the others, his own reputation for witchcraft seems to have developed independently of his wife's and may even have preceded it. Hugh Parsons came to trial in Boston a full year after Mary Parsons: the jury found him guilty in the Court of Assistants, but the General Court subsequently acquitted him of all charges.[77]

New Haven's Elizabeth Godman was suspected of a variety of witchcraft activities in the early 1650s. After clergyman John Davenport mentioned in a sermon "that a forward discontented frame of spirit was a subject fitt for the Devill to worke upon," several of Godman's neighbors decided that she looked and behaved very much as if she was "of such a frame of spirit," and they began to insinuate, both to her and to others, that she was a witch.[78] In 1653, Godman demanded a hearing to clear herself, an act that only served to convince many people that she was indeed one of Satan's associates. Among her other crimes, Godman was suspected of having sexual relations with the Devil; causing miscarriages; knowing things no normal woman could know; bewitching people, cattle, and chickens; and hindering the churning of butter and the brewing of beer. After at least two hearings between 1653 and 1655, the court informed her "that though the evidenc is not sufficient as yet to take away her life," it was strong enough to restrict her movements in the community and to require her to pay £50 security for her good behavior.[79]

The patterns of accusation established in these early witchcraft cases proved durable. The record for the next decade featured a recurring list of witchcraft crimes. Ann Hibbens, the Boston widow hanged for witchcraft in 1656, had faced trial after some of her neighbors accused her of knowing that other people were talking about her.[80] Eunice Cole of Hampton, Massachusetts, a woman who was considered particularly knowledgeable about the activities of witches, was accused that same year of bewitching her neighbors' children and cattle.[81]

Meanwhile, the Boston magistrates also accused as witches two Quaker women, Ann Austin and Mary Fisher, who had come to the colony in 1656 to preach; before they were finally deported, both women were imprisoned for several weeks and searched for witches' marks.[82] The charges brought in 1659 against healer Winifred Holman of Cambridge, Massachusetts, included hindering her neighbor from performing her work at the spinning wheel, possessing the woman's daughter, and harming rather than curing the daughter's child. Holman's own adult daughter was also implicated in her mother's witchcraft.[83]

Ann Hibbens's execution in 1656, however, seems to have begun a hiatus in the actions of the courts. The number and the content of accusations remained similar to those of earlier years, and the number of trials continued apace. But after Hibbens's death there were fewer convictions. Indeed, whereas most of the people tried prior to Hibbens had been found guilty and executed, for five years after she was hanged only one person, Eunice Cole, seems to have been convicted, and even here the evidence concerning the court's decision is ambiguous.[84] Nothing in the actions of New England's magistrates and juries directly explains this change, but it was in any case short-lived. In 1662–63, the first witchcraft outbreak took place, in Hartford, Connecticut.

The origins of the Hartford outbreak are obscure, but the trouble apparently began in the spring of 1662, with the possession and subsequent death of eight-year-old Elizabeth Kelly, who in her fits had cried out on her neighbor, Goodwife Ayres.[85] Convinced that their child had died from bewitchment, her parents demanded an investigation. Ayres was probably the first person named, but two other people, Mary and Andrew Sanford, were brought up for examination not long after. Ayres's husband, who would eventually come under suspicion himself, accused Rebecca Greensmith, who in turn supported accusations against her own husband and implicated several other Hartford residents. And so it went. The community was caught in the grip of a witchcraft fear that would eventually result in accusations against at least thirteen people, and that would take the lives of four of them.

At some point during the early period of the Hartford outbreak, Ann Cole, whom minister Increase Mather described as a "person of real Piety and Integrity," succumbed to possession. She was, he said, "taken with very strange Fits, wherein her Tongue was improved by a Daemon to express things which she her self knew nothing of." In the presence of several local ministers, the demons said "that such and such persons . . . [who were then named and who included some of the people already accused] were consulting how they might carry on mischievous designs against her and several others. . . ."[86] Statements made by Cole that a number of witches were at work in the area seem to have intensified the community's desire to ferret them out.

One of the women mentioned by Cole was her next-door neighbor, Rebecca Greensmith, who was already in prison awaiting trial. When Greensmith was confronted by the ministers and magistrates, she fully admitted her "familiarity with the Devil." She denied making "an express Covenant with him," but said that "at Christmass they would have a merry Meeting" and seal their bargain. She also acknowledged that "the Devil had frequently the carnal knowledge of her Body," and that she and the other accused witches "had Meetings at a place not far from her House." Greensmith was hanged in January 1663, along with her husband, who steadfastly denied his own guilt, and a Farmington woman, Mary Barnes, about whom little is known. According to Mather, Ann Cole was "restored to health" after their executions.[87]

By that time, Mary Sanford had already been convicted of witchcraft and presumably executed. The charges against her husband Andrew had been dismissed, despite some misgivings on the part of the local court. Several other accused people, including Goodwife Ayres and her husband, had escaped and fled before they could be tried. Judith Varlet, one of the women implicated by Ann Cole, was arrested, but she was released from prison after New Netherland governor Peter Stuyvesant sent a letter to the Hartford magistrates attesting to her "known education, Life, Conversation and profession of faith."[88] Another of the accused, Elizabeth Seager, was acquitted, but she was tried again in 1663. This time she was charged with adultery and witchcraft. After a heated controversy over what crime she was actually guilty of, she was convicted of adultery but acquitted of witchcraft. Accused of witchcraft a third time in 1665, she was finally convicted, but Governor John Winthrop, Jr., considered the issues so ambiguous that he asked for a postponement of sentencing. In 1666, a special Court of Assistants called by Winthrop released her because, as they said, the jury's verdict did "not legally answer the inditement." Shortly thereafter, Seager fled to Rhode Island.[89]

Too little is known about Hartford's early history to explain clearly why New England's first witchcraft outbreak occurred there, but like Salem a generation later, it was a community that had suffered years of internal dissension. And like Salem, its people had focused their disagreements on the church and its ministers. By the time the witch panic began, many families in the town had broken away and formed a new community up the Connecticut River valley in Hadley, Massachusetts. For those who stayed behind, the witchcraft testimony suggests, tensions remained high. The outbreak allowed their expression, in attacks against neighbors and people in nearby towns, but it may also have united clergy and townspeople, in their struggle against the Devil and his local supporters.[90]

Whatever the specific causes of the 1662–63 Hartford outbreak, these trials, and most of the witchcraft trials held between 1647 and 1656, signaled the convergence of some of the views held by the ministers with popular opinion—at least about the guilt of *particular* individuals. The feeling among accusers that the trials and executions would bring an end to their personal afflictions seems to have been matched by the clergy's relief in ridding the community of the church's enemies. The confessions of Mary Johnson, Mary Parsons, and Rebecca Greensmith, and the possession of Ann Cole, also show that at least some colonists (even if only confessing witches and the possessed) shared the ministers' preoccupation with the Devil's role in witchcraft. This limited acceptance of the belief in the witch's pact with Satan—as well as the rash of accusations themselves—probably owed something to the massive witch-hunts in England in 1645–47, since it was then that the covenant had first become a central focus of English witchcraft cases.[91]

It is harder to explain the hiatus in witchcraft convictions between 1656 and the onset of the Hartford panic in 1662. The leniency of the high courts during this period seems to have been accompanied by the clergy's reluctance to support witchcraft proceedings actively. Since this official restraint would become even more apparent after the Hartford outbreak, it may be that by 1656 ministers and magistrates had become increasingly uncomfortable with the kinds of people who were being accused of witchcraft. It appears to have been the status of the accused that disturbed colonial leaders, causing them to doubt accusations brought by the populace.

As long as accusations were being directed against women like Margaret Jones, Mary Johnson, and Eunice Cole—women with few economic resources and some taint of disrepute—few people registered discomfort about their fates. These women conformed well to the views settlers brought from England of what witches were like. But in New England, accusations were too frequently being made against women like Elizabeth Godman and Ann Hibbens—women who conformed to established ideas in some respects but not in others. However odious they may have been to some of their neighbors, even some of their most powerful neighbors, women from prosperous families contradicted the inherited assumption that discontent with poverty led women to witchcraft. Prior to Hibbens, most accused witches in New England who had access to substantial financial resources, including Godman, had escaped the fate of poorer witches.[92] But Hibbens did not, and her trial and execution stimulated controversy at the highest levels of New England society. The eminent minister John Norton fought for her release and later said that she had been "hanged for a witch, only for having more wit than her neighbors."[93] This indicates disagreement severe enough to affect official responses to accusations for the next several years— and perhaps much longer. Many of the authorities could justify the execution of Ann Hibbens, but the dissonance seems to have been intolerable for others. Official caution may have been aroused also by the increasing proportion of men appearing in New England courts as witches; this too was higher than it had been in England.

If deviation from inherited English views of witchcraft was at issue here, then the accusations made during the Hartford outbreak must have heightened the concern of many. While two of the convicted witches, Mary Sanford and Mary Barnes, appear to have been poor, the other two, Rebecca and Nathaniel Greensmith, were not. Even more disconcerting, three of the remaining nine people accused were males, and two of the others came from quite prosperous families; none of these people ever came to trial, for the accusations were simply not taken seriously, but that they were accused at all must have given many people pause. However generally New Englanders shared their witchcraft beliefs, there were still areas of considerable disagreement.[94]

The New England experience was slowly redefining the witch. Ann Hibbens may have seemed an improbable witch to John Norton and some others of her peers, as might Elizabeth Godman and even Rebecca Greensmith; in old England, these women's wealth and position would most likely have protected them from suspicion. But in New England economic status was becoming irrelevant to the identity of the witch. Ironically, the clergy's own insistence on the primacy of the witch's relationship with Satan was contributing to that redefinition in ways the clergy never intended.

1664–1688

Following the Hartford outbreak, both official and popular pressure for witchcraft prosecutions waned. The number of accusations dropped from an average of four or five persons each year between 1647 and 1663 to just over three per year during the next twenty-four years. More striking, of the seventy-five people accused in that period, fifty-eight of whom were women, only twelve—nine women and three men—were bound over to higher courts for trial. Only three of these, all women, were convicted, but none of the three was executed. In the wake of the Hartford events, most accusations and trials took place in Massachusetts.

To say that accusations and prosecutions declined and executions ceased is not to say that suspected witches were no longer punished for their behavior. At the very least, having "the Common fame of a witch" was still viewed with considerable hostility by magistrates and jurors.[95] Many of the accused were required to pay the costs of their imprisonments and of the proceedings against them, on the grounds that their behavior at least warranted the charges, even if not the conviction. Some women were punished more severely. Katherine Harrison, a wealthy Wethersfield widow, had been convicted as a witch by a jury in 1669, but the magistrates thought the evidence not convincing enough to hang her. Neither did they release her; instead, they kept her in jail for months while deciding what to do with her. When they finally did free her, it was with the stipulation that she not only pay "her just fees," but remove herself permanently from the colony as well.[96]

If the courts were reluctant to execute witches, members of the community might inflict some punishment of their own.

During Katherine Harrison's imprisonment, her neighbors wounded and killed many of her horses and cattle and destroyed her crops.[97] The acquittal of impoverished Mary Webster of Hadley in 1683 aroused an even more vindictive response from several young men of the Massachusetts town. After she returned from the Boston jail, they "dragged her out of the house . . . hung her up until she was near dead, let her down, rolled her sometime in the snow, and at last buried her in it, and there left her."[98] Apparently, the community considered these reprisals justified. The court ignored Katherine Harrison's petition for redress, and there is no evidence of any action taken against Mary Webster's attackers. Perhaps minister Cotton Mather's interpretation of the "Disturbance" caused to Webster was not uncommon. Mather exonerated the men involved because they were at "their wits end," and because the man she was accused of bewitching was mercifully "at ease" for the duration of their attack against her.[99] Furthermore, the number of witches brought into court more than once to answer to witchcraft charges suggests a strong popular dissatisfaction with the courts' lenient treatment of the accused.[100]

Despite evidence that witches were still objects of community fear and hatred, the years between 1663 and 1687 must be characterized as a time when interest in prosecuting witches sharply diminished, at least among the religious and secular authorities. The end of Puritan rule and the 1660 Restoration of the Stuart monarchy in England may have strongly influenced New England's official responses to witchcraft accusations, especially since witchcraft beliefs came under increasing attack by English intellectuals during the Restoration period.[101] But other factors were at work as well. We have seen that the decline in witchcraft prosecutions began prior to, and was interrupted by, the Hartford outbreak. Another key to the post-Hartford decline seems to have had to do, as before, with the kinds of people being accused in New England.

In the years after the Hartford outbreak the proportion of

men and women among the accused remained constant, but the number of women from the middle and upper ranks of society continued to grow, as did the number of men who were not husbands of witches.[102] At the same time, ministers no longer took responsibility for extracting confessions from the accused, and some of them even discouraged people from filing formal witchcraft complaints.[103] Whatever the other reasons for the clergy's unusually low profile in witchcraft cases during these years, they appear to have been reluctant to trust accusers' judgments about who was responsible for witchcraft afflictions—especially possessed persons, who along with confessing witches were more likely than the other accusers to name people who did not fit the clergy's ideas about who were the witches in their midst.

Although perhaps not entirely typical, the response of minister Samuel Willard to the possession of Elizabeth Knapp in Groton, Massachusetts, in 1671, does suggest a caution not evident two decades earlier. Elizabeth Knapp was sixteen and a servant in the Willard household when she first exhibited signs of possession. In his detailed account of the episode, Willard described his amazement when Knapp suddenly began to behave in "a strange and unwonted manner," giving abrupt shrieks and then bursting into extravagant laughter when asked what was wrong. As her symptoms intensified (she fell into violent fits, complained of being strangled, and attempted to throw herself into the fire), Willard wondered whether she was in genuine distress or merely dissembling. When she responded to questions about the cause of her difficulty by saying that one of her neighbors, or the Devil in her shape, was afflicting her, Willard did not encourage Knapp to file a formal complaint, apparently because he considered the accused "a person . . . of sincere uprightness before God." Knapp shortly "confessed that she believed Satan had deluded her" and never again complained about the woman. When Knapp accused another woman, Willard was similarly wary— even though by the second week of Knapp's possession he felt sure that Satan was responsible for her condition.[104]

The clergy's withdrawal from their former role in witch-craft cases led to a decline in the number of witchcraft confes-sions and possessions. This ministerial retreat also signaled a change (albeit a temporary one) in the public discourse on witchcraft, since the idea of the covenant with Satan had been espoused mainly by religious and secular leaders, confessing witches, and possessed persons; during this period, the cove-nant was only rarely mentioned in witchcraft testimony. Most noticeable is the absence of any explicit discussion of witches' having sexual relations with the Devil. Vivid descriptions of demons sucking on witches' bodies were still submitted as evi-dence against the accused, as were statements about their lewd conduct.[105] But the only direct indication of a demonic sexual alliance is Elizabeth Knapp's temptation to "give herself up [to Satan] soul and body."[106] Witches accused of fornication or adultery were described as having men, not devils, for their partners. One novel sexual crime was introduced at this time, however. Mary Webster had to answer to the authorities for causing a man's breast to swell "like a Womans" and for hav-ing "wounded or burned" his sexual organs.[107]

Otherwise, the testimony presented against witches during this period resembled that submitted in earlier years. In 1669, Susanna Martin of Amesbury, Massachusetts, was bound over to the Court of Assistants on suspicion of witchcraft after sto-ries circulated that her son George Martin was a bastard, that she had attempted to kill him shortly after his birth, and that another son, Richard, was in fact not human at all, but one of her familiars.[108] In 1680, Hampton's Rachel Fuller was exam-ined as a witch for using magic in order to cure a sick child; the death of the child was taken as a sign that she had caused the illness in the first place.[109] Other witches were accused of causing fires, spoiling beer and cows' milk, and bewitching people and cattle—all crimes associated with traditional con-ceptions of witchcraft.

New England's ministers, if more restrained, had not completely abandoned their interest in witchcraft. In 1684, Increase Mather published *An Essay for the Recording of Illustrious Providences,* his lengthy defense of the existence of apparitions, witches, diabolical possessions, and other "Remarkable judgments upon noted sinners." In it, Mather reasserted the Puritan view of witchcraft. He retold the story of Elizabeth Knapp's and Ann Cole's possessions and cited other signs of the Devil's continued efforts to draw people away from God. The book was in part a response to the heretical writings coming out of England, which scornfully denied the reality of witches and the spirit world. The book also reflected Mather's conviction that the sins of the population had brought Indian wars, Quakers, unusual thunderstorms, and other judgments of God on New England in recent years. He wrote, finally, to alert people to the dangers of Satan and their own sinful ways.[110] Those dangers became palpable when Satan returned to New England in 1688. He returned now for both clergy and congregation, and specifically to one of the families in Mather's own church.

1688–1693

In the summer of 1688, Boston ministers and magistrates were suddenly confronted with the possession of four children in the prosperous Godwin family. Soon after, the mother of the Godwins' washerwoman was accused of witchcraft. The official reaction to the accusation was quite different from Samuel Willard's to Elizabeth Knapp's. But then, it was hard to find a more suitable witch than the widow Glover.

Thirteen-year-old Martha was the first of the Godwin children to be possessed. According to Cotton Mather, Increase's son, she was "visited with strange Fits" after a run-in with Glover. Martha had accused Glover's daughter of stealing linens, and the widow was irate. Described by Mather as an "ignorant and a scandalous old Woman" who was already rumored to be a witch, Glover had allegedly "bestowed very bad Language" upon the young girl. Within a short time, three other Godwin children began to show signs of demonic possession. After the magistrates heard the father's testimony, they promptly arrested Glover—not, Mather insisted, because Godwin had any "proof that could have done her any Hurt," but because "the Hag had not power to deny her interest in the Enchantment of the Children."[111]

What Mather meant by these last statements is unclear, but Glover was plainly incensed at the "wrong done to her self and her daughter." Still, she may have found it difficult to defend herself. Glover was Irish, and although Mather claimed that she understood English very well, it seems that she had a hard time comprehending the questions put to her. Because she spoke Gaelic, all communication with her was carried on through interpreters. Glover was also Roman Catholic; she held to a set of religious beliefs that Mather and her other Puritan examiners could hear only as blasphemy. Glover was in turn enraged and bewildered. Mather contended that she never denied her guilt and that she confessed to tormenting the children by stroking small images or puppets. He also implied that she confessed to covenanting with the Devil, but she could as easily have been talking about her God and her saints as about his Satan and his demons. Glover was so confused by the proceedings that even after she had confessed, and after a neighbor had supplied additional testimony that Glover had murdered a woman by witchcraft six years earlier, the magistrates could not be sure whether she "had not procured to her self by Folly and Madness the Reputation of a Witch." However reluctantly, the magistrates consented to her execution after physicians testified that she was "Compos Mentis."[112]

The Godwin children did not recover with the death of their tormentor. They continued to be molested by witches and demons for many months, and two of them, Martha and twelve-year-old John, were still experiencing their afflictions the following year. Apparently no one filed complaints against any of the other women the children named as responsible for their continued agonies. Cotton Mather took Martha into his household to observe her carefully. Soon after her recovery, he published his now famous "Memorable Providences, Relating to Witchcrafts and Possessions," which discussed this case in detail and added several other "proofs" that devils and witches were not only real, but determined to destroy people's souls.[113]

The exposure of Glover's association with the Devil also failed to bring about a reformation of the colonists' sinful ways or an end to God's judgments against them. Community dissension was rife as New England entered the final decade of the century. Social turmoil especially marked eastern Massachusetts, where several generations of settlers were joined by refugees from the continuing Indian wars in the competition over property.[114] There was confusion too over the ways people were expected to behave toward one another. The 1688 Glorious Revolution in England added to the colonists' economic and religious uncertainties. Just four years before, England's Lords of Trade had succeeded in annulling the Massachusetts Bay Colony charter, and in 1688 the Stuarts and their surrogates in Massachusetts were themselves overthrown. No wonder both ministry and populace felt tossed by doubt about the continued existence and direction of their personal and collective enterprise.[115] The tensions of the time surfaced in Salem, where in 1692 Satan returned with a vengeance.

Possession, the signal that witchcraft had come to Salem, was familiar to the townspeople, but this time it occurred on a scale much larger than New England had ever experienced.[116] Apart from its unprecedented scope, what is perhaps most striking about the Salem outbreak was the congruence of belief it featured between Puritan leaders and townspeople. Both feared the witches around them and with fervor set out to destroy them.

The outbreak began in the final weeks of 1691, when several girls and young women in Salem Village began to experiment with magic. Apprehensive about their futures, they clustered around an improvised crystal ball, trying to find out, among other things, "what trade their sweet harts should be of." The image they saw was more frightful than they had imagined— "a spectre in likeness of a Coffin." Before long, a few of them, including the daughter and niece of minister Samuel Parris, began to have fits and exhibit other manifestations of possession. Witchcraft may have been suspected at the outset, but on the advice of local ministers, Parris and the other parents and relatives decided to wait and see if the possessed recovered spontaneously. When the possession spread like a disease to a number of other females in the village, it became impossible to stop talk of the strange distemper. Neighbors became convinced that local physician William Griggs was right when he suggested that the possessed were under the "Evil Hand." Pressure put on the afflicted to name their tormentors did not at first yield results, but by late February 1692, not one but three witches had been named.[117]

All three—Sarah Good, Sarah Osborne, and a Carib Indian woman known only as Tituba—were residents of Salem Village. Tituba was a slave in the Parris household, where the original conjuring took place. Both Good and Tituba were poor women; Osborne was not.

Each of the three women was examined by local officials before being sent off to the Boston jail to await trial. The possessed were present during these initial proceedings, as visible testimony to the torments inflicted upon them by their invisible attackers. All of the accused were presumed guilty, and most of the questions put to them concerned their reasons for these attacks and their association with Satan. "Why do you hurt these children?" they were asked. "Have you made no contract with the devil?" "Hath the devil ever deceived you and been false to you?" Sarah Good maintained throughout that she had been falsely accused and tried to shift the responsibility to Sarah Osborne. Osborne responded with bewilderment that she "was more like to be bewitched than that she was a witch." But Tituba, at least in part out of fear of her master, confessed all. Though contradicting herself, she satisfied her listeners by giving detailed answers to additional queries about the nature of her service to the Devil, the pretty things he offered her in return, the witch meetings she attended, and so forth. She not only implicated Good and Osborne, but alluded as well to other witches still at large.[118]

In the wake of Tituba's confession, the community made every effort to find out from the possessed who these other witches might be. But the afflicted were again at a loss to come up with names. Thirteen-year-old Ann Putnam finally broke the silence by crying out against Martha Corey, a woman from Salem Town who, like Sarah Osborne, was hardly poor. Corey had the temerity to laugh at the questions posed to her during her examination and the naiveté to affirm that she did not know if there were any witches in New England. Though she was, as she herself claimed, a "Gosple-woman," her heretical remarks helped convince many of her neighbors that she was guilty.[119]

After Corey was arrested in March, possessed females had little trouble discovering their attackers. From this point on, the community was faced with unprecedented numbers of accused witches in its midst. Soon, four-year-old Dorcas Good joined her mother and the others in prison: she was accused of taking supernatural revenge on the possessed for taking away her parent. Not long after, seventy-one-year-old Rebecca Nurse and forty-seven-year-old Elizabeth Proctor, both women from quite prosperous families, were also incarcerated. Nurse was a daughter and Proctor a granddaughter of women thought to have been witches in their own lifetimes.[120]

With the naming of Dorcas Good, Rebecca Nurse, and Elizabeth Proctor, the accusations had begun to include relatives of witches, and with those against Proctor and Martha Corey the outbreak had also moved beyond the boundaries of

Salem Village. John Proctor, staunch defender of his wife's innocence and outspoken critic of both the possessed and the proceedings, was the next witch accused and the first male. He was followed by Mary Easty and Sarah Cloyce, both sisters of Rebecca Nurse. Easty, too, had expressed her outrage at what was happening. Also among the accused in those early weeks were Dorcas Hoar of Beverly, Susanna Martin of Amesbury, and Bridget Bishop of Salem Town, all women who had been accused of witchcraft crimes in the 1660s, 1670s, or 1680s. A number of Elizabeth Proctor's children were named, as were her sister and sister-in-law, and Martha Corey's husband, Giles. Most startling of all, so too was George Burroughs, onetime pastor of the Salem Village church; in the minds of many, he would come to be the "Ring Leader of them all."[121]

Almost from the beginning, some people doubted that what was going on was in fact an outbreak of witchcraft. Most considered the whole episode a "delusion of the Devill's," but there were markedly different opinions about whom he was deluding.[122] The early dissidents expressed no complaints about accusations against Tituba, Sarah Good, or other women the community could agree were likely witches; rather, they limited their protests to the naming of those men and prosperous women whom they considered falsely accused.[123] But the protests were only occasionally heard at first. The jails continued to fill and ministers and magistrates persisted in treating most of the accused, even the church members among them, as the Devil's servants.

While originating with the possessed, most of the accusations resonated with at least some other members of the community besides its officials. Before the trials actually began, hundreds of local residents came forward to join the possessed in testifying against dozens of individual witches about crimes committed years, sometimes even decades, before.[124] The primary concern of those non-possessed accusers was *maleficium*, as it had been in earlier witchcraft cases. Also unchanged, the issue for the possessed was the Satanic pact and the torments witches inflicted upon them for refusing to sign it. Confessing witches, who were frequently present at hearings and who were encouraged to implicate others as well as themselves, also continued to stress their experiences with Satan and not their malefic powers.

It was the *number* of people who spoke about witchcraft in the language of the clergy that so distinguished the 1692–93 Salem cases from others. Between the time when the first six witches were sentenced to die and when they were hanged, possession spread beyond the confines of Salem Village to Andover—and from there to other nearby communities. All told, at least forty-eight persons became possessed during this outbreak, either while the trials were still going on or shortly thereafter. Besides this group, another ten cases of possession surfaced during the Salem events: in these instances, the possession was said to have occurred at some time in the past but to have been caused by the witches on trial in 1692. The number of confessions was staggering as well: before the trials were over, at least fifty people admitted to witchcraft practices. The decision of the authorities not to execute confessing women, as they had formerly, doubtlessly augmented this number, especially since so many of those who maintained their innocence found themselves on the gallows.[125]

Virtually all confessing witches during this period were female; they ranged in age from under ten to over seventy. Females also composed the overwhelming majority of the possessed, as they always had in New England. Although most historical studies of the Salem events refer to the possessed as children, girls, or adolescents, these designations are somewhat misleading: forty-four percent of possessed females were between sixteen and twenty, "single-women" or "maids" in seventeenth-century terms, another 38 percent were over twenty, while only 18 percent were under sixteen.[126] These figures make clear, however, what earlier in the century had only been suggested: to the extent that the clergy had been effective in shaping popular conceptions of witchcraft, their success was primarily among the females in their congregations, especially but not exclusively among younger females. Males held more tenaciously to the traditional concern with *maleficium*. Nearly three-fourths of non-possessed accusers in the Salem outbreak, for whom *maleficium* was the central issue, were men.

Ostensibly more pliant, Salem's confessing witches and, particularly, possessed females, were ultimately more subversive—of witchcraft beliefs in general and of witchcraft prosecutions. For they not only persisted in adding names to the lists, but they increasingly named people whose wealth and reputation made them unlikely suspects in the eyes of the authorities and most of their neighbors. Still, these accusations could not be discounted without damaging the whole fabric of witchcraft belief: the people accused conformed to at least some of the many unspoken assumptions about who witches were. Since that fabric of belief was still integral to New England society, it could not be destroyed, at least not yet. After the Salem executions began in June 1692, the authorities dealt with the growing problem of credibility by ignoring accusations against the well-to-do or by allowing, if not encouraging, them to escape. As the number of executions multiplied, however, this solution became an acute embarrassment to the Puritan elite. By late September, the sheer number as well as the unusual stature of some of the accused had generated serious opposition, even among the clergy and magistrates.[127]

Close to two hundred persons were accused of witchcraft during the Salem outbreak, many of them, minister John Hale later noted, people whose "quality . . . did bespeak better things" and whose "blameless and holy lives before did testify for them."[128] Of the 185 witches identifiable by name, more than three-fourths were female. Nearly half the males were husbands, sons, or other male relatives of accused women. Twenty-two women and five men had been tried and convicted before Governor William Phips called a temporary halt to the proceedings in October 1692. Fourteen women and five men, including minister George Burroughs, had already been hanged. Another man, Giles Corey, had been pressed to death after refusing to enter a plea, and several women and men, among them Sarah Osborne, had died in prison awaiting trial.

By the time Governor Phips suspended the trials, most ministers and magistrates probably agreed with him "that the Devill had taken upon him the name and shape of severall persons who were doubtless innocent."[129] One of those innocents whose shape had recently appeared to the possessed was the governor's own wife, Lady Mary Phips. Another was Sarah Hale, who was married to minister John Hale. Margaret Thatcher, one of the wealthiest women in Massachusetts and mother-in-law to Jonathan Corwin, one of the Salem magistrates, was yet another. So, too, was Samuel Willard, by now minister of Boston's Old South Church and among the most prominent clergymen in New England.[130] With the possessed discovering witches at even this level, no one was immune to accusation.

None of these latter accusations was taken seriously, but they could be ignored only by raising questions about the credibility of possessed persons and confessing witches, and about the validity of the "spectral sight" so long allowed these two groups of women. This was done, publicly, by Increase Mather, in his now-famous essay *Cases of Conscience,* presented first as a sermon to other ministers shortly after the governor suspended the proceedings. Stopping short of calling the possessed liars, he described them as "Daemoniacks," as mouthpieces for the "Father of Lyes." He argued that "no *juror* can with a safe Conscience look on the Testimony of such, as sufficient to take away the Life of any Man," even if, as he implied, the possessed normally knew their real tormentors. Thus, whatever special sight these females claimed concerning the identity of their invisible attackers should be ignored, as God "has taught us not to receive the Devil's Testimony in any thing." Confessing witches were also "not such credible Witnesses." They sometimes lied outright, he said, about their own practices and the names of their "Associates in that Trade"; other times they were deluded by Satan "to dream strange things of themselves and others which are not so."[131]

Cases of Conscience signaled not only the end of the Salem outbreak, but the demise of both Puritan and traditional witchcraft beliefs in New England. Ironically, by repudiating the possessed and confessing witches as reliable witnesses, Mather and the other ministers who endorsed his essay were disavowing the most vocal supporters—and supports—of their witchcraft doctrine. If the possessed were no longer credible, there could be no possession. And without the Devil's efforts to recruit more handmaidens, and the integrity of the women who admitted to capitulating, there could be no covenant. Once the validity of spectral sight was denied, even *maleficium* was bound for official extinction. Since *maleficium* was identified as supernaturally inflicted harm, it would become difficult to link it to particular women if, as Mather admitted, the Devil might well be causing that harm in a woman's shape but without her consent.[132] Had the will been there to reconstruct these beliefs, witchcraft might have endured longer. But with the death of innocents acknowledged[133] and criticism intensifying both at home and abroad, no one undertook this task.[134]

After *Cases of Conscience,* we still find considerable support for "clear[ing] the land" of witches, but even stronger feeling that the evidence should be more carefully scrutinized.[135] As a result, the Court of Oyer and Terminer, which had conducted the Salem trials, was dismissed in late October 1692 and a special session of the Superior Court of Judicature called a couple of months later to handle the remaining cases. With the magistrates now reluctant to accept the kind of testimony that had convicted many a New England witch, most of the trials that winter ended with acquittals. Those few women who were convicted, confessing witches all, were soon reprieved by the governor. Despite the discovery of several new cases of possession in other towns, accusations against new witches all

went unheeded. By May, most of the accused had returned to
their families, and the most dramatic episode in New England's
history was for the most part over.

Witchcraft itself had not yet run its full course. During the
early months of the Salem events, witchcraft accusations spread
to Fairfield, Connecticut. In September 1692, Hartford magistrates set up a special Fairfield court to try the growing number of witches there. As in Salem, possession held center stage,
but scores of non-possessed accusers came into court to relate
tales of their ongoing personal disputes with the accused, and
the supernatural vengeance that inevitably followed. Mercy
Desborough, one of the first of at least seven witches named,
was tried and found guilty, but the turn of events in Salem
decisively influenced the handling of her case from then on.
Hesitant to execute her, the magistrates turned to the local
clergy for advice. Taking their cue from their Massachusetts
counterparts, the ministers found the evidence slender and
one of the principal accusers, possessed servant Katherine
Branch, at best unreliable and at worst duplicitous. But the
clergy refused to make a strong recommendation either way,
and the jurors were instructed to reconsider their verdict. When
the jurors returned the same verdict, the magistrates finally
approved it and Desborough was sentenced to hang. Fortu-
nately, Desborough's sentencing came just at the time the
Connecticut Court of Assistants decided to launch its own
investigation of witchcraft evidence and just after Massachusetts Governor Phips pardoned the remaining Salem accused.
Perhaps also because Desborough had the support of one of
Connecticut's most prominent men, the magistrates ordered
her reprieved. All of the other witches were acquitted, or their
cases dismissed without trial.[136]

1694–1725

After the Salem and Fairfield outbreaks, only two people
in New England were sent by local officials to the higher court

to be tried as witches: Winifred Benham of Wallingford and her thirteen-year-old daughter and namesake. The elder Benham, possibly the daughter of an earlier Boston witch, Mary Hale, originally came under suspicion in 1692, but the New Haven County court had dismissed the case for insufficient evidence. Her husband's threat to shoot her accuser did not end the rumors, and the following year she was in court again on the same charge. She was released again, this time required to post bond of £20 for her good behavior. The church soon after added their censure by excommunicating her. When she was accused a third time in 1697, this time of possessing several of her neighbors' children, she was sent to Hartford for trial, along with her daughter, who was by now implicated in her crimes. But the grand jury refused to give credence to the accusation and the cases were dismissed without trials. The court's action failed to clear the Benhams of suspicion, however, and the family soon moved to the less hostile environment of New York.[137]

The Benham cases were unusual. To be sure, some people still believed that witches plagued their communities, but in the aftermath of the Salem outbreak witch trials were no longer countenanced by either ministers or magistrates, nor, it would seem, by the larger community. Many people who had participated in the Salem events still had to reach reconciliations with themselves and their neighbors, so public atonements and justifications continued into the eighteenth century.[138] Formal accusations, however, vanished along with public witchcraft rituals. Women once suspected of using supernatural power to harm, though still objects of fear and hatred, no longer had to fear for their lives. And the many activities once attributed to Satan worship became simply sins against God, crimes against the state, or unwomanly behavior. Considering how long witchcraft beliefs and prosecutions had been regular features of community social relations, it is remarkable that within a very brief period of time most New Englanders stopped believing that their personal and collective misfortunes could be attributed to the malice of witches.

Emblematic of this profoundly altered mood was the response of the Connecticut authorities to the witchcraft accusation lodged against Sarah Spencer of Colchester in 1724. When Elizabeth Ackley said she had been hagridden and pinched by the shape of her sister-in-law, and Ackley's husband threatened to retaliate for his wife's torments, Spencer sued for defamation, arguing that by taking away her reputation, the accusation had "distroyed her Living"—she "being a poor and aged Widow [who] for her Livelyhood . . . did Live by her Labour amongst her Neighbors." The court, as they had done before—though usually not in cases involving indigent women—awarded the plaintiff damages (originally £5, later reduced to one shilling). But for what appears to be the first time in New England's history, the magistrates considered submitting the accusers to a medical examination to determine whether or not they were sane.[139]

TWO

The Demographic Basis
of Witchcraft

Mᴏsᴛ ᴡɪᴛᴄʜᴄʀᴀғᴛ sᴜsᴘɪᴄɪᴏɴs in colonial New England orginated in conflicts among people who knew one another. No one could be certain that an angry encounter with a neighbor would not elicit an accusation. Still, not everyone was equally vulnerable to the accusation of witchcraft. More importantly, not everyone was equally vulnerable to trial, conviction, and execution. For the process by which the community identified the witches in its midst was quite selective. It was informed not only by the witchcraft beliefs described in the first chapter—these could be applied to almost anyone—but also by several widely shared if largely unspoken assumptions about the kinds of people likely to align themselves with Satan.

Some New Englanders were likely witches, others were not. People who did not fit the shared image of the witch could certainly be accused, but except during outbreaks they were almost always vindicated early in the process. Sometimes people in the community simply ignored such accusations or refused to lend them public support. In some cases local authorities prevented further action by dismissing the charges as insubstantial or by punishing accusers for defaming the character of the accused. Even when local courts took an accusation seriously, colony-wide courts responsible for prosecuting witches might refuse to hear the case. By all of these means, accusations against *unlikely* witches were actively discouraged.

But for other townspeople, vindication came grudgingly, if at all. These persons conformed to enough of the accepted notions about witches to be tried, and often convicted and punished, for their alleged crimes. Indeed, it is because of the remarkable regularity with which certain kinds of people came before New England's highest courts on witchcraft charges that we can reconstruct the identity of the colonial witch and understand why witches constituted such a formidable threat to their neighbors. In identifying the colonial witch, however, we will look at the lives of all the accused. For even the most unlikely among the accused usually exhibited some of the characteristics of the witch.

Consider then, in this chapter and two that follow, a collective portrait of New England witches. We will see that whatever else New Englanders explicitly said witchcraft was, their beliefs were most vividly and reliably expressed in action—in the regularity with which they singled out specific kinds of people as their most powerful enemies.

The single most salient characteristic of witches was their sex. At least 344 persons were accused of witchcraft in New England between 1620 and 1725.[1] Of the 342 who can be identified by sex, 267 (78 percent) were female. Roughly half of the seventy-five males accused (thirty-six), as the historian John Demos has pointed out, were "suspect by association": they were the husbands, sons, other kin, or public supporters of female witches.[2]

Although the association of women and witchcraft was evident throughout the period, it was stronger in the ongoing, year-by-year accusations than it was during the Hartford, Salem, and Fairfield outbreaks. Of the 150 persons accused in non-outbreak witchcraft cases, 124 (83 percent) were female. During the Hartford, Salem, and Fairfield outbreaks, when witch fear was particularly intense, and when suspicion extended not only to relatives and associates of witches but to other people in and beyond the community, the proportion of men accused grew. But even during these periods, females made up 156 of the 205 persons named (76 percent).[3] At *all* times, women were much more likely suspects than men.

The idea that witches were women seems to have been more strongly held by local authorities, magistrates, and juries—men who had the power to decide the fates of the accused—than it was by accusers as a whole. This bias is most noticeable in non-outbreak witchcraft cases: although women made up a sizeable 83 percent of the accused in these cases, and although local officials sent roughly the same proportion of female and male suspects to the colony-wide courts for trial, fifteen of the sixteen *convicted* witches (94 percent) were women (see table 1). The only man to be found guilty was Wethersfield carpenter John Carrington, who was hanged with his wife Joan in 1651.[4] Though he was married to a reputed witch and was one of the poorest men in his community, it remains unclear why, leaving outbreaks aside, he was the only man to receive a punishment normally reserved for women.[5] Three of the four women who were convicted but not executed were pun-

TABLE 1.   Sex of Witches, in Non-outbreak Witchcraft Cases, New England, 1620–1725

Action	Female	Male	Total
Accused	124	26	150
Tried	31	6	37
Convicted	15	1	16
Executed	11	1	12

ished by banishment, imprisonment, or house arrest. The fourth woman was released and soon fled to the safety of Rhode Island.[6]

During outbreaks, the reaction of the authorities to witchcraft accusations presents a more complicated, if finally consistent, picture. Though proportionately more men found themselves under suspicion during outbreaks than at other times, officials seem to have been even more reluctant than usual to give credence to these suspicions (see table 2). While they decided to try fifty-eight of the 156 women accused (37 percent), they indicted only eight of the forty-nine men (16 percent). *Once tried*, however, men were in unusually great danger of being convicted and executed. Six of the eight men who were tried were found guilty and hanged. Four of these were related to female witches. Of the other two, one was John Willard, who was a newcomer to Salem Village, and about whom very little is known. The other was former Salem Village minister George Burroughs, who had left the community abruptly nearly a decade before, leaving many enemies behind.[7]

The risks to men during outbreaks can be exaggerated, however. Women were still the primary objects of witch fear. If the overall figures for outbreaks suggest that men who were tried were even more likely to lose their lives than women who were tried, this largely reflects the peculiar dynamics of the Salem episode. First of all, the executions of at least eight con-

TABLE 2.   Sex of Witches, in Outbreak Witchcraft Cases, New England, 1620–1725

Action	Female	Male	Total
Accused	156	49	205
Tried	58	8	66
Convicted	30	6	36
Executed	17	6	23

victed women in Salem were postponed initially, in two cases because the women were pregnant, in most of the others because the women had confessed and were important sources for identifying other witches. Before any of these women could be hanged, opposition to the proceedings had grown so strong that Governor Phips had disbanded the Court of Oyer and Terminer created specifically to handle the Salem cases.

Even more telling, official treatment of the accused during the Salem outbreak changed significantly after the Court of Oyer and Terminer was dismissed in October 1692. Scores of accused witches, many of whom were still housed in local jails, had not yet been tried. The Superior Court of Judicature, designated to deal with the remaining cases, saw reason to indict only twenty-nine of these people, ignoring most of the others and discharging "by proclamation" the rest of those in custody.[8] Of the twenty-nine persons tried in the early months of 1693, twenty-seven (93 percent) were women and young girls. Given widespread opposition at this point to *any* prosecutions, only three of these women were convicted. But in what would be just about the last witchcraft indictments in New England, the courts demonstrated how reluctant they were to consider men as witches.

Indeed, a comparison of the relative treatment of women and men during individual outbreaks reveals that it was only at the height of the Salem outbreak that the secular authorities relinquished to any significant degree their assumption that witches were women (see table 3). Although six of the seven men who were executed for witchcraft in New England died during outbreaks, five of the six were hanged in Salem.

Statistics can establish the extent to which New Englanders considered witchcraft the special province of women, but they cannot convey the vindictiveness that characterized the treatment of female suspects. This sexual double standard is perhaps most vividly seen in the different punishments meted out to confessed witches outside of the Salem outbreak.

Deeming voluntary confession one of the best "proofes

TABLE 3. Sex of Witches, by Individual Outbreak, New England, 1620–1725

Outbreak	Action	Female	Male	Total
Hartford	Accused	9	4	13
(1662–63)	Tried	4	1	5
	Convicted	3	1	4
	Executed	3	1	4
Salem	Accused	141	44	185
(1692–93)	Tried	52	7	59
	Convicted	26	5	31
	Executed	14	5	19
Fairfield	Accused	6	1	7
(1692–93)	Tried	2	0	2
	Convicted	1	0	1
	Executed	0	0	0

sufficient for Conviccon,"[9] ministers and magistrates put considerable pressure on women to admit they had covenanted with the Devil.[10] No comparable coercion was used with men. When Wethersfield's Mary Johnson succumbed to this insistence in 1648, admitting that she and the Devil provided many services for one another, she was convicted of familiarity with Satan and hanged.[11] After Rebecca Greensmith described the nature of her covenant with Satan in Hartford in 1662, she too was executed.[12] Similarly, confession doomed the widow Glover in Boston in 1688.[13] Except during the Salem events, when the magistrates decided to put off the executions of people who admitted their guilt until all local witches were discovered, women who incriminated themselves were almost all punished in accordance with the biblical injuction, "Thou shall not suffer a witch to live."[14]

Men who incriminated themselves were treated quite differently. When John Bradstreet of Rowley confessed in 1652 to having familiarity with Satan, the Essex County court ordered him whipped or fined "for telling a lie."[15] In 1674, Christopher Brown was also released by Essex County magistrates, on the grounds that *his* confession seemed "inconsistent with the truth," despite his admission that he had been "discoursing with . . . the devil."[16] Though Hugh Crosia of Stratford confessed in 1692 that he had "signed to the devells book and then seald it with his bloud" five years earlier, and that ever since he had "been practising Eivel against Every man," the Connecticut Court of Assistants refused to try him, discharging him upon payment of his jail fees and the costs of bringing him to Hartford.[17] Men who confessed to witchcraft outside of the Salem outbreak were punished, to be sure—but whereas most confessing women were taken at their word and executed, confessing men were almost all rebuked as liars.[18]

Even when the courts took charges against individual men more seriously, their responses to these men were noticeably less severe than were their responses to the women whose cases they acted upon. As the following accounts illustrate, the repercussions of an accusation were likely to be far graver and longer lasting for a woman than for a man, even when their personal circumstances and the evidence were strikingly similar.

Both Eunice Cole of Hampton and John Godfrey of Essex County had long-standing reputations for witchcraft practices, and both were rumored to be particularly powerful witches. Both appear in New England court records several times in this connection over a period of many years—Cole between 1656 and 1680, Godfrey between 1659 and 1669. Both were indicted on charges much like those brought against other witches: consulting with familiar spirits, covenanting with the Devil, bewitching their neighbors and their neighbors' cattle.

In spite of widespread assumptions about their guilt, however, their confrontations with the New Hampshire and Massachusetts authorities and the subsequent reactions of their communities were markedly dissimilar.

Eunice Cole was first tried for witchcraft crimes in Boston in the fall of 1656. It was not her first court appearance; she had been brought before local magistrates in Essex and Norfolk counties on several occasions for lesser crimes, the first time in 1645, when she was charged with making "slanderous speeches."[19] Her reckless speech also figured strongly in the evidence presented in her witchcraft trial. Goodwife Marston and Susanna Palmer testified "that goodwife Cole said that shee was sure there was a witche in the towne, and she knew where hee dwelt" and that Cole had also said that she had known somebody years before who was "bewitched as goodwife marston's childe was." Thomas Philbrick, who had lost two calves, deposed that Goody Cole had let him know that if his calves ate "any of hir grass she wished it might poyson them or choke them." Richard Ormsby, constable of Salisbury, said that when he had stripped Cole for whipping he saw "under one of hir brests . . . a bleu thing like unto a teate hanging downeward about thre quarters of an inche longe . . . [with] some blood with other moystness [which she said] was a sore."[20]

On this and other like testimony, Cole was apparently convicted. The magistrates were reluctant to execute her, however. Instead, they sentenced her to what she afterwards called a "duble" punishment: both to be whipped and to be imprisoned "during [her] life or the pleasure of the court."[21] She spent most of the next twelve to fifteen years incarcerated in the Boston jail.

Probably within the first year of her imprisonment, Eunice Cole petitioned the General Court for her release, pleading her own "aged and weake . . . condition" and the infirmities of her husband, William Cole, who, "being 88 yeeres of Age," needed the kind of care that "none but a wife would" provide.

She also asked the magistrates to consider the condition of "that little estate" she and her husband had accumulated in Hampton, which, she averred, she had been "the greatest instrument under God to get us" but which "all goes to ruine" in her absence. Alluding to the criminal behavior that had brought her to her present straits, she promised "for the future . . . to behave [herself] both in word and deed towards those amongst whom" she dwelt.[22] Although the magistrates' response to Cole's plea has not survived, they were evidently unwilling to release her at this time.

In 1659, William Cole sent a petition of his own to the General Court, describing the predicament both he and the town of Hampton were in because of his wife's imprisonment, and asking the magistrates for "some relief in the case." He could not farm the land alone, he said, and could not afford to hire someone to assist him because he had signed his estate over to his wife sometime previously, "to keep her from going away from him." Unable to eke out a subsistence and on the verge of perishing, he had had to call upon the town for relief, which had been suppplied. But, he added, "without recourse to a lawsuit . . . , the town could recover nothing for the assistance rendered."[23]

Goodman Cole does not seem to have been disingenuous about his or the town's plight. He and his wife had no children to assist them with the farm labor, and in 1658, at least, the town apparently provided him with some aid.[24] In 1656, moreover, the same year that Goodwife Cole was tried for witchcraft, he had signed a deed of gift, transferring "all his estate" to his wife—though years later witnesses testified that the transfer was to occur "at his death."[25] Whatever significance this 1656 deed had for William Cole or his community, the General Court invalidated it in 1659. In response to William Cole's petition, they ordered "that the town of Hampton should take into their possession all the estate belonging to the said Cole, or his wife—as was pretended—and out of said estate, or otherwise, as they should see cause, supply the said

Cole's and his wife's necessities during their lives."[26]

If William Cole specifically requested his wife's liberty in his 1659 petition, his words went unrecorded. But within a year, Eunice Cole was back in Hampton. Despite her earlier promise to watch her tongue, she was soon presented at the county court for "unseemly speeches."[27] By 1662, whether for this reason or some other, she had been returned to the Boston prison. In that year, her husband died and she petitioned again for her freedom.[28]

Shortly before his death, William Cole had written a will that voided his earlier transfer of his property to his wife and left his £59 estate (minus debts) to his neighbor Thomas Webster, with the stipulation that Webster provide for him "Comfortably" for the duration of his life.[29] The Hampton selectmen, who officially controlled the Cole estate, were not happy with this will; nor were they pleased with the possibility that Eunice Cole might be allowed to return again to their town. Boston jailer William Salter, who had not been paid, at least not in full, by the selectmen for Eunice Cole's prison maintenance, was also upset. When the General Court met on 8 October 1662, they had to consider not only Eunice Cole's petition but one from Salter and one from the town of Hampton. In answer to all three, the magistrates ordered "that the said Unice Cole pay what is due on arreares to the keeper, and be released the prison, on condicion that she depart, within one month after her release, out of this jurisdiction, and not to returne againe on poenalty of hir former sentenc being executed against hir."[30]

Cole was released at this time, but she did not leave the colony within the month. Almost immediately upon her return to Hampton, witchcraft suspicions resurfaced and before long she found herself back in prison.[31] Meanwhile, William Cole's estate was being settled: by October 1663, the county court had divided the remaining Cole property between Thomas Webster and Eunice Cole, but arranged for Cole's share—by now only £8—to be paid to the Hampton selectmen "for her use."[32] Evidently, the town had still not completely paid the costs of keeping her in prison, because in 1664 William Salter had one of the Hampton selectmen arrested for ignoring his demand for Cole's fees.[33] In 1665, Cole petitioned yet another time for her release. And again the court consented, this time stipulating only that she give security for her permanent departure from the colony.[34] With little or nothing left of her estate, she could not meet the requirements and remained in jail.

At some point between 1668 and 1671, Eunice Cole was discharged from the Boston prison, but by 1671 she was back in Hampton, completely destitute. The selectmen arranged for her maintenance by providing her with what, according to the folklore of the region, was a "hut" along the Hampton River, and by requiring that a different family supply her with food and fuel each week.[35] In 1673, however, she was back in front of the Boston court facing another witchcraft charge. This time she was accused of appearing in various human and animal shapes to entice a young girl "to come to live with her," of "inchanting [the] oven" of the constable who was responsible for bring her the provisions her neighbors supplied, and of committing many other crimes, both recent and long-standing.[36] She was acquitted of all specific charges, but with the strong reservations of the court: "In the case of unis cole now prisoner att the Bar—not Legally guilty according to Inditement butt just ground of vehement suspissyon of her having had famillyarryty with the devill."[37] In spite of the court's reluctance, Cole was allowed to return again to Hampton.

There is little information on how Cole fared the next several years, but clearly her reputation as a witch did not diminish. By 1680, she was in prison again, awaiting the decision of the Hampton court as to whether she should be tried a third time. After hearing testimony, the court decided the evidence was insufficient for indictment—but not for punishment. The presiding magistrate allowed that there was "not full proofe" that she was a witch but, he added, "the Court vehemently suspects her so to be." He ordered her imprisoned again "until this Court take further order," this time "with a lock to be kept on her legg" to prevent her escape.[38]

Little else about Cole's life can be verified. According to local legend, she was released from prison one more time and lived out her last days in the hovel by the river, completely ostracized by the community. When she died, it is said, her body was dragged outdoors, pushed into a shallow grave, and a stake driven through it "in order to exorcise the baleful influence she was supposed to have possessed."[39]

John Godfrey, it would seem, was a no less troubling figure to his Essex County neighbors than was Eunice Cole to the people of Hampton. Beginning in 1648, when he was indicted for "subborning a witness," until his death in 1675, Godfrey was brought before the magistrates for minor criminal offenses numerous times, and sometimes to answer to more serious charges.[40] Single, without family,[41] a herdsman by occupation, he had no permanent residence or employment; he lived and worked where he could and was repeatedly involved in litigation with his more stable neighbors. Though by no means prosperous, he had some resources. He supported himself in part by lending small sums of money at rates considered usurious by at least some men in the community.[42]

Like Eunice Cole, Godfrey was known for coarse language and frequent talk of witches. When he was first brought into local court on witchcraft charges in 1659, several members of the Tyler family accused him of saying to Job Tyler that an animal familiar had come "to suck your wife," a statement tantamount to calling her a witch.[43] Perhaps more serious in the eyes of his neighbors, Godfrey was said to have been in the habit of "speakeing about the power of witches." Witness Charles Browne testified that

the sayd Godfrye spoke that if witches were not kindly
entertayned the devill will apeare unto them and aske them
if they were greeved or vexed with any body and aske them
what he should do for them. And if they would not give
them beer or victalls, they might let all the beere run out
of the cellar. And if they lookt steadfastly upon any creature it would dye. And it were hard to some witches to take
away life either of man or beast, yet when they once begin
it then it is easye to them.[44]

In addition, Godfrey was accused of carrying out his thinly
veiled threats by causing "strange losses in . . . swine and cows
and calves," as well as afflicting the bodies of his neighbors.[45]

Godfrey had not taken these charges lightly. In fact, he
had initiated a defamation suit against two of his twenty-four
accusers, and it appears from the records that the local
authorities dealt with both Godfrey's and his neighbors' grievances at the same time. They found Godfrey justified in his
complaint that William Simmons and his son had slandered
him by "charging him to be a witch." But they also added that
"the jury notwithstanding doe conceive that by the testimo-
nyes he is rendered suspicious."[46] On this basis, they bound
him over to one of the higher courts for trial.[47] The official
proceedings against him have been lost, but the evidence suggests that the higher court either refused to try the case or
acquitted him. Shortly thereafter, he was back home among
his Andover, Haverhill, and other Essex County neighbors.[48]

In 1663, Godfrey lodged a slander suit against Jonathan
Singletary, a young adversary who had gone to prison rather
than pay Godfrey what the county court had determined was
a fair settlement of a protracted financial disagreement between
them.[49] According to Godfrey, Singletary had defamed him
by "calling him a witch," by saying "is this witch on this syde
Boston Galloes yet," and by "reporting that [Godfrey] went
into Ipswich prison in the night when the doors were locked
and when [Singletary] was in the prison."[50] The court found
in Godfrey's favor, both that year and the next, when the case
was appealed. Singletary responded to the charges by relating

again how Godfrey had several times appeared to him in jail, frightening him, threatening him, and urging him to resolve their dispute and end his imprisonment by paying Godfrey the court-affirmed debt.[51]

Although this accusation does not seem to have led to a witchcraft prosecution, Singletary's testimony may have been added to the mass of evidence presented against Godfrey during his only recorded trial early in 1666; it is clear that evidence from his 1659 hearing was resubmitted along with depositions concerning his more recent crimes.[52] The new testimony confirmed the message of the old. For years Godfrey and his neighbors had been in open and often bitter conflict, and Godfrey more often than not came out ahead. His enemies had come to see him both as having an advantage that could only come from the Devil, and as a cause of their other troubles as well.

After deliberation, the jury acquitted him, albeit with strong misgivings: "Wee finde him not to have the feare of God in his heart. He have made himself . . . suspitiously Guilty of witchcraft, but not legally guilty, according to lawe and evidence wee have received."[53] Repeated suspicion was enough to require him to pay the costs of his trial; it was not sufficient to inflict upon him the kind of retaliatory measures executed against Eunice Cole. Godfrey was allowed to return to his established—if marginal—way of living.

Consider this final note on Godfrey and the relative complacency with which the authorities viewed accusations against him. In 1669, Godfrey appeared in the county court for the last time in connection with witchcraft. The case was another slander suit, this time brought by Godfrey against Daniel Ela of Haverhill "for reporting that he, the said Godfrey, was seene at Ipswich, and at Salisbury, at the same time"—a feat that presumably only a witch could perform.[54] This time the court found not for Godfrey but for his accuser. Moreover, the testimony of the slander trial suggests that the decision was not simply about whether Ela had indeed spread the story, but

whether or not it was true. What is striking here is that the
verdict in favor of Ela was not followed by an attempt to institute proceedings against Godfrey—even though this man was
widely believed to be in league with the Devil.[55] It appears
that he, and men like him, were considered much less dangerous to the community than were women like Eunice Cole. The
threat these men posed was of a type different from that
understandable as witchcraft.

The dissimilar treatment accorded Cole and Godfrey by
their respective communities was by no means unusual. In
general, among witchcraft suspects reluctantly released by
the authorities, women could expect that community reprisals against them would be harsher than those against
men.

For example, when seaman Caleb Powell was brought
before the Essex County court in the winter of 1679–80 for
"working with the devil to the molesting of William Morse and
his family," he was told to post a £20 bond "for the answering
of the . . . complaint" against him at the next county court,
"or else he was to be carried to prison." After local magistrates
heard the testimony against him, they decided that he had
"given such ground of suspicion of his so dealing, that we cannot so acquit him, but that he justly deserves to beare his owne
shame and the costs of the prosecution of the Complaint."[56]
Women were also required to post security bonds for their
appearance in court and to pay court costs when the evidence
was found strong but insufficient, but many times they were
subjected to additional punishments as well. When the New
Haven General Court decided that the evidence presented
against Elizabeth Godman in 1655 was "not sufficient as yet
to take away her life, yet the suspitions are cleere and many,"
they threatened to return her to prison if she did not "for-
beare from goeing from house to house to give offenc, and
cary it orderly in the family where she is"—and they insisted

that she post a £50 bond for her continuing good behavior.[57] Similarly, in 1680, when the Hampton court decided that the testimony submitted against Rachel Fuller and Isabella Towle was not strong enough to try them as witches, it ordered "that they still continew in prisson till bond be given for theire good behavior of £100 apeece during the Courts pleasure"[58] Overall, the initial bonds required of women were considerably higher that those required of men,[59] and men rarely if ever had to provide security for their behavior *after* they were acquitted or the prosecution of the complaint had been dropped.

The need to post substantial security bonds could disrupt the lives of accused women in ways not immediately obvious. Witchcraft suspicions, as we shall see, very often originated in property disputes, and the additional burden of posting a bond for their good behavior seems to have made it difficult if not impossible for women to pursue their claims against their adversaries. At least this was the perception of Portsmouth's Hannah Jones, who had been quarreling for years with her next-door neighbor George Walton over land that both maintained was legally their own.[60] Her 1682 petition to the New Hampshire Provincial Council suggests the restraining effect of a bond in such cases:

> . . . that your Honors would please to take into your consideration her present strait, which is in regard of George Walton's dealing with her, who falsely accuseth her of what she is clear of, and hath so far prevailed that upon that account your humble petitioner is bound in a bond of the peace; since which said Walton's horse breaks into her pasture and doth her damage; and your petitioner, being under bond, knows not what to do to help herself, fearing lest any ways advantage may be taken against her for breaking her bond.[61]

Since most Portsmouth residents supported Jones's claim to the parcel of land in contention in 1682, Walton had not been successful in establishing his right to it—at least not before his political allies came to power in New Hampshire. Apparently it was the newly appointed Secretary of the Province, who boarded in the Walton household, who decided that Walton's accusation warranted the stipulation that Jones put up part or all of her estate as security for her good behavior.[62]

The burden of accusation fell especially hard on women in other ways as well. Once formally accused, they often found themselves faced with repeated witchcraft charges, even if they were fully exonerated by the courts (in itself a much rarer occurrence for women than for men). When Portsmouth's Jane Walford was first named as a witch in 1648, the county court demanded that her accuser, Elizabeth Row, publicly acknowledge her slanderous remarks and that she and her husband, Nicholas Row, pay Walford £2 damages as well as the costs of court.[63] Eight years later, in 1656, Nicholas Row was one of at least seven persons to come forward to testify about Jane Walford's witchcraft. This time local magistrates seem to have taken the matter more seriously, putting Walford under a £20 bond for her appearance at the next court. Still, when they reviewed the evidence against her the following year, they discharged her "by three times proclamation."[64] In 1669, she was awarded £5 in a slander suit she initiated against physician Robert Couch for saying "the said Jane was a witch and he would prove her one."[65] In spite of repeated acknowledgments of her innocence, however, the stigma of witchcraft continued for the rest of Walford's life—and even after her death. This stigma was apparently passed on to all five of her daughters, including the same Hannah Jones mentioned above. Among Jones's complaints against George Walton in 1682 was that he defamed not only Hannah herself, but her deceased mother as well.[66]

Mary Staplies' history in Fairfield was similar to Walford's. Concluding that they saw "no cause to lay any blemish of a witch upon Goodwife Staplies" in 1654, the New Haven court awarded Thomas Staplies £10 "for reparation of his wives name" and £5 for "his trouble and charge" in prosecuting his complaint against her accuser, Roger Ludlow.[67] But Mary Staplies' name was never fully repaired. In 1692, she was again accused of witchcraft—this time along with her daughter and granddaughter, Mary and Hannah Harvey.[68] While many other women shared Staplies' and Walford's fate, only two men seem to have lived in the shadow of recurrent suspicion, one of whom was John Godfrey, whose history we have recounted.[69]

A 1663 slander suit brought by Hartford merchant John Blackleach, Jr., exhibits some measure of the unequal impact accusations had on men and women. Charging that witchcraft allegations originating with his neighbor John Stedman had injured both himself and his wife, Elizabeth Blackleach, he asked the court to award *him* £80 "for unjust molestation" and "defamation." In addition, he asked for £40 "in behalf of his wife" for unjust molestation, and a more substantial £200 for defamation of his wife's character.[70] Perhaps Elizabeth, as a woman, had been more severely slandered; perhaps also, John perceived the long-term damage to her reputation to be much more serious than to his. Jane Walford of Portsmouth set the cost imposed by the suspicions and fears of her neighbors even higher: in 1669, she asked the county court for a whopping £1000 damages from her accuser, Robert Couch.[71] Though the courts rarely awarded a plaintiff in a witchcraft defamation suit more than £15 (and usually much less), these suits suggest that to the accused themselves no amount of reparation seemed too much to ask.

As we have seen, the damage from which people like the Blackleaches, Jane Walford, and Mary Staplies sought relief could range from the simple enmity of one's neighbors to the loss of property, of freedom of movement, and of life itself. Though the burden of accusations fell disproportionately on women in colonial New England, not all women were equally vulnerable. Other demographic characteristics affected the likelihood, first, that a particular woman would be accused of witchcraft, and second, that the accusation would have serious ramifications. Age was one of the most important of these characteristics.

For women born in England or in the colonies during the early years of settlement, records regarding age are scarce. Still, of the 267 females known to have been accused of witchcraft in New England in the seventeenth and early eighteenth centuries, 156 can be identified by approximate age, and an additional forty-eight can be described as under forty, over forty, or over sixty (see table 4). At first glance, these figures suggest that the popular image of the witch as an old woman does not conform to the evidence. Although 119 (58 percent) of the accused witches were over forty, only thirty-seven (18 percent) are known to have been over sixty, what we—or our colonial New England ancestors—might consider "old."[72] And what seems more striking is the extent to which females of *all* ages were susceptible to witchcraft allegations—from four-year-

TABLE 4.   Age of Female Witches, New England, 1620–1725

Age	Females
Under 10	3
10–19	23
20–29	26
30–39	23
40–49	31
50–59	23
60–69	19
70–79	7
Over 80	1
Under 40 (exact age unknown)	10
Over 40 (exact age unknown)	28
Over 60 (exact age unknown)	10
TOTAL	204

old Dorcas Good of Salem to twenty-eight-year-old Elizabeth Blackleach of Hartford, to forty-seven-year-old Isabella Towle of Hampton, to seventy-five-year-old Margaret Scott of Rowley.[73]

But a closer look at the evidence suggests that women under forty were, in fact, unlikely witches in Puritan society (see table 5).[74] Though frequently suspected of witchcraft, only a quarter of those accused women under forty eventually faced trial. More significantly, women under forty were rarely found among convicted witches. Two-thirds of the females in this age group (fifty-seven of eighty-five), moreover, were named during a single event, the Salem outbreak. Most of the Salem accused in this group never came to trial, and almost all those who did were tried in the early months of 1693, when the outbreak was essentially over. Only five women under forty were convicted in 1692–93, and just *one*—thirty-eight-year-old Sarah Good—was executed.[75] Of the twenty-eight females in this younger age group who were accused outside of Salem, only two were ever indicted. If the identification of a witch was a process of social consensus that reached beyond the simple leveling of a charge—that required enough community support to warrant a bill of indictment—then women under forty cannot be considered part of the population most at risk.

Females under forty are perhaps best characterized as a

TABLE 5. Female Witches under Forty, New England, 1620–1725

Action	Females, Salem Cases	Females, All Other Cases	Total
Accused	57	28	85
Tried	19	2	21
Convicted	5	0	5
Executed	1	0	1

group analogous to the male relatives of female witches. Indeed, like these men, roughly half of the females in this younger group (forty-six of eighty-five) *were* related to (older) female witches. Also like these men, women under forty were most vulnerable to accusation, trial, and conviction during outbreaks (particularly the one at Salem), when established notions about who could be a witch broadened temporarily to include individuals under the potential influence of witches. Seventeen of the nineteen women under forty tried in Salem in 1692–93 (close to 90 percent) were daughters, granddaughters, or other relatives of female witches. The aged Lydia Dustin of Reading, for instance, was called into court along with her two daughters, thirty-nine-year-old Sarah Dustin and forty-two-year-old Mary Colson (her granddaughter, sixteen-year-old Elizabeth Colson was also accused, but she escaped before she could be prosecuted).[76] Only three women in this under-forty group, two of whom were between thirty-five and thirty-nine, seem to have been the main targets of accusations in 1692.

Women over forty, on the other hand, were consistently more vulnerable to accusation, whether or not the community was in the grips of an outbreak, and they fared much worse once charged (see table 6). Almost 40 percent of older accused women (47 of 119) were brought to trial and well over half of those tried were convicted. Women over forty were in greater

TABLE 6. Female Witches over Forty, New England, 1620–1725

Action	Females, Salem Cases	Females, All Other Cases	Total
Accused	66	53	119
Tried	28	19	47
Convicted	19	8	27
Executed	12	5	17

danger during the Salem outbreak than they were at other times, but at any time they had much more to fear from an accusation than did women under forty.

But what about women over sixty years of age? Were accusations lodged against these women as likely to be taken as seriously as accusations against women who were between forty and fifty-nine? The question is particularly important in light of recent research on New England witchcraft, which suggests that contrary to the popular stereotype, middle-aged rather than old women were the prime targets of accusation.[77]

I have located fifty-three women over forty who were accused of witchcraft apart from the Salem events. The ages of thirty-three of these women can be fixed closely enough to classify them as either middle-aged or old: twenty-three were between forty and fifty-nine, and ten were sixty or over (see table 7). Of the twenty-three middle-aged women, nine were tried and two found guilty. One of the convicted women was Elizabeth Kendall of Cambridge, who was in her mid-forties when she was executed in 1651.[78] The other was fifty-two-year-old Mercy Desborough of Fairfield, who was tried and

TABLE 7. Age Groups, Female Witches over Forty, New England, 1620–1725

	Action	Women 40–59	Women over 60	Total
Non-Salem Cases	Accused	23	10	33
	Tried	9	3	12
	Convicted	2	1	3
	Executed	1	0	1
Salem Cases	Accused	31	17	48
	Tried	15	13	28
	Convicted	8	11	19
	Executed	4	8	12

sentenced to die in October 1692—at the height of the Fairfield outbreak—but was reprieved the next year, at about the
same time that the remaining women condemned at Salem
were pardoned.[79] Of the ten old women accused as witches
outside of Salem, three were tried and one was convicted. The
woman who was found guilty, sixty-five-year-old Elizabeth
Morse, was not executed, though she was punished. After
spending almost a year in prison, and after her husband had
sent two petitions to the Boston magistrates, Morse was allowed
to return home in 1681, "Provided she goe not above sixteen
Rods from hir Oune house and land at any time except to the
meeting house."[80] Although in the non-Salem cases, women
over sixty made up only about 30 percent of accused women
over forty, *once accused,* old women seem to have been treated
comparably to their middle-aged counterparts.

During the Salem outbreak, old women who were accused
of witchcraft were in noticeably greater danger than middle-
aged suspects: composing only a slightly higher proportion of
accused witches over forty (35 percent) than in other years,
once accused, old women at Salem were more likely than middle-aged women to be tried, convicted, and executed (see table 7). Of the sixty-six women over forty accused at Salem,
forty-eight can be identified as either middle-aged or old: thirty-
one were between forty and fifty-nine, while seventeen were
sixty or over. Just about half of the middle-aged women were
prosecuted, half of the prosecuted women were found guilty,
and half of those found guilty were hanged. Among the seventeen old women who were accused, three-quarters were
prosecuted, four-fifths of the prosecuted women were found
guilty, and close to three-quarters of those found guilty were
hanged. In contrast to the non-Salem cases, the older the
woman at Salem, the more likely that she would suffer the
most serious consequences of a witchcraft reputation.

Because age data for New England witches born in the late
sixteenth and early seventeenth centuries are scarce, it is difficult to know whether the special vulnerability of old women

we find in Salem was peculiar to that outbreak. Cotton Mather suggested that it was not when he wrote, just before the Salem events, of the tendency of some colonists "to traduce for, A Witch, Every Old Woman, whose Temper with her Visage is not eminently Good."[81] He and other writers sometimes referred to accused witches in terms such as "an ignorant and a scandalous old woman" or "a lewd, ignorant, considerably aged woman."[82] And to be sure, throughout the century, the words "old" and "witch" or "old" and "hag" rolled together off the tongues of accusers.[83] In the absence of specific age information, however, we cannot simply assume that these women really were old.

Nevertheless, when we look at the period after about 1680, when more reliable information on the ages of older women becomes available, we find women over sixty appearing more frequently among those accused of witchcraft. Old women could have been prosecuted more often in earlier decades than the figures indicate, or their numbers among likely witches could have grown over the course of the century. I suspect both to have been the case—the former because of the relative lack of information on older women prior to 1680, the latter because the early settlers were a predominantly young and middle-aged group and the problems old women presented to their communities, as we shall see, grew as the early settlers aged. In any event, the evidence suggests that the heightened vulnerability of old women as targets of witchcraft fear was not limited to the Salem episode. They may have been in considerably greater danger of losing their lives in 1692 than at other times, but unlike women under forty and men, old women had become increasingly visible among witches in the decade or so before the Salem outbreak, and this visibility continued after the outbreak came to an end.

This picture becomes clearer when we place the proportions of middle-aged and old women accused, tried, convicted, and executed for witchcraft in the framework of the overall age structure of seventeenth-century New England. Age structure data are rare for the colonial period, but the material we have suggests that by the latter part of the seventeenth century, in settled communities, there were at least 2.5 times as many women between forty and fifty-nine as there were women sixty and over.[84] (The ratio would have been much higher earlier in the century and in newer settlements.) Based on this community age structure for women between forty and fifty-nine and women sixty and over, table 8 illustrates that old women were overrepresented among females over forty who were accused, tried, convicted, and executed as witches at Salem. At every stage of the process, women over sixty were at high risk during the outbreak. Especially notable is their disproportionate representation among the women found guilty and executed. For the non-Salem cases, the large number of women for whom age cannot be determined leaves the figures on women over forty who were accused prior to

TABLE 8. Proportionate Representation among Female Witches of Women between Forty and Fifty-nine and Women over Sixty by Community Age Structure, New England, 1620–1725

	Action	Women 40–59 (Actual)	Women over 60 (Predicted on 1:2.5 Age Ratio)	Women over 60 (Actual)
Non-Salem Cases	Accused	23	9.2	10
	Tried	9	3.6	3
	Convicted	2	.8	1
	Executed	1	0.0	0
Salem Cases	Accused	31	12.4	17
	Tried	15	6.0	13
	Convicted	8	3.2	11
	Executed	4	1.6	8

1692 little more than suggestive. But what they suggest is that old women were just as much at risk then, given their numbers in the larger population, as were middle-aged women.[85]

More important than whether the main targets of witchcraft fears were middle-aged or old is the fact that they were almost all over forty.[86] The women in both of these groups had reached the point in their lives when they were no longer performing what Puritans considered to be the major role of women: they were no longer bearing children. The older women among them, moreover, were not only beyond their childbearing years but were also no longer likely to be responsible for the care and maintenance of children. Indeed, in some cases, the roles of mother and child had been reversed: the accused were being cared for and maintained by their adult children. These life cycle questions bear upon other characteristics of witches as well—particularly marital status.

Single, married, and widowed women are all found in significant numbers among accused witches in early New England (see table 9). Married women predominated, however, both during the Salem events and at other times. Women who were married also made up the majority of women prosecuted, convicted, and executed for witchcraft throughout the century.

Within this larger picture, certain patterns emerge. Most noticeably, during the Salem outbreak, the proportion of married women among suspected women dropped, from a little less than three-quarters of the total in non-Salem cases to just over half. This difference is attributable to the increase, in Salem, of accusations against reputed witches' daughters and granddaughters, most of whom were both young and unmarried. *All* of the fourteen single women tried in 1692–93 fit into this category. With a few exceptions, their presence among prosecuted and convicted witches probably had more

TABLE 9. Marital Status of Female Witches, New England, 1620–1725

	Action	Single	Married	Widowed	Divorced/Deserted	Total
Non-Salem Cases	Accused	11	80	16	2	109
	Tried	1	25	5	0	31
	Convicted	0	13	3	0	16
	Executed	0	9	2	0	11
Salem Cases	Accused	40	68	22	2	132
	Tried	14	27	9	1	51
	Convicted	3	16	6	1	26
	Executed	0	10	4	0	14

to do with their relationships to older women in their families than with their marital status. At other times, when relatives of witches were less susceptible to witchcraft suspicion, all but one of the accusations against young, single women were ignored by the authorities (only thirteen-year-old Winifred Benham of Wallingford was prosecuted, along with her mother).[87]

More significant is the treatment accorded widows by the men who determined witches' fates. Although widows accounted for only about 15 percent of the accused, unlike young, single women, *once accused* they could expect to be treated much as married women were: as a group, they were tried, convicted, and executed in roughly the same proportions as their married counterparts. They resembled married witches as well in that while they were more likely to be prosecuted and convicted during the Salem events than at other times, the difference is not striking: at all times, widows who were named as witches had as much to fear from an accusation as women whose husbands were still alive.[88]

The presence of divorced and deserted women among the accused, though in itself numerically insignificant, raises questions about whether the absence of a husband rather than widowhood *per se* was at issue in some witchcraft cases. This line of inquiry is encouraged as well by certain ambiguities in the marital status statistics shown in table 9. The figures on unmarried females, for instance, mask the presence of several women (such as Sarah Dustin of Reading[89]) who were in their late twenties or thirties but who had remained single. Other women (Elizabeth Godman of New Haven, for example[90]) are not included in these figures at all because it is unclear whether they were widows or spinsters. Among those counted as married, moreover, were many women who were temporarily living apart from their husbands: these women were either itinerant Quaker preachers or the wives of soldiers, fishermen, merchants, or mariners.[91] Eliminating from discussion unmarried women under thirty (because their marital status may have reflected age rather than choice or circumstance) and married women temporarily living alone (because they were seldom prosecuted as witches), we can compare the witchcraft experience of married women and women alone. As in our discussion of age factors, we will make that comparison in light of the relative numbers of both groups in the larger population.

If we cannot fix precisely the proportion of women alone in colonial New England, we can conservatively estimate a ratio of women alone over thirty to married women over thirty as 1:4. That is to say, we may reasonably calculate that widows, spinsters, and separated, divorced, and deserted women constituted no more than 20 percent of the female population over thirty.[92] Based on that calculation, table 10 illustrates the overrepresentation of women alone among females accused, tried, convicted, and executed for witchcraft. Although the evidence for the non-Salem cases is less marked (especially for convicted and executed witches), the number of women alone over thirty among each of the categories is larger than we might

TABLE 10. Proportionate Representation among Female Witches of Married Women over Thirty and Women Alone over Thirty, New England, 1620–1725

	Action	Married Women over Thirty (Actual)	Women Alone over Thirty (Predicted on 1:4 Ratio)	Women Alone over Thirty (Actual)
Non-Salem Cases	Accused	50	12.5	20
	Tried	17	4.3	6
	Convicted	8	2.0	3
	Executed	5	1.3	2
Salem Cases	Accused	57	14.3	25
	Tried	26	6.5	10
	Convicted	16	4.0	7
	Executed	10	2.5	4

expect, given their numbers in the total population. In spite of the noticeable predominance of married women among accused witches, women alone seem to have been at greater risk.[93] Ironically, even during the Salem outbreak, when husbands themselves were most vulnerable to witchcraft suspicion, marriage seems to have offered women some measure of protection.

Husbands shielded their wives against the danger of accusation in several ways. In some cases, they appealed to the authorities directly on behalf of their wives. Nicholas Rice of Reading, for instance, petitioned the Massachusetts General Court to release his wife from the Boston jail in 1692, pleading that he had lived with his "ancient decriped" spouse, Sarah Rice, "above Tweinty years, in all which time he never had reason to accuse her for any Impietie or witchcraft, but the Contrary, shee lived with him as a good Faithfull dutifull wife and alwise had respect to . . . the ordinances of God while her strength Remained."[94] Other men instituted slander proceedings against their wives' accusers, calling witnesses to testify to the godly character of the women in question. Sometimes, however, simply the presence of a husband appears to have staved off a formal complaint or influenced the response of the court. A number of women, including Katherine Harrison of Wethersfield, Ann Hibbens of Boston, and Bridget Oliver of Salem, were formally accused for the first time within a year or two after they became widows—although in some cases it is clear that their reputations as witches predated their widowhood.[95] Other women, officially cleared of witchcraft charges while their husbands were still alive, found themselves in greater peril after their husbands' deaths.[96]

It was not merely the absence of a protector that made women alone more susceptible than married women to witchcraft prosecutions. Like their age, the marital status of women was crucial in determining their relationship to their families and to their society. In the eyes of her community, the woman alone in early New England was an aberration: the fundamental female role of procreation was at best irrelevant to her. At worst, of course, she might be performing this function outside the institution of marriage. Moreover, women alone no longer performed—perhaps never had performed—the other main function of women in New England society: they were not the "helpmeets" to men Puritans thought women should be. Even more than women over forty, women alone could not legitimately "answer the end in [woman's] creation."[97]

The greater vulnerability of women without husbands can easily be overstated, however. The protection marriage offered some women should not obscure the fact that a woman's marital status was much less significant in predicting the likelihood and impact of a witchcraft accusation than her sex and age. If we can describe a community consensus about the kinds of people who were witches in colonial New England, it seems that there was widespread agreement that witches were women, and that they were over forty years of age. Because the evidence is not conclusive, we can argue (though not firmly establish) that women alone and women over sixty were in even greater danger than married women and women between forty and sixty.

But these are simply the demographic outlines of a more complex portrait. There was much more to the making of a witch in New England than we have seen so far. Though we cannot know how many older women were considered witches by their neighbors, only some colonial women in this age group were complained of publicly. A closer look at the material conditions and behavior of the accused reveals other characteristics—intimately related to their sex, age, and marital status—that set witches apart from other older women in their communities.

THREE

The Economic Basis
of Witchcraft

MOST OBSERVERS NOW agree that witches in the villages and towns of late sixteenth- and early seventeenth-century England tended to be poor. They were not usually the poorest women in their communities, one historian has argued; they were the "moderately poor." Rarely were relief recipients suspect; rather it was those just above them on the economic ladder, "like the woman who felt she ought to get poor relief, but was denied it."[1] This example brings to mind New England's Eunice Cole, who once berated Hampton selectmen for refusing her aid when, she insisted, a man no worse off then she was receiving it.[2]

Eunice Cole's experience also suggests the difficulty in evaluating the class position of the accused. Commonly used class indicators such as the amount of property owned, yearly income, occupation, and political offices held are almost useless in analyzing the positions of women during the colonial period. While early New England women surely shared in the material benefits and social status of their fathers, husbands, and even sons, most were economically dependent on the male members of their families throughout their lives. Only a small proportion of these women owned property outright, and even though they participated actively in the productive work of their communities, their labor did not translate into financial independence or economic power. Any income generated by married women belonged by law to their husbands, and because occupations open to women were few and wages meager, women alone could only rarely support themselves. Their material condition, moreover, could easily change with an alteration in their marital status. William Cole, with an estate at his death of £41 after debts, might be counted among the "moderately poor," as might Eunice Cole when he was alive. But the refusal of the authorities to recognize the earlier transfer of this estate from husband to wife ensured, among other things, that as a widow Eunice Cole was among the poorest of New England's poor.

The distinction between the economic circumstances of wife and widow here may not seem particularly significant, but in other cases the problem is more complicated. How, for instance, do we classify the witch Ann Dolliver? The daughter of prominent Salem minister John Higginson, who was well above most of his neighbors in wealth and social status, she was also the deserted wife of William Dolliver, and lived out her life without the support of a husband, dependent first on her father and then on the town for her maintenance.[3] Even if we were willing to assume that the accused shared the class position of their male relatives, the lack of information on so many of the families of witches makes it impossible to locate even the males on an economic scale.

Despite conceptual problems and sparse evidence, it is clear that poor women, both the destitute and those with access to some resources, were surely represented, and very probably overrepresented, among the New England accused. Perhaps 20 percent of accused women, including both Eunice Cole and Ann Dolliver, were either impoverished or living at a level of bare subsistence when they were accused.[4] Some, like thirty-seven-year-old Abigail Somes, worked as servants a substantial portion of their adult lives. Some supported themselves and their families with various kinds of temporary labor such as nursing infants, caring for sick neighbors, taking in washing and sewing, or harvesting crops. A few, most notably Tituba, the first person accused during the Salem outbreak, were slaves. Others, like the once-prosperous Sarah Good of Wenham and Salem, and the never-very-well-off Ruth Wilford of Haverhill, found themselves reduced to abject poverty by the death of a parent or a change in their own marital status.[5] Accused witches came before local magistrates requesting permission to sell family land in order to support themselves, to submit claims against their children or executors of their former husbands' estates for nonpayment of the widow's lawful share of the estate, or simply to ask for food and fuel from the town selectmen. Because they could not pay the costs of their trials or jail terms, several were forced to remain in prison after courts acquitted them. The familiar stereotype of the witch as an indigent woman who resorted to begging for her survival is hardly an inaccurate picture of some of New England's accused.

Still, the poor account for only a minority of the women accused. Even without precise economic indicators, it is clear that women from all levels of society were vulnerable to accusation. If witches in early modern England can accurately be described as "moderately poor," then New Englanders deviated sharply from their ancestors in their ideas about which women were witches. Wives, daughters, and widows of "middling" farmers, artisans, and mariners were regularly accused, and (although much less often) so too were women belonging to the gentry class. The accused were addressed as Goodwife (or Goody) and as the more honorific Mrs. or Mistress, as well as by their first names.[6]

Prosecution was a different matter. Unless they were single or widowed, accused women from wealthy families—families with estates valued at more than £500—could be fairly confident that the accusations would be ignored by the authorities or deflected by their husbands through suits for

slander against their accusers. Even during the Salem outbreak, when several women married to wealthy men were
arrested, most managed to escape to the safety of other colonies through their husbands' influence. Married women from
moderately well-off families—families with estates valued at
between roughly £200 and £500—did not always escape prosecution so easily, but neither do they seem, as a group, to have
been as vulnerable as their less prosperous counterparts. When
only married women are considered, women in families with
estates worth less than £200 seem significantly overrepresented among *convicted* witches—a pattern which suggests that
economic position was a more important factor to judges and
juries than to the community as a whole in its role as accuser.[7]

Without a husband to act on behalf of the accused, wealth
alone rarely provided women with protection against prosecution. Boston's Ann Hibbens, New Haven's Elizabeth Godman, and Wethersfield's Katherine Harrison, all women alone,
were tried as witches despite sizeable estates. In contrast, the
accusations against women like Hannah Griswold of Saybrook, Connecticut, Elizabeth Blackleach of Hartford, and
Margaret Gifford of Salem, all wives of prosperous men when
they were accused, were simply not taken seriously by the courts.
The most notable exception to this pattern is the obliviousness
of the Salem judges to repeated accusations against Margaret
Thatcher, widow of one of the richest merchants in Boston
and principal heir to her father's considerable fortune. Her
unusual wealth and social status may have kept her out of jail
in 1692, but more likely it was her position as mother-in-law
to Jonathan Corwin, one of the Salem magistrates, that accounts
for her particular immunity.[8]

Economic considerations, then, do appear to have been at
work in the New England witchcraft cases. But the issue was
not simply the relative poverty—or wealth—of accused witches
or their families. It was the special position of most accused
witches vis-à-vis their society's rules for transferring wealth from
one generation to another. To explain why their position was

so unusual, we must turn first to New England's system of inheritance.

Inheritance is normally thought of as the transmission of property at death, but in New England, as in other agricultural societies, adult children received part of their father's accumulated estates prior to his death, usually at the time they married.[9] Thus the inheritance system included both pre-mortem endowments and post-mortem distributions. While no laws compelled fathers to settle part of their estates on their children as marriage portions, it was customary to do so. Marriages were, among other things, economic arrangements, and young people could not benefit from these arrangements unless their fathers provided them with the means to set up households and earn their livelihoods. Sons' portions tended to be land, whereas daughters commonly received movable goods and / or money. The exact value of these endowments varied according to a father's wealth and inclination, but it appears that as a general rule the father of the young woman settled on the couple roughly half as much as the father of the young man.[10]

Custom, not law, also guided the distribution of a man's property at his death, but with two important exceptions. First, a man's widow, if he left one, was legally entitled "by way of dower" to one-third part of his real property, "to have and injoy for term of her natural life." She was expected to support herself with the profits of this property, but since she held only a life interest in it, she had to see that she did not "strip or waste" it.[11] None of the immovable estate could be sold, unless necessary for her or her children's maintenance, and then only with the permission of the court. A man might will his wife more than a third of his real property—but not less. Only if the woman came before the court to renounce her dower right publicly, and then only if the court approved, could this principle be waived. In the form of her "thirds," dower was meant to provide for a woman's support in widowhood. The inviolability of dower protected the widow from the claims of her children against the estate and protected the community from the potential burden of her care.

The second way in which law determined inheritance patterns had to do specifically with intestate cases.[12] If a man died without leaving a will, several principles governed the division of his property. The widow's thirds, of course, were to be laid out first. Unless "just cause" could be shown for some other distribution, the other two-thirds were to be divided among the surviving children, both male and female.[13] A double portion was to go to the eldest son, and single portions to his sisters and younger brothers. If there were no sons, the law stipulated that the estate was to be shared equally by the daughters. In cases where any or all of the children had not yet come of age, their portions were to be held by their mother or by a court-appointed guardian until they reached their majorities[14] or married. What remained of the widow's thirds at her death was to be divided among the surviving children, in the same proportions as the other two-thirds.

Although bound to conform to laws concerning the widow's thirds, men who wrote wills were not legally required to follow the principles of inheritance laid out in intestate cases. Individual men had the right to decide for themselves who would ultimately inherit their property. As we shall see later, will-writers did sometimes deviate sharply from these guidelines, but the majority seem to have adhered closely (though not always precisely) to the custom of leaving a double portion to the eldest son. Beyond that, New England men seem generally to have agreed to a system of partible inheritance, with both sons and daughters inheriting.

When these rules were followed, property ownership and control generally devolved upon men. Neither the widow's dower nor, for the most part, the daughter's right to inherit signified more than *access to* property. For widows, the law was clear that dower allowed for "use" only. For inheriting daughters who were married, the separate but inheritance-related principle of coverture applied. Under English common law, "feme covert" stipulated that married women had no right to own property—indeed, upon marriage, "the very being or legal existence of the woman is suspended."[15] Personal property which a married daughter inherited from her father, either as dowry or as a post-mortem bequest, immediately became the legal possession of her husband, who could exert full powers of ownership over it. A married daughter who inherited land from her father retained title to the land, which her husband could not sell without her consent. On her husband's death such land became the property of her children, but during his life her husband was entitled to the use and profits of it, and his wife could not devise it to her children by will.[16] The property of an inheriting daughter who was single seems to have been held "for improvement" for her until she was married, when it became her dowry.[17]

This is not to say that women did not benefit when they inherited property. A sizeable inheritance could provide a woman with a materially better life; if single or widowed, inheriting women enjoyed better chances for an economically advantageous marriage or remarriage. But inheritance did not normally bring women the independent economic power it brought men.

The rules of inheritance were not always followed, however. In some cases, individual men decided not to conform to customary practices; instead, they employed one of several legal devices to give much larger shares of their estates to their wives or daughters, many times for disposal at their own discretion. Occasionally, the magistrates themselves allowed the estate to be distributed in some other fashion. Or, most commonly, the absence of male heirs in families made conformity impossible. In all three exceptions to inheritance customs, but most particularly the last, the women who stood to benefit economically also assumed a position of unusual vulnerability. They, and in many instances their daughters, became prime targets for witchcraft accusations.

Consider first the experience of five witches who came from families without male heirs. Together with the story of Hampton's Eunice Cole, these histories begin to illuminate the subtle and often intricate manner in which anxieties about inheritance lay at the heart of most witchcraft accusations.

Katherine Harrison

Katherine Harrison first appears in the Connecticut colonial records in the early 1650s, as the wife of John Harrison, a wealthy Wethersfield landowner.[18] Her age is unknown[19] and her family background is obscure. We know that she called John, Jonathan, and Josiah Gilbert, three prominent Connecticut Valley settlers, her cousins, but her actual relationship to them is ambiguous: one Gilbert family genealogist lists her as their sister, while another denies any family relationship altogether.[20] She may have been the daughter or niece of Lydia Gilbert, who was executed as a witch in Hartford in 1654, but we can be reasonably certain only that the two women were members of the same Connecticut family.[21] Also unclear is the exact sequence of events that led to Katherine Harrison's conviction as a witch and to her subsequent expulsion from Connecticut. The following, therefore, must be read as an attempt to reconstruct these events.

It has been said that Katherine Harrison was first tried as a witch in October 1668.[22] If so, then she must have been acquitted, because she was indicted in the Court of Assistants in Hartford on 25 May 1669, on the same charge.[23] The jury was unable to agree upon a verdict, however, and the court adjourned to the next session. Meantime, Harrison was supposed to remain in jail, but for some reason she was released in the summer or early fall, and she returned home to Wethersfield. Shortly thereafter, thirty-eight Wethersfield townsmen filed a petition, complaining that "shee was suffered to be at libertie," since she "was lately prooved to be Deaply guiltie of *suspicion* of Wichcrafte" and that "the Juerie (the greater part of them) judged or beleaved that she was guilty of such high crimes" and "ought to be put to death." Among the petition's signers were several of the town's most prominent citizens, including John Blackleach, Sr., who had "taken much paines in the prosecution of this cause from the beginninge," and John Chester, who was then involved in a legal controversy with Harrison concerning a parcel of land.[24] When the Court of Assistants met again in October, all of the jury members found her guilty of witchcraft.[25]

The Hartford magistrates, however, were reluctant to accept the verdict. Perhaps remembering how accusations had gotten out of hand during the Hartford outbreak seven years before, they put Harrison back in prison and appealed to local ministers for advice on the use of evidence. The response was ambiguous enough to forestall execution.[26] At a special session of the Court of Assistants the following May, the magistrates reconsidered the verdict, determined that they were not able to concur with the jury "so as to sentance her to death or to a longer continuance in restraynt," and ordered Harrison to pay her fees and leave the colony for good.[27]

If witnesses testifying against her in her 1669 trial can be believed, Katherine Harrison's neighbors had suspected that she was a witch sixteen or eighteen years earlier. Elizabeth Simon deposed that as a single woman, Harrison was noted to be "a great or notorious liar, a Sabbath breaker and one that told fortunes"—and that her predictions frequently came to pass. Simon was also suspicious of Harrison for another reason: because she "did often spin so great a quantity of fine linen yarn as the said Elizabeth did never know nor hear of any other woman that could spin so much."[28] Other witnesses testified to the more recent damage she did to individuals and their property. Harrison was also a healer, and although many of her neighbors called upon her skills, over the years some of them came to suspect her of killing as well as curing.[29] Or so they said in 1668–69; she was not formally accused of any witchcraft crimes until after her husband's death.

John Harrison had died in 1666, leaving his wife one of the wealthiest, if not *the* wealthiest woman in Wethersfield. In his will he bequeathed his entire estate of £929 to his wife and three daughters. Rebecca, age twelve, was to have £60, and his two younger daughters, eleven-year-old Mary and nine-year-old Sarah, were to have £40 each. The remaining £789 was to go to his widow.[30] Unlike many widows in colonial New England, Katherine Harrison chose not to remarry. Instead she lived alone, managing her extensive holdings herself, with the advice and assistance of her Hartford kinsman, Jonathan Gilbert.

In October 1668, not long after her adversaries began gathering their witchcraft evidence against her, Harrison submitted a lengthy petition to "the Fathers of the Comonweale" asking for relief for the extensive vandalism of her estate since her husband's death. Among other damage, she spoke of oxen beaten and bruised to the point of being "altogether unserviceable"; of a hole bored into the side of her cow; of a three-year-old heifer slashed to death; and of the back of a two-year-old steer broken. Her corn crop was destroyed, she said, "damnified with horses, they being staked upon it," and "30 poles of hops cutt and spoyled." Twelve of her relatives and neighbors, she said, including Jonathan and Josiah Gilbert, could testify to the damage done. The response of the court went unrecorded, but there is no indication that provision was made for the "due recompense" Harrison requested or that her grievances were even investigated.[31]

The Court of Assistants also seems to have been unsympathetic to another petition Harrison submitted in the fall of 1668, in which she complained that the actions of the magistrates themselves were depleting her estate.[32] Indeed, the local court had recently fined her £40 for slandering her neighbors, Michael and Ann Griswold—a fine greatly in excess of the normal punishment in such cases.[33] The exact circumstances of the incident are unknown, but the Griswolds were among Harrison's witchcraft accusers, and she apparently considered Michael Griswold central in the recruiting of additional witnesses against her, for she said that "the sayd Michael Griswold would Hang her though he damned a thousand soules," adding that "as for his own soule it was damned long agoe." Griswold, a member of Wethersfield's elite, but not as wealthy as Harrison, sued her for these slanderous remarks and for calling his wife Ann "a savadge whore."[34] Besides levying the fine, the court ordered Harrison to confess her sins publicly.[35] She made the required confession, but she appealed the exorbitant fine.

Harrison's petition, which she filed within the month, was a peculiar mixture of justification for her actions, concession to the magistrates' insistence on deference in women, determination in her convictions, and desperation in her attempt to salvage her estate. Acknowledging herself to be "a female, a weaker vessell, subject to passion," she pleaded as the source of her frustration and anger the vicious abuse to which she had been subjected since her husband's death. She admitted her "corruption," but pointed out that it was well known that she had made "a full and free confession of [her] fault" and had offered "to repair the wound that [she] had given to [the Griswolds'] names by a plaster as broad as the sore, at any time and in any place where it should content them." At the same time, she indicted Michael Griswold for being less interested in the reparation of his name than in her estate and did not hesitate to call the fine oppressive, citing the laws of God and the laws of the commonwealth as providing "that noe mans estate shal be deminished or taken away by any colony or pretence of Authority" in such an arbitrary manner. In her final statements, however, she returned to a more conciliatory stance: "I speake not to excuse my fault," she said, "but to save my estate as far as Righteousness will permit for a distressed Widdow and Orphanes."[36]

Fear of losing her estate is a recurring theme in the records of Harrison's life during this period. Almost immediately after her husband's death in 1666, she petitioned the court to change the terms of her husband's will. Arguing that the bequests to the children were "inconsiderate" (by which she probably meant inconsiderable), she asked that the magistrates settle on her eldest daughter £210, and £200 on each of her younger daughters, reserving the house and lot for herself during her lifetime.[37] Since her husband had left her full ownership of most of his estate, she could simply have given her daughters larger portions, but she must have felt that the court's sanction rendered the inheritances less vulnerable. Several months later, she appealed directly to Connecticut's governor, John Winthrop, Jr., requesting that Hartford's John and Jonathan Gilbert, and John Riley of Wethersfield, be appointed overseers of her estate.[38] Winthrop must not have granted her request because in 1668 Harrison signed over the rest of the estate she had inherited from her husband to her daughters and appointed Jonathan and John Gilbert her daughters' guardians.[39] By the following year, her neighbors reported, she had "disposed of great part of her estate to others in trust."[40]

In June 1670, Katherine Harrison moved to Westchester, New York, to begin her life anew. Her reputation for witchcraft followed her, however, in the form of a complaint, filed in July by two of her new neighbors, that she had been allowed to resettle in Westchester. Noting that suspicion of her in Connecticut "hath given some cause of apprehension" to the townspeople, in order to "end their jealousyes and feares" a local New York magistrate told her to leave the jurisdiction.[41] Harrison refused. Before any action could be taken against her, her eldest daughter was fortuitously betrothed to Josiah Hunt, a son of Thomas Hunt, one of the men who had protested her presence in Westchester. The elder Hunt became a supporter and appeared in court on her behalf, with his son and three other influential men. Though she was required to give security for her "Civill carriage and good behaviour," the

General Court of Assizes in New York ordered "that in regard there is nothing appears against her deserving the continuance of that obligacion shee is to bee releast from it, and hath Liberty to remain in the Towne of Westchester where shee now resides, or any where else in the Government during her pleasure."[42]

Evidently Harrison continued to live with recurring witchcraft suspicion, but after 1670 there is no further evidence of official harassment.[43] Early in 1672, she reappeared in Hartford to sue eleven of her old Connecticut Valley neighbors, in most cases for debt, and to release her "intrusted overseer" Jonathan Gilbert from his responsibilities for her estate (although he continued to act as guardian to her two younger daughters).[44] A month later, she signed at least some of her remaining Wethersfield land over to Gilbert.[45] After that, she fades from view. She may have returned to Connecticut for good at that time, for some evidence suggests that she died at Dividend, then an outlying section of Wethersfield, in October 1682.[46]

Susanna Martin

Born in England in 1625, Susanna North was the youngest of three daughters of Richard North. Her mother died when Susanna was young and her father subsequently remarried. The family migrated to New England in or just prior to 1639, the year in which Richard North was listed as one of the first proprietors of Salisbury, Massachusetts. Susanna's sister Mary had married Thomas Jones and was living in Gloucester by 1642. Of her sister Sarah we know only that she married a man named Oldham, had a daughter named Ann, and died before the child was grown. In August 1646, at the age of twenty-one, Susanna married George Martin, a Salisbury man whose first wife had recently died. In June of the following year, she gave birth to her son Richard, the first of nine children. One of these children, a son, died in infancy.[47]

During the first twenty-two years of her marriage, Susanna Martin emerged from obscurity only twice in the town and colony records. In 1647 or 1648, she was fined 20 shillings for some unnamed offense.[48] In 1667, perhaps because this offense (or some other) lingered in the minds of her neighbors, she was assigned a seat in the meetinghouse which her husband, who was on the committee that made the seating arrangements, apparently found beneath her station.[49] Although the family's social and economic status is not clear, George Martin was as active in the economic life of his community during this period as he was in its religious affairs. Local records reveal that he bought, mortgaged, and deeded property with some frequency.[50]

Early in 1668, less than a year after the birth of her last child, Susanna Martin's father died, leaving a modest estate of about £150. As the only surviving children, the then forty-three-year-old Susanna and her sister Mary anticipated receiving a major portion of the property, to possess either immediately or after the death of their stepmother, Ursula North. They were disappointed. According to the will probated shortly after he died, Richard North had voided all previous wills and written a new one—*nearly two decades* before his death. In this document, dated January 1649, he left all but £22 of his estate directly to his wife. Twenty-one pounds was to be divided among Mary Jones, Susanna Martin, and Ann Bates (Sarah Oldham's daughter). Susanna's share was 20 shillings and the cancellation of a £10 debt George Martin owed his father-in-law. Listed as witnesses to this will were Thomas Bradbury of Salisbury and Mary Jones's daughter, Mary Winsley.[51] But the will raised problems. In 1649, Ann Bates was still Ann Oldham (she did not marry Francis Bates until 1661) and the Mary Winsley listed as witness to the will was still Mary Jones, at most eleven or twelve years old when it was allegedly written.[52] Despite the obvious irregularities, Thomas Bradbury and Mary Winsley attested in court that this was indeed Richard North's last will and testament.

Whether Susanna Martin and her sister saw or protested this will when it was probated cannot be determined. Susanna, at least, may have had more pressing concerns on her mind. In April 1669, a bond of £100 was posted for her appearance at the next Court of Assistants "upon suspicion of witchcraft." That was the same day that George Martin sued William Sargent for slandering his wife. According to George Martin, Sargent had not only said that Susanna "was a witch, and he would call her witch," but also accused her of having "had a child" while still single and of "wringing its neck" shortly after. George Martin also sued William Sargent's brother Thomas for saying "that his son George Marttin was a bastard and that Richard Marttin was Goodwife Marttin's imp." The response of the Salisbury court is more than a little confusing. Although George Martin withdrew his charges against Thomas Sargent, the jury found William Sargent guilty of accusing Susanna of fornication and infanticide; but in what appears to have been a public insult, the magistrates awarded George Martin a mere "white wampam peague [colonial currency] or the eighth part of a penny damage." In the matter of witchcraft slander, the jury brought in an acquittal for William Sargent, in which the "Court did not concur."[53]

Meanwhile, the magistrates bound Susanna Martin over to the higher court to be tried for witchcraft. Although the records have not survived, she must have been acquitted, because several months later she was at liberty. In October 1669, George Martin was again bound for his wife's appearance in court, not for witchcraft this time but for calling one of her neighbors a liar and a thief.[54]

By April 1671, George and Susanna Martin (Susanna's sister Mary Jones would later join them) were involved in what would become protracted litigation over the estate of Susanna's father. Ursula North had died a month or two before, leaving a will, dated shortly after her husband's death, that effectively disinherited her two stepdaughters by awarding them

40 shillings apiece. She left the rest of the original North estate first to her granddaughter, Mary Winsley, and secondarily to Mary and Nathaniel Winsley's only child, Hepzibah.[55]

The exact sequence of the numerous court hearings that followed is less clear. Evidently, Susanna and George Martin initiated legal proceedings against Mary and Nathaniel Winsley in April 1671, for unwarranted possession of the North estate. They based their suit on the illegality of Richard North's (and therefore Ursula North's) will. Despite testimony that Ann Bates was still Ann Oldham in the late 1650s and the claim of two neighbors that "they heard old North severrall times say that Nathaniel Winsl[ey] should never bee the better for his estate if hee Could helpe itt," the county court, when it met again in October, apparently decided in the Winsleys' favor.[56] Susanna Martin appealed this judgment, first to the Court of Assistants and later, along with her sister, to the General Court, stressing the "sundry inconsistencies if not impossibilities" of their father's alleged will.[57] In October 1672, the General Court responded, giving Susanna Martin liberty to sue for her inheritance a second time at the local level.[58]

In April 1673, the recently widowed Mary Jones and George Martin, acting for his wife, sued Nathaniel Winsley "for withholding the inheritance of housing, lands and other estate . . . under color of a feigned or confused writing like the handwriting of Mr. Thomas Bradbury and seemingly attested by him, and Mary Winsly."[59] The court declared the case nonsuited, and again Susanna Martin appealed to the General Court, requesting that the case be reheard at the local level.[60] The General Court consented in May 1673, and the following October, Susanna and George Martin instituted proceedings against the Winsleys for the third time. Again the county court decided for the defendants, and the Martins appealed to the Court of Assistants.[61] For a while it looked as though things were finally going their way. The higher court, which "found for the plaintiff there being no legall prooffe of Richard North's will," ordered that "the estate the said North left be left to the disposall of the county court."[62] When Susanna Martin and Mary Jones applied to the county court in April 1674, for "the division of the estate of Richard North between them," the court "affirmed that [the will] had been legally proved." Thomas Bradbury testified "that he was one of the witnesses before the court and at that time [Richard North] was compos mentis."[63]

The following month, Susanna, George, and Mary appealed a final time to the General Court, this time for "a hearing of the whole case" by the highest court itself. The magistrates agreed to hear the case, remitting the usual court fees, as they had done before, on the basis of Susanna's pleas of poverty.[64] But in October 1674, after "perusall of what hath binn heard and alleadged by both parties," the court found for Nathaniel Winsley.[65] In what Susanna Martin and Mary Jones believed was a flagrant miscarriage of justice, they had lost what they considered their rightful inheritances.

For almost the next two decades, Susanna Martin's name rarely appears in the public records of the colony. Her sister Mary died in 1682, followed by her husband George in 1686.[66] Early in 1692, she was again accused of witchcraft, this time by several of the possessed females in Salem. They claimed that her apparition "greviously afflected" them, urging them to become witches themselves. Summoned before the court as witnesses against her were eleven men and four women, all old neighbors of the now sixty-seven-year-old widow.[67]

Unnerved by either the agonies of the possessed or the magistrates' obvious belief in her guilt, Martin insisted that she was innocent. To Cotton Mather, she "was one of the most impudent, scurrilous, wicked Creatures in the World," who had the effrontery to claim "that she had lead a most virtuous and holy life."[68] Years of living as a reputed witch had left Martin well-versed on the subject of the Devil's powers. "He that appeared in sam[uel]s shape, a glorifyed saint," she said, citing the Bible in her own defense, "can appear in any ones shape." She laughed at the fits of her young accusers, explaining: "Well I may at such folly." When asked what she thought the possessed were experiencing, she said she did not know. Pressed to speculate on it, she retorted: "I do not desire to spend my judgment upon it" and added (revealing what must have been her long-standing opinion of the magistrates' bias), "my thoughts are my own, when they are in, but when they are out they are anothers."[69]

If her impertinence did not convict her, her neighbors' allegations of more than thirty years of evildoing surely did. Robert Downer of Salisbury testified that after he told her that he believed what people said about her—that she was a witch— Martin threatened that "some shee devel woold fech him away shortly," and that night "the likness of a catt" had assaulted him in his bed.[70] William Browne's testimony had another kind of sexual overtone. His wife Elizabeth, he said, had been a rational, sober, God-fearing woman, "prudently Carefull in her family," until Martin had possessed her more than thirty years before. A day of fasting and prayer appointed by the Salisbury church on Elizabeth's behalf seemed to be speeding her recovery, he continued; but Martin threatened her again— at which point Elizabeth began to insist that she and her hus- band were no longer married, that they had in fact been divorced in England many years earlier.[71] According to John and Mary Pressy, Martin had taken vengeance on *them* because John had testified against her at her last witchcraft trial. At the time Martin had threatened that "we shoold never pros- per . . . p[ar]ticulerly that we should never have but too cows," John recalled, and "from that time to this day we have never exeeded that number."[72]

Susanna Martin was found guilty of witchcraft and was one of five women executed on 19 July 1692. One week later, another Salisbury woman was indicted on the same charge. She was Mary Bradbury, the now elderly wife of the man Susanna Martin believed had written her father's "will" nearly twenty-five years before. Mary Bradbury was sentenced to hang too, but friends helped her to escape. No explicit connection between the accusations of the two women is discernible.

Rumors circulated, however, that because Thomas Bradbury had friends in positions of authority, there had been little real effort to capture his fugitive wife.[73]

Joan Penney and Mehitabel Downing

Aged widow Joan Penney of Gloucester, Massachusetts, was one of the many women arrested but not prosecuted during the Salem outbreak, the trials having come to an end before the judges heard their cases. She had been accused of committing "severall acts of witchcraft" on the body of twenty-five-year-old Mary Hill, an unmarried Salem woman. The complaint against Penney was filed by Mary's father, Zebulon Hill, a former resident of Gloucester.[74] Zebulon's wife, Elizabeth, was the stepdaughter of Joan Penney's deceased spouse, Thomas Penney.[75] Thomas had died in August 1692, shortly before the accusation had been lodged, leaving all but £7 of his estate to his "Beloved Wife Joan Pinny."[76] Though Thomas Penney had been married twice before and had both children and grandchildren, only two members of this branch of the family—Joan Kent, a daughter from his first marriage and her thirty-two-year-old son, Josiah—were mentioned at all in his will. After Joan Penney was arrested, Josiah Kent appealed to local magistrates to grant him administration of Thomas Penney's estate, on the grounds that his grandfather had promised him the whole estate and that he was the sole male heir.[77]

Joan Penney's history can be traced back to 1652, when she was Joan Braybrook, wife of forty-year-old Richard Braybrook of Ipswich. That year, Richard appeared in local court, along with Alice Ellis, to answer to charges of fornication. Ellis was at that time working as a servant in the Braybrook household. The Essex County magistrates found them both guilty and ordered them whipped. They also freed Ellis from her service and insisted that Richard bring up the child of their illicit union.[78] The child, Mehitabel, came to be viewed as the daughter of both Joan and Richard Braybrook. She was the only child the couple had, although they also raised a nephew, John Bayer, who was a few years older than his cousin.

The social status of the Braybrook family in Ipswich is ambiguous. Richard and Joan were ambitious settlers who prospered, despite Richard's affront to community sexual standards. In 1665, Richard was called upon to serve on a grand jury, indicating that he was a man of some recognized position in the town.[79] By 1669 he owned at least two farms, rented a third, and was able to hire people to work the various properties.[80]

But there are indications that the Braybrooks' ambitions overstepped the bounds of acceptable behavior in their neighbors' eyes. Joan Braybrook was brought into the county court in 1653 for "wearing a silk scarf," a crime in Massachusetts if her husband's property was valued at less than £200.[81] That the charge was not proved suggests that the family may have been more economically successful than their neighbors knew or, possibly, approved. In 1668, during a dispute about some leased property, Richard Braybrook sued Thomas Wells for calling him a liar, a "damned wrech and a lim of the Divell," and for saying "his wife was as bad as he."[82] Four years later, Joan Braybrook was brought into court for "breach of the Sabbath"—for "carrying a half bushel of corn or pease" on her way to church.[83]

Mehitabel Braybrook was an even greater problem for the community than were her parents. At the age of sixteen, while working as a servant to Jacob Perkins, she was accused of setting her master's house on fire. Though Mehitabel testified that she had accidentally dropped her pipe, not realizing that there were coals still in it, the court convicted her "of extreme carelessness if not wilfully burning the house," and ordered her to be severely whipped and to pay £40 to Perkins. The court's decision was no doubt influenced by the testimony of a neighbor who claimed that Mehitabel was a spiteful young woman.[84] Other neighbors, some of whom attributed their impressions to conversations with Joan Braybrook, described Mehitabel as a liar, a thief, and an "unchaste creature."[85]

If Joan Braybrook was indeed hostile to Mehitabel (and it is not at all clear that she was), Richard Braybrook was not. In 1669, "in considderation of a mariage" to be "solemnized between John Downeing of Ipswich . . . and [his] daughter," Richard signed a deed giving the young couple the half of his Ipswich farm that bordered on Gloucester, reserving the other half, his Wenham farm, and six other acres of Ipswich land for himself. As part of the marriage agreement, John and Mehitabel were to "carry on the business and Imployment of the whole farme . . . dureing the naturall lives of the sayd Richard and Joane . . ." and with "the payment of one hundred pounds att or before the decease of the sayd Richard and Joane," they would "possess and enjoy the benefitts and preveledges of the whole farm."[86] As his only child, seventeen-year-old Mehitabel had been given a dowry by her father which far exceeded the marriage portions of most of her female contemporaries.

Richard Braybrook died in 1681 without leaving a will. The administration of his estate was granted to John Downing, and the following year Downing and Joan Braybrook confirmed in court an agreement they had made as to the disposition of the estate. They presented the original deed establishing Downing's interest in the inheritance and allowed what must have been Richard Braybrook's desire concerning his Wenham farm—that the widow Braybrook retain a life interest in the property but that it eventually go to his nephew, John Bayer.[87] She had by then signed over the other half of the Ipswich farm to John Downing.[88] The estate was settled in what seems to have been an amicable manner.

A week later, Joan Braybrook married Thomas Penney. In the Penneys' attempt to claim a third of the remaining six acres of Richard Braybrook's Ipswich land as part of Joan's dower, they, like John Downing, ran into the opposition of Joan's former next-door neighbor, John Burnam, who insisted that the property was not part of the Braybrook estate. Both the Penneys and John Downing took Burnam to court, but for some reason the Penneys withdrew their suit. Local magistrates eventually resolved the dispute between Downing and Burnam in Burnam's favor.[89]

Joan Penney fades from the public records after 1682, only to reemerge as an accused witch after her second husband's death in 1692. Mehitabel and John Downing appeared in court several times in the 1670s and 1680s—she for excessive drinking and "neglecting their children some days and nights, often leaving them alone," he for excessive drinking, stealing, "threatening of his co-inhabitant to burn the house," and other misdemeanors.[90] Ultimately, Mehitabel's behavior was the more serious. Though no evidence remains about who accused her or of what crimes, the then forty-year-old Mehitabel Downing's name appears, along with the widow Penney, as one of ten witches petitioning for their release from the Ipswich jail in the fall of 1692.[91]

Martha Carrier

Like most women in seventeenth-century New England, Martha Allen grew up in a large household. She was one of six children of Andrew and Faith Allen, two of the original settlers of Andover, Massachusetts. The birth dates of Martha and her sisters, Mary and Sarah, are unknown, but a sister Hannah was born in 1652, a brother Andrew in 1657, and a brother John in 1662.[92] The Allens were "middling" folk, not among the most wealthy residents, but well enough off to have two house lots and several hundred acres of land—most of which the senior Andrew Allen reserved to settle on his two sons. He gave substantial portions of this land to Andrew and John at their marriages in the 1680s, also promising his eldest son that he would eventually inherit the town house and lot.[93]

In this way he assured both sons a livelihood, and economically advantageous marriages as well.

The portions given to the four daughters when they married in the 1660s and 1670s have not been recorded, but they were probably not equal to even the younger son's share. Nevertheless, Sarah and Hannah Allen had, in the eyes of their community, married well. Sarah had married Samuel Holt, eldest son of one of Andover's most prosperous residents, and Hannah had married Samuel's brother James. Although there were five sons in their family to inherit, the Holt sons' portions were comparable to if not larger than those settled on Andrew and John Allen.[94] Mary and Martha Allen, however, had not lived up to community expectations for young women of their station. Mary, probably the eldest Allen child, had married Roger Toothaker of Billerica, a man whose father had died young and who owned only a small parcel of land deeded to him by his stepfather.[95] Martha had married Thomas Carrier in 1674, after naming him the father of her first child. Thomas was a young Welsh servant, with hardly any resources at all.[96]

Martha and Thomas Carrier lived in Billerica (and possibly other towns as well) during the early years of their marriage. How they survived is unclear, but in the late 1680s they arrived in Andover—destitute and with four children. A fifth child was born soon after. Fearful that the Carriers' support would become the responsibility of the community, the Andover selectmen had initially warned them out of town, a move which officially precluded application for relief. But for some reason the selectmen changed their minds, even going so far as to grant Thomas Carrier land. The action did not presage community acceptance, however. On the contrary, Martha Carrier's independent spirit and lack of deference for her more prosperous neighbors seems to have intensified community hostility to the family. When Martha and several of her children came down with smallpox late in 1690, the town responded as if she had deliberately created an epidemic. The selectmen notified Martha's brothers and brothers-in-law that the town abnegated all responsibility for her and her children. They would only "take care," they said, that the Carriers did not "spread the distemper with wicked carelessness which we are afraid they have already done," and they insisted that the family provide for the infected members "out of their own estates."[97]

The disease spread nonetheless. Hardest hit was the Allen family itself, especially the male line. Martha's father and both of her brothers died that winter. So too did her brother Andrew's youngest son and several of her in-laws, including her sister Hannah's husband and eldest son.[98] Rumor had it that Martha Carrier was a witch.

No one formally accused her of demonic activities until 1692, when the possessed females in Salem saw her shape among other witches. Carrier was arrested soon after, and brought before the magistrates to be examined. Several of the possessed complained that she was trying to make them witches too, almost killing them because they refused. Several reminded the court "that she had killed 13. at Andover." A young confessing witch from Andover was more specific. Martha Carrier, she said, had murdered her brothers, her brother-in-law Holt, and her two nephews.[99]

Martha Carrier was as unyielding during her pre-trial examination as Susanna Martin had been, and the enemies of Satan were just as vindictive. Many of her old Billerica and Andover neighbors came forward to testify about the sudden and strange accidents to their persons and cattle which followed upon their past disputes with this woman. They described her as angry, envious, and malicious. On the basis of this testimony, the judges decided that she should be put to death, and on 19 August 1692, maintaining her innocence to the last, she was hanged. Cotton Mather, one of the witnesses to her execution, would later immortalize her as the very "Queen of Hell."[100]

Martha Carrier's sister and brother-in-law, Mary and Roger Toothaker, their daughter, and four of Martha's children were all named as witches during the Salem outbreak.[101] Roger Toothaker died in prison before he could be tried. The rest of the family, including eight-year-old Sarah Carrier, confessed. Whether they believed they were witches or simply confessed to save their lives is not certain, but according to John Proctor, one of the men executed in 1692, Martha's sons Richard and Andrew incriminated themselves only after they were "tyed . . . Neck and Heels till the Blood was ready to come out of their Noses."[102] They all retracted their confessions once it was clear that the lives of the accused were no longer endangered by pleas of innocence.

These five short histories—and the earlier profile of Eunice Cole—suggest the diverse economic circumstances of witches in early New England. If this were all the histories revealed, we would be justified in concluding that material conditions had little to do with the dynamics of witchcraft accusations. But these stories reveal much more. The six women featured in these histories were either (1) daughters of parents who had no sons (or whose sons had died), (2) women in marriages which brought forth only daughters (or in which the sons had died), or (3) women in marriages with no children at all. These patterns had significant economic implications. Because there were no legitimate male heirs in their immediate families, each of these six women stood to inherit, did inherit, or were denied their apparent right to inherit substantially larger portions of their fathers' or husbands' accumulated estates than women in families with male heirs. Whatever actually happened to the property in question—and in some cases we simply do not know—these women were aberrations in a society with an inheritance system designed to keep property in the hands of men.

These six cases also illustrate fertility and mortality patterns widely shared among the families of accused witches. A substantial majority of New England's accused females were women without brothers, women with daughters but no sons, or women in marriages with no children at all (see table 11). Of the 267 accused females, enough is known about 158 to identify them as either having or not having brothers or sons to inherit: only sixty-two of the 158 (39 percent) did, whereas ninety-six (61 percent) did not. More striking, *once accused,* women without brothers or sons were even more likely than women with brothers or sons to be tried, convicted, and executed: women from families without male heirs made up 64 percent of the females prosecuted, 76 percent of those who were found guilty, and 89 percent of those who were executed.

These figures must be read with care, however, for two reasons. First, eighteen of the sixty-two accused females who *had* brothers or sons to inherit were themselves daughters and granddaughters of women who did not. If, as we argued earlier, these eighteen females, most of whom were young women or girls, were accused because their neighbors believed that their mothers and grandmothers passed their witchcraft on to them, then they form a somewhat ambiguous group. Since they all had brothers to inherit, it would be inaccurate to exclude them from this category in table 11, yet including them

TABLE 11. Female Witches by Presence or Absence of Brothers or Sons, New England, 1620–1725 (A)

Action	Women without Brothers or Sons		Women with Brothers or Sons		Total
Accused	96	(61%)	62	(39%)	158
Tried	41	(64%)	23	(36%)	64
Convicted	25	(76%)	8	(24%)	33
Executed	17	(89%)	2	(11%)	19

understates the extent to which inheritance-related concerns were at issue in witchcraft accusations. At the same time, the large number of cases in which the fertility and mortality patterns of witches' families are unknown (109 of the 267 accused females in New England) makes it impossible to assess precisely the proportion of women among the accused who did not have brothers or sons.[103]

Table 12 helps clarify the point. It includes as a separate category the daughters and granddaughters of women without brothers or sons and incorporates the cases for which this information is unknown. Although inclusion of the unknowns renders the overall percentages meaningless, this way of representing the available information shows clearly the particular vulnerability of women without brothers or sons. Even if *all* the unknown cases involved women from families *with* male heirs—a highly unlikely possibility—women from families without males to inherit would still form a majority of convicted and executed witches. Were the complete picture visible, I suspect that it would not differ substantially from that presented earlier in table 11—which is based on data reflecting 60 percent of New England's witches and which indicates

TABLE 12. Female Witches by Presence or Absence of Brothers or Sons, New England, 1620–1725 (B)

Action	Women without Brothers or Sons	Daughters and Grand-daughters of Women without Brothers or Sons	Women with Brothers or Sons	Unknown Cases	Total
Accused	96 (36%)	18 (7%)	44 (16%)	109 (41%)	267
Tried	41 (48%)	6 (7%)	17 (20%)	22 (26%)	86
Convicted	25 (56%)	0 (0%)	6 (13%)	12 (27%)	45
Executed	17 (61%)	0 (0%)	2 (7%)	9 (32%)	28

that women without brothers and sons were more vulnerable than other women at all stages of the process.

Numbers alone, however, do not tell the whole story. More remains to be said about what happened to these inheriting or potentially inheriting women, both before and after they were accused of witchcraft.

It was not unusual for women in families without male heirs to be accused of witchcraft shortly after the deaths of fathers, husbands, brothers, or sons. Katherine Harrison, Susanna Martin, Joan Penney, and Martha Carrier all exemplify this pattern. So too does elderly Ann Hibbens of Boston, whose execution in 1656 seems to have had a profound enough effect on some of her peers to influence the outcome of subsequent trials for years to come.[104] Hibbens had three sons from her first marriage, all of whom lived in England; but she had no children by her husband William Hibbens, with whom she had come to Massachusetts in the 1630s. William died in 1654; Ann was brought to trial two years later. Although her husband's will has not survived, he apparently left a substantial portion (if not all) of his property directly to her: when she wrote her own will shortly before her execution, Ann Hibbens was in full possession of a £344 estate, most of which she bequeathed to her sons in England.[105]

Similarly, less than two years elapsed between the death of Gloucester's William Vinson and the imprisonment of his widow Rachel in 1692. Two children, a son and a daughter, had been born to the marriage, but the son had died in 1675. Though William Vinson had had four sons (and three daughters) by a previous marriage, the sons were all dead by 1683. In his will, which he wrote in 1684, before he was certain that his last son had been lost at sea, William left his whole £180 estate to Rachel for her life, stipulating that she could sell part of the lands and cattle if she found herself in need of resources. After Rachel's death, "in Case" his son John "be Living and returne home agayne," William said, most of the estate was to be divided between John and their daughter Abigail. If John did not return, both shares were to be Abigail's.[106]

Bridget Oliver (later Bridget Bishop) was brought into court on witchcraft charges less than a year after the death of her husband Thomas Oliver in 1679. He had died intestate, but since the estate was worth less than £40 after debts, and since Bridget had a child to raise, the court gave her all but £3 of it during her lifetime, stipulating that she could sell a ten-acre lot "towards paying the debts and her present supply." Twenty shillings went to each of her husband's two sons by his first wife, and twenty shillings to the Olivers' twelve-year-old daughter Christian, the only child of their marriage.[107]

In other cases, many years passed between the death of the crucial male relative and the moment when a formal witchcraft complaint was filed. Twenty years had elapsed, for instance, between the death of Adam Hawkes of Lynn and the arrest of his widow and daughter. Adam had died in 1672, at the age of sixty-four, just three years after his marriage to the much-younger Sarah Hooper and less than a year after the birth of their daughter Sarah. He had died without leaving a will, but his two principal heirs—his widow and his son John from his first marriage—said they were aware of Adam's intentions concerning his £772 estate. The magistrates responsible for distributing Adam's property took their word, allowing "certain articles of agreement" between the two to form the basis of the distribution. As a result, the elder Sarah came into full possession of 188 acres of land and one-third of Adam's movable property. Her daughter was awarded £90, "to be paid five pounds every two years until forty pounds is paid, and the fifty pounds at age or marriage."[108]

It was just about the time young Sarah was due to receive her marriage portion that she and her mother, then Sarah Wardwell, were accused of witchcraft. Named with them as witches were the elder Sarah's second husband, carpenter Samuel Wardwell, their nineteen-year-old daughter Mercy, and the mother, two sisters, and brother of Francis Johnson, the younger Sarah's husband-to-be.[109] It is not clear whether when

Sarah Hawkes became Sarah Johnson she received the balance of her inheritance, but £36 of Sarah and Samuel Wardwell's property was seized by the authorities in 1692. Massachusetts passed a law at the height of the Salem outbreak providing attainder for "conjuration, witchcraft and dealing with evil and wicked spirits."[110] Attainder meant the loss of civil, inheritance, and property rights for persons like Sarah Wardwell who had been sentenced to death. Not until 1711 was restitution made to Sarah Wardwell's children.[111]

Margaret Thatcher was not formally accused of witchcraft until more than thirty years after she became an heiress. Merchant Jacob Sheaffe, Margaret's first husband, may have been the richest man in Boston when he died in 1659, leaving only his thirty-four-year-old widow and two daughters, Elizabeth and Mehitabel, to inherit.[112] What disposition was made of the estate is not clear, but the following year witnessed the death of Margaret's father, merchant Henry Webb, a man whose wealth nearly equaled that of his son-in-law, and whose highly detailed will is extant. Margaret was Webb's only child (his wife had died only months before) and he left most of his £7819 estate to her and his two granddaughters, with alternative bequests in several places in the event that Margaret had male heirs by a "second or other marriage."[113] Margaret *was* married again, to Thomas Thatcher, minister of Boston's Old South Church, but no male heirs were born.[114] Though Margaret was not named a witch until the Salem outbreak, her cousin Elizabeth Blackleach was accused in 1662, two years after Henry Webb's death.[115] Henry had left Elizabeth £140 in his will, £40 of which was to go to her then only child after Elizabeth's death.

Mary English of Salem was charged with witchcraft seven years after she came into her inheritance. Her father, merchant William Hollingworth, had been declared lost at sea in 1677, but at that time Mary's brother William was still alive. Possibly because the younger William was handling the family's interests in other colonies, or possibly because the father's estate was in debt for more than it was worth, the magistrates gave the widow Elinor Hollingworth power of attorney to salvage what she could.[116] With her "owne labor," as she put it, "but making use of other mens estates," the aggressive and outspoken Mistress Hollingworth soon had her deceased husband's debts paid and his wharf, warehouse, and tavern solvent again.[117] She had no sooner done so, however, than she was accused of witchcraft by the wife of a Gloucester mariner.[118] Though the magistrates gave little credence to the charge at the time, they may have had second thoughts later. In 1685, her son William died, and Elinor subsequently conveyed the whole Hollingworth estate over to Mary English, who was probably her only surviving child.[119]

Elinor Hollingworth had died by 1692, but Mary English was one of the women cried out upon early in the Salem outbreak. Her husband, the merchant Philip English, was accused soon after. Knowing their lives were in grave danger, the Englishes fled to the safety of New York. But as one historian of witchcraft has pointed out, flight was "the legal equivalent of conviction."[120] No sooner had they left than close to £1200 of their property was confiscated under the law providing attainder for witchcraft.[121]

Not all witches from families without male heirs were accused of conspiring with the Devil *after* they had come into their inheritances. On the contrary, some were accused prior to the death of the crucial male relative, many times before it was clear who would inherit. Eunice Cole was one of these women. Another was Martha Corey of Salem, who was accused of witchcraft in 1692 while her husband was still alive. Giles Corey had been married twice before and had several daughters by the time he married the widow Martha Rich, probably in the 1680s. With no sons to inherit, Giles's substantial land holdings would, his neighbors might have assumed, be passed on to his wife and daughters. Alice Parker, who may have been Giles's daughter from a former marriage, also came before the magistrates as a witch in 1692, as did Giles himself. Martha Corey and Alice Parker maintained their innocence and were hanged. Giles Corey, in an apparently futile attempt to preserve his whole estate for his heirs, refused to respond to the indictment. To force him to enter a plea, he was tortured: successively heavier weights were placed on his body until he was pressed to death.[122]

What seems especially significant here is that most accused witches whose husbands were still alive were, like their counterparts who were widows and spinsters, over forty years of age—and therefore unlikely if not unable to produce male heirs. Indeed, the fact that witchcraft accusations were rarely taken seriously by the community until the accused stopped bearing children takes on a special meaning when it is juxtaposed with the anomolous position of inheriting women or potentially inheriting women in New England's social structure.

Witches in families without male heirs sometimes had been dispossessed of part or all of their inheritances before—sometimes long before—they were formally charged with witchcraft. Few of these women, however, accepted disinheritance with equanimity. Rather, like Susanna Martin, they took their battles to court, casting themselves in the role of public challengers to the system of male inheritance. In most instances, the authorities sided with their antagonists.

The experience of Rachel Clinton of Ipswich is instructive. As one of five daughters in line to inherit the "above £500" estate of their father, Richard Haffield,[123] Rachel had been reduced to abject poverty at least eighteen years before she came before county magistrates in 1687 as a witch. Richard Haffield had bequeathed £30 to each of his daughters just before his death in 1639, but since Rachel was only ten at the time, and her sister Ruth only seven, he stipulated that their shares were to be paid "as they shall com to the age of sixteen yeares old."[124] While he had not made other bequests, he made his wife Martha executrix, and so the unencumbered portions of the estate were legally at her disposal. In 1652, since Rachel and Ruth were still unmarried (Rachel was twenty-three at the time), local magistrates ordered Martha Haffield to pay one of her sons-in-law, Richard Coy, the £60 still due Rachel and Ruth, to "improve their legacy."[125]

When Martha Haffield wrote her own will in 1662, six years before her death, she bequeathed the still-single Rachel the family farm, valued at £300, with the proviso that she share the income it produced with her sisters, Ruth (now Ruth White) and Martha Coy. The household goods were to be divided among the three. Martha had effectively disinherited her two oldest children (children of her husband's first marriage) with ten shillings apiece.[126] This will, though legal, would never be honored. In 1666, the county court put the whole Haffield estate into the hands of Ruth's husband, Thomas White, whom they named as Martha Haffield's guardian and whom they empowered to "receive and recover her estate." They declared Martha Haffield "non compos mentis."[127]

The issue that seems to have precipitated this court action was Rachel's marriage to Lawrence Clinton several months before. Lawrence was an indentured servant and fourteen years younger than his wife. Perhaps even more offensive to community standards, Rachel had purchased Lawrence's freedom for £21, with money she said her mother had given her. Once Thomas White had control of the Haffield estate, he immediately sued Lawrence's former master, Robert Cross, for return of the £21.[128]

Several issues were raised in the almost four years of litigation that followed, but arguments focused on the legality of Rachel's access to and use of the money. Never explicitly mentioned by White, but clearly more important to him than the £21, was Rachel's sizeable inheritance. For Rachel, the stakes were obvious: "my brother [in-law] White . . . is a cheaten Rogue," she insisted, "and [he] goese about to undoe mee. He keeps my portion from me, and strives to git all that I have."[129] The case was complicated by a number of factors, including Lawrence Clinton's desertion of his wife.[130] White did at last gain full control of the Haffield estate, however, and retained it for the rest of his life.[131]

Martha Haffield died in 1668. Shortly before, Rachel, then thirty-nine, had been forced to petition the court for relief, "being destitute of money and friends and skill in matters of Law." The house where she and her mother had lived, she said, had been sold by White, and its contents seized. Even her marriage portion, she averred, was still withheld from her "under pretence of emprovement."[132] Giving up her attempt to claim her inheritance, she subsequently tried to make her estranged husband support her. Though the court made several halfhearted attempts to compel Lawrence to live with his wife, or at least to maintain her, by 1681 they had tired of the effort: "Rachel Clinton, desiring that her husband provide for her, was allowed 20 shillings," they declared, "she to demand no more of him."[133] No doubt Rachel's adulterous involvement with other men influenced the court's decision, although Lawrence's sexual behavior had been even more flagrant.[134] In 1677, Rachel had petitioned for, but had been denied, a divorce.[135] When she appealed again in late 1681, it was granted her.[136] From then on, she was a ward of the town.[137] In 1687, and again in 1692, she was accused of malefic witchcraft. The second time she was tried and convicted.[138]

Sarah Good's plight resembles that of Rachel Clinton, even in some of the particulars. Sarah's father, John Solart, a prosperous Wenham innkeeper, had taken his own life in 1672, leaving an estate of about £500 after debts. He left a widow, Elizabeth, and nine children—seven daughters and two sons. The court accepted testimony from three witnesses concerning an oral will he had made, and awarded the widow £165, and the eldest son, John, a double share of £84. Since two of the daughters had already received their shares as marriage portions, the other six children, including Sarah, were to receive £42 each when they came of age.[139] Sarah was then seventeen or eighteen. That same year, the widow Solart married Ezekiel Woodward, who upon this marriage came into possession of the £165 and the unpaid childrens' portions.[140]

More than a decade later, the surviving daughters peti-
tioned the court for the inheritances left them by their father.
By that time their mother and both of their brothers had died.
After the death of their mother, they said,

> . . . Ezekill Woodward, that maryed with our mother, did
> Refuse to enter into any obligation to pay our portions.
> Our brother Joseph, whoe would have bien of Age the last
> Winter, is dead, and your Honores have declared the last
> court at Salem, that his portion shall be devided amongst
> us. But except your honnours will be pleased to put us into
> som capacity to gitt it, we know not well how to gitt it that
> soe we may divid it.

Most wronged, they added, was their sister Sarah, then wife
of former indentured servant, Daniel Poole:

> . . . she is 28 yers of age and she is yett without her portion.
> And except that she will accept of a parcell of land which
> our father bought at a very deare Rate for his conve-
> nience, which was well fenced, and she alow the same price
> for it now, the fenc is taken off, she is not like to have
> anything. . . .

The court responded that the daughters "could recover their
right from any person withholding it," but made no provision
for them to do so.[141] Twenty-three years later, litigation over
the Solart estate was still going on.[142]

Sarah, at least, never did recover what she felt was right-
fully hers. By 1686, the little she had was gone. Her first husband, Daniel Poole, had died sometime after the 1682 petition
was filed, leaving only debts for which Sarah and her second
husband, William Good, were held responsible. Two men presented testimony in court that Poole "had been his own man
several years before he was married unto Sarah Solah," and
that Sarah "did enjoy and dispose of [his] whole estate . . . viz.
a horse, 2 cows, and all his moveable goods." Ezekiel Woodward came into court to testify that one month earlier he had
delivered to William Good three acres of the Solart land—

land that the Goods should have had many years before. The court ordered William and Sarah Good to satisfy Poole's creditors. When the couple could not pay, the magistrates put William Good in jail and ordered seized about £9 worth of the Goods' Wenham land. Shortly thereafter, the Goods sold the rest of their Wenham property for £5, apparently out of dire necessity.[143]

From then on Sarah and her husband were reduced to begging work, food, and shelter from their neighbors. By the time of the 1692 outbreak, they were living in Salem, where Sarah Good was one of the first witches named. Within a month, her four-year-old daughter Dorcas, evidently her only living child, was jailed as well.[144]

As these last two cases suggest, the land and other property of witches or their families could be confiscated in ways that went beyond the 1692 attainder law. The property of women in families without male heirs was vulnerable to loss in a variety of ways, from deliberate destruction by neighbors (as Katherine Harrison experienced) to official sequestering by local magistrates. In nearly every case, the authorities themselves seem hostile or at best indifferent to the property claims of these women. One final example deserves mention here, not only because it indicates how reluctant magistrates were to leave property in the control of women, but because it shows that the property of convicted witches was liable to seizure even without the benefit of an attainder law.

Rebecca Greensmith had been widowed twice before her marriage to Nathaniel Greensmith. Her first husband, Abraham Elsen of Wethersfield, had died intestate in 1648, leaving an estate of £99. After checking the birth dates of the Elsens' two children, three-year-old Sarah and one-year-old Hannah, the court initially left the whole estate with the widow.[145] When Rebecca married Wethersfield's Jarvis Mudge the following year, the local magistrates sequestered the house and land Abraham Elsen had left, worth £40, stating their intention to rent it out "for the Use and Benefit of the two daughters."[146] The family moved to New London shortly after, but Jarvis Mudge died in 1652 and Rebecca moved with Hannah and Sarah to Hartford. Since Rebecca was unable to support herself and her two daughters, the court allowed her to sell the small amount of land owned by her second husband (with whom she had had no children) "for the paing of debts and the Bettering the Childrens portyons."[147]

Sometime prior to 1660, Rebecca married Nathaniel Greensmith. During the Hartford outbreak, Rebecca came under suspicion of witchcraft. After Nathaniel sued his wife's accuser for slander, Nathaniel himself was named. Both husband and wife were convicted and executed.[148]

Respecting Nathaniel's £182 estate, £44 of which was claimed by the then eighteen-year-old Sarah and seventeen-year-old Hannah Elsen, the court ordered the three overseers "to preserve the estate from Waste" and to pay "any just debts," the only one recorded being the Greensmiths' jail fees. Except for allowing the overseers "to dispose of the 2 daughters," presumably to service, the magistrates postponed until the next court any decision concerning the young women's portions. First, however, they deducted £40 to go "to the Treasurer for the County."[149] No reason was given for this substantial appropriation and no record of further distribution of the estate has survived.

Aside from these many women who lived or had lived in families without male heirs, there were at least a dozen other witches who, despite the presence of brothers and sons, came into much larger shares of estates than their neighbors would have expected. In some cases, these women gained full control over the disposition of property. We know about these women because their fathers, husbands, or other relatives left wills, because the women themselves wrote wills, or because male relatives who felt cheated out of their customary shares fought in the courts for more favorable arrangements.

Grace Boulter of Hampton, one of several children of Richard Swain, is one of these women. Grace was accused of witchcraft in 1680, along with her thirty-two-year-old daughter, Mary Prescott. Twenty years earlier, in 1660, just prior to his removal to Nantucket, Grace's father had deeded a substantial portion of his Hampton property to her and her husband Nathaniel, some of which he gave directly to her.[150]

Another witch in this group is Jane James of Marblehead, who left an estate at her death in 1669 which was valued at £85. While it is not clear how she came into possession of it, the property had not belonged to her husband Erasmus, who had died in 1660, though it did play a significant role in a controversy between her son and son-in-law over their rightful shares of both Erasmus's and Jane's estates. Between 1650 and her death in 1669, Jane was accused of witchcraft at least three times by her Marblehead neighbors.[151]

A third woman, Margaret Scott of Rowley, had been left most of her husband Benjamin's small estate in 1671. The land and most of the cattle were hers only "dureing hir widdowhood," but approximately one-third of the estate was "to be wholy hir owne." Margaret did not remarry. By the time she was executed as a witch in 1692, twenty-one years after her husband's death, she was seventy-five years old and little remained of the estate for the next generation to inherit.[152]

In each of these last few cases, the women came into property through the decision of a father or husband. Only occasionally, however, do we find the courts putting property directly into the hands of women subsequently accused of witchcraft. Mary English's mother, Elinor Hollingworth, was one of these exceptions. In this situation, as in the others, the unusual decision of the magistrates can be attributed to the small size of the estate involved. These particular inheriting women were widows, usually with young children to support.

Looking back over the lives of these many women—most particularly those who did not have brothers or sons to inherit—we begin to understand the complexity of the economic dimension of New England witchcraft. Only rarely does the actual trial testimony indicate that economic power was even at issue. Nevertheless it is there, recurring with a telling persistence once we look beyond what was explicitly said about these women as witches. Inheritance disputes surface frequently enough in witchcraft cases, cropping up as part of the general context even when no direct link between the dispute and the charge is discernible, to suggest the fears that underlay most accusations. No matter how deeply entrenched the principle of male inheritance, no matter how carefully written the laws that protected it, it was impossible to insure that all families had male offspring. The women who stood to benefit from these demographic "accidents" account for most of New England's female witches.

The amount of property in question was not the crucial factor in the way these women were viewed or treated by their neighbors, however. Women of widely varying economic circumstances were vulnerable to accusation and even to conviction. Neither was there a direct line from accuser to material beneficiary of the accusation: others in the community did sometimes profit personally from the losses sustained by these women (Rachel Clinton's brother-in-law, Thomas White, comes to mind), but only rarely did the gain accrue to the accusers themselves. Indeed, occasionally there was no direct temporal connection: in some instances several decades passed between the creation of the key economic conditions and the charge of witchcraft; the charge in other cases even anticipated the development of those conditions.

Finally, inheriting or potentially inheriting women were vulnerable to witchcraft accusations not only during the Salem outbreak, but from the time of the first formal accusations in New England at least until the end of the century. Despite

Thus there is no evidence of causation for economics-based accusations

sketchy information on the lives of New England's early witches, it appears that Alice Young, Mary Johnson, Margaret Jones, Joan Carrington, and Mary Parsons, all of whom were executed in the late 1640s and early 1650s, were women without sons when the accusations were lodged. Elizabeth Godman, brought into court at least twice on witchcraft charges in the 1650s, had neither brothers nor sons.[153] Decade by decade, the pattern continued. Only Antinomian and Quaker women, against whom accusations never generated much support, were, as a group, exempt from it.

The Salem outbreak created only a slight wrinkle in this established fabric of suspicion. If daughters, husbands, and sons of witches were more vulnerable to danger in 1692 than they had been previously, they were mostly the daughters, husbands, and sons of inheriting or potentially inheriting women. As the outbreak spread, it drew into its orbit increasing numbers of women, "unlikely" witches in that they were married to well-off and influential men, but familiar figures to some of their neighbors nonetheless. What the impoverished Sarah Good had in common with Mary Phips, wife of Massachusetts's governor, was what Eunice Cole had in common with Katherine Harrison, and what Mehitabel Downing had in common with Ann Hibbens. However varied their backgrounds and economic positions, as women without brothers or women without sons, they stood in the way of the orderly transmission of property from one generation of males to another.

a conspiratorial interpretation psycho-social and freudian but conspiratorial nonetheless

FOUR

Handmaidens of the Devil

MOST WITCHES IN New England were middle-aged or old women eligible for inheritances because they had no brothers or sons. But not all women who shared these demographic and economic characteristics were accused of witchcraft. It was Rachel Clinton rather than her mother or her sisters whom neighbors saw as casting spells on themselves and their children. It was Susanna Martin rather than her sister or stepmother whom neighbors said appeared to them in animal shapes, bewitched their cattle, and prevented them from prospering. Many female relatives of reputed witches were eventually found among the accused, especially during the Salem outbreak, but many others seem to have escaped the stigma of suspicion. So too, apparently, did other inheriting or potentially inheriting women in New England who had passed their childbearing years. What was it about the accused that set them apart even from other women in similar positions?

The answer most likely to emerge from recent historical accounts of New England witchcraft is that the character or personalities of New England's witches made them suspect in

obviously

their neighbor's eyes. Although some scholars are more sympathetic than others to the plight of their subjects, witches are generally portrayed in the literature as disagreeable women, at best aggressive and abrasive, at worst ill-tempered, quarrelsome, and spiteful. They are almost always described as deviants—disorderly women who failed to, or refused to, abide by the behavioral norms of their society. In two accounts, at least some of the accused *were* witches: that is to say, they are described as actually practicing the black arts in order to harm or kill their adversaries.[1]

Key

Drawn primarily from descriptions left to us by witches' accusers, this portrait conforms to the popular stereotype of the witch.[2] Like other stereotypes, it contains enough truth to mask the interests it serves. By suggesting that their disagreeable personalities separated the accused from "ordinary" colonists, even the most sympathetic accounts encourage us to conclude that New England witches, to a greater or lesser extent, brought the accusations upon themselves.[3] In accepting their adversaries' views of how these women ought to have behaved, these descriptions overlook the variety of norms that guided behavior in early New England. These norms varied with prevailing class, gender, and racial assumptions, which construed behavior appropriate for some social groups as inappropriate for others. And the social assumptions that prevailed in early New England accurately measure the distribution of power at the time.

In their behavior or character, New England witches were in fact not very different from their neighbors. Some were disagreeable and quarrelsome, others were not. All may have occasionally been outspoken and abrasive, but that simply shows how much they resembled the people around them. New Englanders were an aggressive, contentious, disorderly lot, no more willing or able than people in other times and places to live up to their own ideals of familial or neighborly harmony. Yet not all colonists—not even all ill-tempered and contentious colonists—were vulnerable to witchcraft accusations. What made witches unusual was not how they behaved but how their behavior was understood in New England's hierarchical society. As older women, in most cases as poor, middling, or unexpectedly well-off women, some of their attitudes and actions were construed not simply as unneighborly or sinful—as were similar attitudes and actions in other people—but as evidence of witchcraft, as signs of women's refusal to accept their "place" in New England's social order.

The social process that transformed women into witches in New England required a convergence of belief on the part of both the townspeople and the religious and secular authorities that these women posed serious threats to society. For most people that threat lay in the subversion of the sexual order, but the clergy articulated the threat of witchcraft as the subversion of the order of Creation. Not surprisingly, then, the behaviors that brought witches to the attention of their community were not simply random lapses from social norms. They were two types of dangerous trespass: challenges to the supremacy of God and challenges to prescribed gender arrangements.

Distinguishing between the two in colonial New England is not always easy. Puritan beliefs were the most powerful determinants of acceptable female behavior, while religious ritual and symbolism continually reinforced behavioral distinctions between the sexes. Gender issues *were* religious issues, and perhaps nowhere is that more vivid than in the case of witchcraft. In Puritan thought, the witch-figure was a symbol of the struggle between God and Satan for human souls. In Puritan society, witches (who as we have seen were usually female) were known by behavior closely or exclusively associated with the female sex. Often implicit and seldom measurable, official religious beliefs were nonetheless central in determining who witches were and what witches did.

Bearing these considerations in mind, we now turn to the specific sins of New England witches: discontent, anger, envy, malice, seduction, lying, and pride. Recognizing that all actions associated with witches were ultimately offenses against God and the order of Creation, and that all had repercussions for community social and economic relations, we can for conve-nience' sake divide the range of sins into roughly three groups of transgressions, running along a continuum, differentiated according to the primary object of the activity: (1) explicitly religious sins directed against God or his emissaries on earth—the church and its ministers, (2) sins of a mixed religious and sexual nature committed against other members of the com-munity, and (3) predominantly sexual sins against the order and processes of nature. Lying and pride will be discussed last because they are of such a general character as to permeate and inform the full range.

Witchcraft was rebellion against God, and among the grounds for examining a witch were signs that she had trans-ferred her allegiance from God to Satan. Neighbors testifying against the accused often cited hostility to the Puritan God, church, or clergy as evidence of witchcraft. Anything from sabbath-breaking to overt repudiation of ministerial authority to blasphemy could be interpreted as signifying a covenant with the Devil. When, for instance, John Brown presented his testimony against Sarah Cole of Lynn in 1692, he charged her with once having said that "all Church members were Devills."[4] James Kettle came into the Salem court to accuse Elizabeth Hubbard of speaking "severall untruthes in denying the sabath day and saying she had not ben to meting that day."[5] And Andrew Elliott thought the court might want to know that a man who had once lived with Susannah Roots of Beverly had said that "she was a bad woman . . ." who "would withdraw and absent herselfe" from family prayer.[6]

Confessing witches and defenders of the accused also acknowledged a connection between a woman's attitude toward the church and her witchcraft. After detailing her many witchcraft practices in Andover, Ann Foster said in 1692 that "she formerly frequented the publique metting to worship god, but the divill had such power over her that she could not profit there and that was her undoeing."[7] As evidence of Winifred Holman's innocence, several of her Cambridge neighbors averred in 1660 that they never had "any grounds or reasons to suspect her for witchery," adding that "she is diligent in her calling and frequents public preaching, and gives diligent attention there unto."[8]

Mockery of established religion, either by word or deed, does not seem to have constituted sufficient proof of witchcraft, however. Stronger evidence of a deliberate pact with Satan was normally required for conviction. Even in those cases where indications of religious recalcitrance were submitted as evidence and where a verdict of guilty was found, the magistrates' decisions appear to have been based primarily on testimony concerning supernatural harm done or intended to individuals or their property.[9] Still, the association of women, religious dissent, and witchcraft aided the process of witch identification. Witches were thought to be clever and powerful hags whose supernatural practices were hard to prove. A woman's opposition to the church, on the other hand, was "knowable." Like her other sins against God, it indicated that there was at least reason to suspect that she was in league with the Devil.

The significance of witches' real or perceived enmity to the church is best seen in the experiences of women for whom religious crimes were clearly major causes for suspicion. Unlike Sarah Cole and the other women mentioned above, most of these latter witches were tried for heresy, not *maleficium*.

As we have seen, witchcraft-as-heresy was a belief held by a few influential men but not shared by most colonists. During the Antinomian crisis in the late 1630s, witchcraft fear surfaced among some of Massachusetts' leaders, but their accusations never reached the level of formal complaints. Besides indicating that popular as well as elite support was necessary for trials to take place, accusations brought against women for religious crimes highlight the underlying gender issues in most other witchcraft cases.

Women in Boston, Salem, New Haven, and other Puritan communities continued to play prominent roles as religious dissenters for several years after the Antinomian crisis.[10] Once witchcraft trials became regular features of the social environment in the late 1640s, however, women became less vocal about their beliefs and less assertive in their doubts about their religious leaders.[11] By the late 1650s, however, a new group of female religious activists, the Quaker testifiers, had aroused witchcraft alarm among the authorities.

From almost the beginning of their movement in the 1640s, English Quaker women openly assumed what New England's Antinomian women had claimed only indirectly—the right to female spiritual leadership. Female preachers and "publishers of truth" were numerous among the Quakers in the years following England's civil war. Once the sect was organized in New England, its female adherents there became immediately visible as active proselytizers of the faith. Rejecting Pauline proscriptions against women speaking in church, Quakers, with their insistence on a lay ministry and their emphasis on the "inner light," took the Protestant principle of the "priesthood of all believers" to its logical conclusion. Because God revealed his word to all, there was no need for an ordained ministry. Women as well as men, the uneducated with the educated, could know—and teach—divine truth.[12]

To Puritan opponents in both old and New England, Quaker doctrine smacked of blasphemy. Its practice evoked images of chaos in the social order. As Puritan clergyman Hugh Peter had made clear to Anne Hutchinson during her church trial, women who assumed to preach God's word called into question not only the hierarchical relations between preacher and hearer but the ordered relations between husband and wife, and magistrate and subject.[13] When the first Quaker preachers arrived in Boston harbor in 1656, the authorities were prepared. Ann Austin and Mary Fisher were arrested as witches before they even reached shore.[14]

Acting Governor Richard Bellingham ordered both Austin and Fisher stripped naked on board ship and their bodies examined for signs of Devil worship. Their possessions were searched for books containing "corrupt, heretical, and blasphemous Doctrines."[15] Apparently the incriminating evidence was found, for the literature they brought with them was burned and the women incarcerated in the Boston jail. So dangerous were these two women to Puritan society that the windows of their cells were boarded up and a fine of £5 was levied on anyone who tried to speak with them. After five weeks of confinement, they were thrown out of the colony without a trial.

Not all were convinced by the allegations that Quakers practiced witchcraft. Austin and Fisher had immediately found supporters among local residents, and the next group of Quakers, who arrived in Boston just two days after Austin and Fisher left, were not treated as witches. These eight men and women were simply detained in prison for eleven weeks as members of that "cursed sect of hereticks" and then shipped back to England.[16] By the time they were gone, Massachusetts magistrates had passed legislation that allowed them to punish Quakers *as Quakers,* for 'tak[ing] uppon them to be imediately sent of God, and infallibly asisted by the spirit": for holding "blasphemouth opinions, despising government and the order of God in church and comonwealth, speaking evill of dignities, reproaching and reviling magistrates and ministers, seeking to turne people from the faith, and gaine proselytes to theire pernicious wayes."[17]

With this and subsequent laws providing legal grounds for confronting the fast-growing population of Quakers and Quaker sympathizers, witchcraft allegations may have become unnecessary. For almost the next four years (the period in which the Society of Friends grew most quickly in New England), no such charges seem to have been lodged against them. Even Mary Dyer, who had returned to Massachusetts in 1657 and three years later was hanged as a Quaker, escaped public accusation as a witch.

With the Restoration of Charles II to the throne in England, witchcraft themes reappeared in public attacks on Quakers. Charles was known to disapprove of the persecution of Quakers in Massachusetts, and this may have affected their treatment there. When Long Island's Mary Wright came before the Massachusetts General Court in 1660, she came as a suspected witch, and as a witch she may even have been tried. Yet the only surviving evidence speaks to the matter of her having entered Massachusetts to protest the execution of Quakers, for which she was subsequently banished from the colony.[18]

No other Quaker was tried as a witch, yet the informal connection between witchcraft and Quaker belief persisted. Mary Tilton was exiled in 1662 for "having like a sorceress gone from door to door to lure and seduce people, yea even young girls, to join the Quakers," but in this as in other cases, witchcraft was merely implied and the accusation was never formalized.[19] When a Boston constable could not identify Margaret Brewster among several Friends who disturbed a Puritan congregation in 1677, he blamed her for his confusion, explaining that during her crime Brewster had been disguised "in the shape of a Devil."[20] According to Cotton Mather, when Mary Ross fell into the hands of Quakers in the early 1680s, she became possessed with demons. Mather did not accuse the man who converted her of being a witch, but he did suggest that Satan had had a hand in the business. "The stories Recorded by my Father," he said, "(plainly enough) demonstrate, That Diabolical Possession was the Thing which did dispose and encline Men unto Quakerism." Claiming that their "quaking" was a symptom of possession, he suggested that the first Quaker was a female oracle of Delphi who, when possessed by a demon, "was immediately taken with an extraordinary *trembling* of her whole body." Her *"prophesies,"* Mather added, ". . . *enchanted* all the world into a veneration of them."[21] A similar connection among Quakers, "diabolical practices," and possession had been drawn by minister John Norton in 1659 in *The Heart of New England Rent,* the sole full-length orthodox Puritan response to the Quaker threat.[22]

Mather's and Norton's writings reveal that the idea of witchcraft-as-heresy remained an element in Puritan belief for most of the century. However limited, it evidently had some impact on popular belief, since opposition to the established church was mentioned in witchcraft testimony against twenty-eight women. Only ten of these seem to have been accused primarily because of their religious dissent: their witchcraft is best understood in terms of the centuries-long tendency of Christian authorities to see their adversaries—especially their female adversaries—as witches.[23] The significance of accusations against the other eighteen women lies less in their heresies, blasphemies, or other church-related crimes than in the sin of discontent. It was their perceived dissatisfaction with the religious system—and by extension with the religiously defined social system—that linked them to their sister witches.[24]

In the early 1650s, when New Haven minister John Davenport preached in a sermon on witchcraft that "a forward discontented frame of spirit was a subject fitt for the Devill to work upon," he was both expressing and reinforcing one of the most common assumptions about witches in New England.[25] When members of his congregation went into court in 1653 to explain why they considered Elizabeth Godman a witch, only one woman alluded directly to Davenport's words, but it was on Godman's many discontents that the rest of them focused. New Haven's deputy governor, Stephen Goodyear, in whose household Godman resided, talked of her flinging herself out of a room after his "exposition of a chapter" of the Bible because "she liked [it] not but said it was against her." According to William Hooke, Godman was also annoyed that "witches" were not allowed to "come into the church." Kept out of the church herself, Godman was particularly sensitive on this issue.[26]

But there were other manifestations of her discontent besides those directly connected with the church and its doctrines. Hooke said she was bitter because a man for whom she had "some affection" married another woman. Another witness, Goodwife Thorpe, testified to Godman's irritation when Thorpe was unable to sell her the chickens she sought. By the subsequent hearing of the case in 1655, both Hooke and Goodyear had more to say. Hooke described how, after begging beer from him, Godman had gone away "in a muttering discontented manner" when she could not have it "newly drawne," and Goodyear added a tale of Godman's displeasure when he "warned her to provide her[self] another place to live in."[27] To be sure, Godman may have expressed considerable discontent. A woman from a family with no male heirs, she had seen her estate turned over to Goodyear. Hardly a poor woman, and clearly not young, she was compelled to ask, even beg, for her needs.[28]

Godman was not the only witch whose discontent was traced, in the testimony, to her perception that her neighbors were against her. Like Godman, many women were accused of witchcraft after relatives or neighbors gained possession of all or part of their estates or otherwise intervened in their affairs in ways they interpreted as hostile. According to two accusers, newly widowed Dorcas Hoar of Beverly expressed dissatisfaction with them when they came to her house in 1691 to examine her husband's body because she knew they suspected her of killing him.[29]

The irritants were sometimes less explicitly threatening to the long-term well-being of the witch herself. In 1654, Roger Ludlow accused Mary Staplies of witchcraft, citing as evidence that she was unwilling to accept the opinion of the New Haven court that her Fairfield neighbor Goody Knapp was a witch; another colonist added that Staplies was not satisfied that "their were any witches" at all.[30] But witches' discontent was com-

monly described as the result of some real or imagined personal slight, as when Henry Herrick told the Salem court that
Sarah Good was annoyed with him when he refused her lodging in his father's house.[31]

Confessing witches often confirmed the belief shared by
ministers, magistrates, and witnesses that dissatisfaction led
women to join Satan's forces. According to Hartford minister
Samuel Stone, Mary Johnson admitted that it was because of
her discontent with her work as a servant that she became a
witch in 1648; yearning to escape from her many chores, she
resorted to calling on Satan to perform them for her.[32] Nineteen-year-old Mercy Wardwell of Andover confessed during
the Salem outbreak that she became dissatisfied after people
told her that "she should Never hath such a Young Man who
loved her"; it was for this reason, she said, that she decided to
take Satan as a lover.[33] Implicit in these and other statements
of guilt was the women's unhappiness with the material conditions of their lives. They were drawn to Satan, they said, by
promises of prosperity, fine clothes, future husbands, and
security.[34]

Puritans defined discontent as thinking oneself above one's
place in the social order, as "better then some whom God hath
preferred to us, either in honour, esteem, preferment, or
wealth."[35] When Elizabeth Godman disagreed with decisions
of New Haven church members as to who could or could not
join the church, she was asserting the right of individuals (as
opposed to the congregation of God's elect) to pass on their
own spiritual states. Anne Hutchinson and the Quaker witches,
of course, claimed for themselves the clergy's privilege both
to interpret and to teach the word of God. Mary Johnson's
displeasure with her role as a servant amounted to an unwill-
ingness to subordinate her will to that of a master. By challenging the right of the New Haven court to determine a witch's
innocence or guilt—or even to try women as witches—Mary
Staplies usurped the role of magistrate. Sarah Good, by her
disgruntled response to Herrick's refusal of aid, revealed that

she accepted neither her poverty nor his prosperity with the proper spirit of humility. To her accusers, Dorcas Hoar was guilty of killing her husband, the ultimate expression of insubordination in a wife.

Dissatisfaction with one's lot was one of the most pervasive themes of witches' lives. We find that women accused of witchcraft were involved in petitions and court suits involving property, mistreatment, even divorce. A few women, Katherine Harrison and Rachel Clinton being the most obvious examples, repeatedly took their grievances to court for redress—although legal channels seem to have provided little satisfaction. Of course, the witches themselves did not always initiate the official process that expressed their dissatisfaction. Dorcas Hoar and Mary Johnson, to name only two of at least fourteen women, had been charged with stealing prior to being accused of demonic activities.[36] Hoar was later accused of bewitching a child who threatened to reveal the theft, while another witch, Margaret Jones, was asked whether she did not think the witchcraft accusation God's way of punishing her for taking what was not hers.[37] The connections between the two crimes—or between the witch's earlier appearance in court and her later identification as a witch—were rarely so clearly drawn.

If a woman's discontent was a sign of an alliance with Satan, an even stronger indication, as John Davenport implied, was evidence that she in some way acted upon it. While discontent was sinful in itself, it might pass unnoticed in a person struggling for acceptance. But witches were "forward" about their complaints. Mary Staplies not only refused to accept the magistrates' decision that her neighbor was a witch, a decision based in part on the discovery of a "witch's teat" on the woman's body, but according to witnesses Staplies insisted upon examining the body herself after the execution and publicly announced that these teats were "no more teates then I myselfe have, or any other women."[38] Mary Johnson was not just displeased with having to take out the ashes and chase hogs from the fields, Samuel Stone said, she wished the Devil would do it for her.[39] Dorcas Hoar was more than just unhappy about the investigation into her husband's death, she was incensed: according to the two men appointed by local authorities to look into the "untimely death," Hoar broke out "in a very greate pashtion," wringing her hands, stamping her feet, and calling them "wiked wretches" for assuming her guilty of murder.[40] Submissiveness, a quality expected of women in Puritan society, appears to have been characteristic of none of these three women. Nor was it common among other witches, most of whom were decidedly assertive.

Self-assertion could take a variety of forms, but most often witches were said to have expressed their dissatisfaction in the manner of Dorcas Hoar—with anger. When Sarah Good was refused aid, several of her neighbors attested, she went "muttering away . . . and scolding extreamly."[41] Similarly, Sarah Holton deposed that witch Rebecca Nurse "continewed Railing and scolding agrat while" after the Holtons' pigs got into the Nurses' field.[42] John Winthrop claimed that Margaret Jones persisted in her "railing upon the jury and witnesses" until the moment her life was taken away.[43] Almost as recurrent an image in the witchcraft documents as the discontented woman is the furious hag. So fused was this figure with that of the witch that neighbors sometimes felt it unnecessary to cite specific instances of a witch's rage. It was evidence enough to testify that a given woman was often angry.[44]

The anger did not have to be intense. According to Cotton Mather, the complaint against the aged Lydia Dustin of Reading was that she had merely uttered a "Christian admonition": "God would not prosper them," she told some of her neighbors, "if they wronged the Widow."[45] Ann Pudeator's crime was scolding. John Best, speaking about how he had several times found Pudeator's cow among his father's when he rounded up the herd, explained that the reason he "did ConClude said pudeater was a wich" was that she "would Chide me when I Came houm for turning the Cow bak."[46] Anger, no matter how mild, was viewed with deep suspicion when the person expressing it was a woman. Even the word "scold," practically a synonym for "witch" in the European witchcraft tradition, was defined as an angry woman. No comparable word for an angry man existed in the language.[47]

In Puritan thought, anger, like discontent, was evil in and of itself. If not "speedily repressed," it also soon spawned two additional sins, envy and malice.[48] No creatures were so fully inclined to these offenses as witches, who were said to have so resented the place and possessions of their neighbors that they called upon Satan for the power to avenge themselves. If not guilty of actually murdering their enemies by supernatural means, then witches were presumed responsible for numerous lesser crimes—all injuries inflicted on their neighbors to even the score for their own hard lot.

Envy was often invoked by ministers as a motive for witchcraft, but it was rarely mentioned directly by witches' opponents or by confessed witches. Jealousy and envy were certainly implicit in accusers' descriptions of witches' discontent and anger, especially when, like Sarah Good or Mary Johnson, the accused women were poor. Malice, on the other hand, was openly and repeatedly talked about—every time an accuser said that a witch threatened, cursed, or cast spells upon someone. In each case, witnesses made clear, the witch intended to cause her neighbors harm.

It has so far been possible to discuss the sins attributed to witches without questioning their plausibility. Other sources support the testimony of accusers that witches were frequently unhappy about the treatment they received from family members, neighbors, or the authorities, and often discontented with the overall conditions of their lives. We cannot be sure that Rebecca Nurse was angry when the Holtons' pigs damaged her crops, or that Ann Pudeator was annoyed at having her cow driven off, or that Dorcas Hoar was furious at the insinuation that she had done away with her husband; but these reactions are plausible. Nor is it hard to believe that Sarah Good or Rachel Clinton, both deprived of their inheritances and reduced to the most demeaning poverty, were the embittered and resentful women their neighbors said they were: the conditions of their lives, like those of so many other witches, were hardly more conducive to cheerfulness than they were to submissiveness.

What we know about witches comes largely from accusers' depositions concerning their quarrels with the accused, but the impression accusers intended to create—one of responsible and righteous persons in conflict with discontented, angry, and contentious women—is in fact not supported by the evidence. At the very least, the testimony reveals mutual displeasure, hostility, and resentment between the disagreeing parties, and many times prior animosity on the part of accuser. It was in some cases not the witch's ire that generated the accusation, but the accusation that generated her ire. When Elizabeth How was tried in 1692, witnesses indicated that for more than a decade she had been kept from joining the Ipswich church and had repeatedly been subjected to harassment because her neighbors thought her a witch. Yet as support for his belief that she was in league with the Devil, one witness specifically cited anger that was clearly a response to his suspicion.[49] Without discounting the emotions women like How must have expressed, we cannot uncritically accept their adversaries' view of them. Elizabeth How was also a woman without sons and likely to inherit a substantial portion of her husband's estate; on that score alone she could have been the object of her neighbors' deep-seated resentment.

The dynamics of accusations become even more complicated when we try to sort out whether the accused were guilty of the sin of malice. If we accept their detractors' statements, witches' malice was expressed in *maleficium*, the supernatural harm they inflicted on others. In light of the prevalent belief that such practices worked, some women may have responded to their enemies in this manner, especially when there were few other avenues of redress for their grievances. But the evidence that some New England witches resorted to black magic is inconclusive.[50] Did Elizabeth Godman "cast a fierce looke upon" Stephen Goodyear with the intention of causing him to fall into a "swonding fitt"—or did she merely look at him fiercely?[51] Did Rebecca Nurse call upon the Devil to kill Benjamin Holton—or did the Holtons simply believe that she did? Godman and Nurse, like most other witches, said they were innocent of the sin of *maleficium,* and we have only their accusers' word that they were not. Short of accepting their enemies' versions of their actions, we can only acknowledge the possibility of witches' guilt. ⟩ *as is the case in almost every trial*

For the witch herself, the malevolence lay with her accusers, who knew the effect of an accusation on a woman's life. Perhaps, as some writers have intimated, *she* was right.[52] It is difficult to read about Roger Ludlow's intense battles with Fairfield's Mary Staplies, or George Walton's long-standing property dispute with Hannah Jones in Portsmouth, without recognizing the deep animosity these men felt toward their respective neighbors. But the evidence writers have cited against accusers is no more compelling than that presented against the accused. Witches' adversaries may have been guilty of malice, but their testimony indicates that they lodged their complaints out of a firm conviction that their neighbors were practicing *maleficium* and were therefore a serious menace to them, their families, and their society.

This is not to say that people were not injured. Clearly, the accused suffered. Most convicted witches lost their lives, and many of them their property; others lost their freedom of movement within the community or were forced to leave families and friends to find homes in other colonies. Their families also endured the consequences of conviction, both emotional and financial. Even those women were were acquitted (if they escaped Eunice Cole's experience of being punished anyway) lived in the shadow of renewed accusation, shunned by some of their neighbors and provoked by others. So too did many women who were never tried.

Accusers were harmed as well. Whether or not the accused believed that they could inflict supernatural damage, or acted upon that assumption, other people were convinced that witches could and did affect their health and prosperity. To presume that in lodging their complaints accusers exploited the witchcraft belief system for sinister ends overlooks the enormous power of religious conviction and cultural ideology to shape social behavior. The harm attributed to witches appears to have been real—in the sense that people who believe in the efficacy of witchcraft and think themselves the objects of a witch's malice can suffer and even die as a result of their fears. Anthropologists studying witchcraft in other societies have many times noted that in this particular sense, witchcraft exists.[53] There seems little reason to doubt that in colonial New England, where witchcraft beliefs constituted one of several explanatory systems for natural and social misfortunes, people could be genuinely afflicted.

The experience of Elizabeth How and Hannah Perley illustrates well both the power of belief and the harm inflicted by witchcraft.[54] In 1682, Elizabeth How and her husband had "a faling out" with their Topsfield neighbor, Samuel Perley. Soon after, Perley's ten-year-old daughter Hannah fell into a "sorowful condition." At the suggestion of other family members, apparently made out of genuine conviction, Hannah began to see herself as a victim of Elizabeth How's anger and malice. Her affliction may have been a natural illness for which possession was the explanation, or it may have been brought on by the belief that she was possessed. In either case, she alternated between affirming and denying that How was responsible. So too did her parents. For two or three years she suffered "dredful fits," and eventually "so Pined awai to skin and bone" that she died.

Elizabeth How's fate was similarly tragic. Guilty probably

of little more than discontent and anger, she was suspected of malefic witchcraft. None of the Perley family or any of the other neighbors who came to see themselves as How's victims brought their accusations to the magistrates over the next few years, but they made their feelings known. How was not allowed to become a church member and was subjected to numerous smaller indignities because of her reputation. Stories of her deeds surfaced in Salem in 1692, just as witchcraft accusations spread out from the village to nearby communities. At least nine Salem people came to believe themselves under her spell and "cried out" on her. Topsfield and Ipswich residents, confirmed in their long-held suspicions, came forward to testify about Hannah Perley's death and How's other malicious activities. Despite the testimony of several witnesses for the defense, and despite How's unwavering protestations of innocence, she was convicted and executed. Like Hannah Perley, her life came to a premature end not because of calculated attempts to harm her but because of a profound fear of witchcraft. Still to be explained is why the fear was there in the first place, and why it was so intense. That explanation, as we will see, ultimately requires an understanding of the relationship between witchcraft beliefs and accusations and the social structure of early colonial New England.

The witch's power to avenge her discontent by inflicting harm upon her neighbors was intimately connected, in the perception of New Englanders, to her more general powers to disrupt the social and natural order. These more general powers carried an implicit sexual content, often made explicit in the specific behaviors attributed to witches and the language of these allegations.

Of witches' many sins, the most clearly sexual was the sin of seduction. For Puritans, seduction was "improving of [one's] wit to draw others into sin, to study devices, and lay snares to entrap their souls withal."[55] As this definition suggests, witches were all deemed guilty of this sin because they attempted to entice people away from their worship of God to the worship of the Devil. Indeed, the destruction of their neighbors' souls was yet another form of witches' malice.

In descriptions of witches' attempts to lead others into sin, Puritan ministers focused most frequently on cases of possession—the most visible sign that witches were working to increase their numbers. During the initial stages of possession, the clergy argued, witches enticed their victims with material rewards, spouses, relief from labor, and so forth. (Only after seductive methods failed did they begin to employ their powers of torture.) For reasons never explained, witches who supposedly recruited others into the Devil's service focused their attention on other women. Eighty-six percent of possession cases on record in colonial New England are female.[56] When Massachusetts magistrates banished Mary Tilton "for having like a sorceress gone from door to door to lure and seduce people, yea even young girls, to join the Quakers," or when they tried Eunice Cole for "enticing Ann Smith to come to live with her," they were only expressing less obliquely what ministers implied in their sermons and published works: witches were most dangerous as seducers of other females, and they were especially given to working on the young. More than half of the New England possessed were under twenty.

Possession behavior, as scholars have noted, contains elements that suggest repressed erotic impulses.[57] But the erotic power witches were thought to wield over possessed females was only rarely explicit during possession; when openly mentioned, it was not the witch but the Devil himself who seduced female bodies and promised to satisfy women's carnal desires. Witches' attempts to seduce women and girls tended to be described as the seduction of souls.

An erotic dimension, however, was often implicit in witches' seduction of other females. Descriptions of witches successful in luring women into their ranks sometimes implied that they accomplished this end by appealing to other women's licentiousness. In trying to account for Anne Hutchinson's appeal to the "Femall Sex," one Puritan writer described her followers as "silly Women laden with diverse lusts."[58] Referring to Hutchinson as an "American Jesabel" and associating her with "Harlots" and religious groups rumored to be unchaste, John Winthrop and Thomas Weld also insinuated that she was seducing more than souls.[59] Clergyman John Cotton was more direct about the implications of Hutchinson's seductive powers. "That filthie sinne of the Comunitie of Woemen," he told her publicly, "and all promiscuus and filthie cominge togeather of men and Woemen without Distinction or Relation of Marriage, will necessarily follow."[60] Hutchinson's enemies were evidently convinced that women led astray by her would eventually be adulterous.

Witches were also described as seducers of men, but this sin took a very different form from witches' seduction of other women. Witches lured women through the process of possession, but New England males were seldom described as possessed. The few cases of male possession—almost all of which occurred during the Salem outbreak—were largely ignored. When men confessed to becoming witches, they almost always implied that they had bypassed women in the process, claiming that the Devil himself was responsible for their enticement.[61] Thus we find little direct evidence for men of the kind of seduction most often and most directly attributed to witches—that of leading others into deliberate alliances with Satan.

For men, the closest parallel to being possessed was being bewitched in the night. Coming into their bedrooms uninvited, witches were said to attack men while they slept. Although men rarely referred to these nocturnal visits as sexual aggression on the part of witches, those who left detailed descriptions of these attacks suggested precisely that. Bernard Peach, for instance, claimed as evidence of Susanna Martin's witchcraft that

> being in bed on a lords day night he heard a [scratching]
> at the window. He this deponent saw susana martin . . .
> com in at the window and jumpt downe upon the flower.
> Shee was in her hood and scarf and the same dress that
> shee was in before at metting the same day. Being com in,
> shee was coming up toward this deponents face but turned
> back to his feet and took hold of them and drew up his
> body into a heape and Lay upon him about an hour and
> half or 2 hours, in all which taim this deponent coold not
> stir nor speake. . . .[62]

Peach did not interpret Martin's supernatural appearance as
an inducement to sign a covenant with the Devil or even as a
torment inflicted for that purpose. Rather he offered it merely
as additional evidence of Martin's malice. Yet for Peach as for
some other New England men, witches seem to have been
particularly seductive figures.

Implicit in these tales of witches' night wandering is not
just that they forced themselves sexually on unwilling men but
that witches' carnal appetites were both internally uncontrolled and externally uncontrollable. The testimony implied
that these women were dissatisfied with—indeed had no respect
for—their society's rules governing sexual behavior. Like the
animals with which they were associated, and in whose shape
they more often than not seduced their unsuspecting prey,
witches made no attempt to restrain their sexual impulses. Since
most of the accused were beyond their childbearing years, they
lacked the "natural" control pregnancy provided; those who
were single or widowed, moreover, lacked even the restraint
of a husband's presence.

Nowhere are their excesses more apparent than in accounts
of witches' intimate contact with their animal familiars. The
teats upon which these demon-animals sucked were invariably
searched for (and found) on parts of the body where women
experience the greatest erotic pleasure, suggesting that the
witch may have symbolized forbidden impulses for women as
well as men. For while women were only rarely disturbed in

their sleep by witches, female accusers frequently testified about witches' contact with familiars, and women were the ones who conducted most of the searches for evidence of it.

Most witches were guilty of seduction only in the minds of their accusers, but the erotic content of witchcraft is also indicated by the presence among the accused of twenty-three women who were explicitly charged with sexual excesses, either during their witchcraft trials or during the years preceding the accusation. When Elizabeth Seager was tried as a witch in Hartford in 1662, she was simultaneously charged with adultery (and blasphemy as well).[63] Her situation paralleled that of Susanna Martin, who in 1669 was also accused of witchcraft and sexual crimes with men. In both cases the magistrates insisted on separating the two issues.[64] More commonly, when direct charges of sexual misbehavior were lodged against an accused witch, it was the Devil who was the alleged partner and the two crimes were treated as one. Sometimes witnesses simply referred vaguely to the Devil's coming "bodyly unto" the woman at night;[65] sometimes they submitted more explicit testimony that the Devil had had carnal knowledge of her. In New Haven in 1653, Elizabeth Godman complained that some neighbors had said that she "had laine with" the Devil and that "Hobbamocke [supposedly an Indian 'devil god'] was her husband."[66]

Testimony presented against Seager, Martin, and Godman was unusual in that during actual witchcraft trials accusers seldom linked licentious acts and witchcraft so blatantly. Witches were sometimes denounced as bawds or lewd women in the course of their trials, but rarely were the sexual charges specified. Yet when we look at the lives of the accused prior to the accusation, we sometimes find evidence of real or alleged sexual offenses. Like women's crimes against the church, these sins seem to have played a role in generating the accusation in the first place. Citing English opinion, Cotton Mather noted that a "lewd and naughty kind of Life" was a sign of "probable" witchcraft.[67]

Margaret Jennings's situation is instructive. Jennings had been tried and convicted of fornication in 1643, when she was "Margerett Poore, alias Bedforde" of New Haven, an indentured servant to Captain Nathaniel Turner. She had run away with Nicholas Jennings, evidently taking some of her master's possessions with her. She must have been pregnant when the authorities apprehended her, since among their other actions they ordered the couple to marry and Nicholas to give satisfaction to Turner for the service Margaret owed him.[68] The record is silent until eighteen years later when Margaret (now living in Saybrook, Connecticut) came before the magistrates a second time: she had been ordered to appear with her daughter Martha, both of them to answer a neighbor's complaint. The exact charge was not recorded, but the court ordered young Martha to submit to a physical examination. Finding her not to be "with child but rather the contrary," the magistrates released both her and her mother.[69] Soon after, Margaret and her husband Nicholas were on trial for their lives, accused of murdering several persons, including a young child, by witchcraft. Many of the jurymen believed them both guilty but hesitated to convict them. The only apparent action taken against them was the removal of their two youngest children from their care.[70]

Mercy Desborough's experience suggests another variation on the way sexual themes appear in the life histories of the accused. Desborough was convicted of witchcraft during the Fairfield outbreak in 1692–93, but like Jennings she was not explicitly accused of any licentious behavior.[71] Connecticut legal records reveal, however, that she had been punished in 1661, along with Joseph James, for an unspecified offense.[72] At that time she was Mercy Holbridge, servant to the prominent Gershom Bulkeley of New London. Bulkeley played a central role in getting Desborough reprieved in 1693,[73] and with the court granting her a full pardon it appeared that she was safe from further prosecution. But in 1696, Desborough was brought before the magistrates a third time, not for witchcraft but for fornication and infanticide. James Redfin of Fairfield (formerly of New London) accused her of having done away with an illegitimate child when she worked for Bulkeley nearly thirty-five years before. He implied that Bulkeley (not Joseph James) had fathered the child.[74]

If, as in the cases of Desborough, Jennings, and Susanna Martin, witchcraft suspicion was aroused at the time the sexual misconduct allegedly took place—when these women were all young—there is no sign of it. They were all considerably older when accused of demonic practices. Twenty-one in 1661, Desborough was fifty-two when specifically charged with fornication and infanticide. Many times the sexual sin itself was said to have been committed when the woman was of mature years. Seager's and Godman's exact ages are unknown, but both seem to have been in their late thirties at least, and possibly much older, when their sexual behavior was publicly called into question. Rachel Clinton was thirty-eight when first charged with adultery; when first accused of witchcraft she was fifty-eight. Neighbors sometimes informed a young woman that her "nightwalking" or "wicked carriages" would lead people to think "the devil was in her,"[75] but usually a woman had to pass her childbearing years before suspicions of licentiousness took the form of suspicions of witchcraft. The men said to have been involved with these women, it is worth noting, were often considerably younger.

Women who confessed to witchcraft during the early years of witchcraft prosecutions tended to make the erotic content of witches' seduction more obvious than their accusers did. Admitting carnal knowledge of both men and devils, these women seldom cloaked their descriptions in vague language. Mary Johnson and Rebecca Greensmith provided detailed accounts of their relationships with devils, and Johnson further confessed to more earthly sexual encounters.[76] After the 1660s, the sexual content of confessions became more muted. During the Salem outbreak, many women confessed that Satan had them "soul and body," but only occasionally during the latter part of the century did accused women offer specific sexual information. When fifty-three-year-old Rebecca Eames of Andover admitted in 1692 that she had given herself soul and body to the Devil, she made it clear that she considered herself an adulterer—but she was a rare exception.[77]

Accusations of Devil worship were sometimes viewed as God's way of punishing women for illicit sexual behavior, as is evident in the response of Margaret Lakes of Dorchester to her witchcraft conviction. When, just before she was hanged, both a minister and her former master tried to convince her to confess, she refused, saying that she "owned nothing of the crime laid to her charge." At the same time, according to John Hale, she fully justified God for bringing her out as a witch, saying that "she had when a single woman played the harlot, and being with Child used means to destroy the fruit of her body to conceal her sin and shame."[78]

As the words of Margaret Lakes might suggest, New Englanders associated witchcraft not just with sexual fantasy, fornication, and adultery, but also with bearing illegitimate children, with abortion, and with infanticide—sins attributed to women almost exclusively. At least fourteen women were suspected of one of these three sins prior to their witchcraft accusations. Such crimes (whether committed by these women or not) might have been understood as evidence of dissatisfaction with the social rules governing female sexuality and reproduction, but for many New Englanders these sins carried greater import. They stamped the witch as guilty of interfering with the natural processes of life and death.. A woman guilty of these crimes took it upon herself to decide who should live and who should die, the prerogative of God alone. Even if, like Boston's Jane Hawkins, she was thought to have helped generate life, or like Rachel Fuller had cast spells to prolong life, her transgression was just as heinous.[79] For women even to possess knowledge so critical to the existence of their families and neighbors seems to have been at the heart of many witchcraft accusations.

Some witches were midwives and healers, women whose work involved them daily in matters of life and death. We cannot determine precise numbers—or how explicit a woman's identification as healer had to be to render her vulnerable to suspicion—because all colonial women were responsible for the health of their families. Attendance at childbirth and provision of medical care were two of the many services colonial women provided for their neighbors as well. Medical knowledge and skills were handed down from mother to daughter, in much the same way colonists thought witchcraft arts were passed on. The few published housewifery manuals of the day included not only cooking recipes but "Receipts of Medicines" for "Distempers, Pains, Aches, Wounds, Sores, etc."[80]

Witches such as Ann Burt of Lynn, Elizabeth Morse of Newbury, and Wethersfield's Katherine Harrison all seem to have been paid for their medical services.[81] But the professional status of most of the twenty-two midwife / healers who were accused of witchcraft is more ambiguous. Ann Burt's granddaughter, Elizabeth Proctor of Salem, was accused of killing her neighbors in 1692 because they would not take her medical advice, but it is unclear whether she was a self-identified healer or simply one of thousands of New England women who nursed others through childbirth and illnesses.[82] The problem is further complicated by the presence among witches of women like Ann Pudeator, who turned these housewifery skills to profit when widowed or at other times of economic need.[83] If, as is likely, midwives and healers were particularly susceptible to witchcraft suspicion, we must also recognize that the skills that made them suspect were possessed by most women, if not to the same extent.

Whether paid for their services or not, midwives and healers were in direct competition with the few male medical practitioners, in much the same way that Antinomian and Quaker women vied with ministers for spiritual leadership. Men had already succeeded in denigrating women's medical learning in early seventeenth-century England by designating male healers "doctors," by barring women from "professional" training, and, it seems, by accusing female practitioners of witchcraft.[84] In early New England, however, doctors were still scarce and male control over medical services was not established. Most towns relied on women's medical skills throughout the century. The frequency with which doctors were involved in witchcraft cases suggests that one of the unspoken (and probably unacknowledged) functions of New England witchcraft was to discredit women's medical knowledge in favor of their male competitors.

Physician Phillip Read of Lynn was connected with at least two separate episodes, testifying in 1669 that Ann Burt caused an illness for which there was "noe Natural caus," and filing an unspecified complaint against Margaret Gifford in 1680.[85] Ministers and magistrates wanting confirmation that individuals were either bewitched or possessed did not rely on the medical knowledge of women, but sought instead the medical advice of men. Hartford magistrates were so reluctant to trust local women on these issues that, lacking doctors in the vicinity, in 1662 they sent for Bray Rossiter of Guilford to corroborate townspeoples' suspicions concerning the death of young Elizabeth Kelly.[86] Midwives were called upon as "juries" to examine the bodies of the accused for signs of devil worship, but this very intimate procedure was as far as the authorities trusted women's medical judgments in witchcraft cases, even though many of the same men relied on women for their own and their families' medical needs. Not surprisingly, only one "doctor" seems to have been accused of witchcraft in New England. Not only was he the husband of one witch and the brother-in-law of another, but he seems to have taken on the title of doctor simply by virtue of his sex.[87]

Just as the witch was a symbol of unrestrained lust to her neighbors, she also symbolized women's control over the health and well-being of others. Most witches, as we have seen, were accused of causing illnesses, accidents, or deaths among family members or neighbors. Infants and young children—those physically most dependent upon women—were known to be the most vulnerable to attack. Midwives and healers, like women accused of abortion and infanticide, could have been likely suspects simply because they were ever-present reminders of the power that resided in women's life-giving and life-maintaining roles. ⟩ flimsy

When ministers and magistrates discussed the seductive power of witches they often linked it—albeit covertly—to women's functions not only as midwives and healers but also as childbearers and childrearers. The procreative, nurturing, and nursing roles of women were *perverted* by witches, who gave birth to and suckled demons instead of children and who dispensed poisons instead of cures. The "Poisonous Insinuations" of witches, Cotton Mather wrote, spread like a "terrible Plague" through communities, causing them to become "Infected and Infested" with evil.[88] John Winthrop told his readers that Anne Hutchinson "easily insinuated her selfe into the affections of many" because she was "a woman very helpfull in the times of child-birth, and other occasions of bodily infirmities." Those who "tasted of [the Antinomians'] Commodities. . . ," Thomas Weld added, "were streight infected before they were aware, and some being tainted conveyed the infection to others: and thus that Plague first began amongst us." Winthrop and others referred to Hutchinson's seduction of other women in terms of her power to "hatch," "breed," and "nourish" heretical opinions much as she (and other witches) hatched, bred, and nourished monsters.[89] Similar metaphors were employed in discussions of the Quaker menace. Minister John Norton described the influence of the Quakers as a "contagion," arguing that the Puritans must save their "nurse-lings from the poyson of the destroyer."[90]

Besides affecting conception, childbirth, and people's emotional and physical well-being, witches were regularly accused of interfering with domestic processes and harming domestic animals—accusations that reflected prevailing gender assumptions. Witches were said to have thwarted the making of butter, cheese, beer, and clothing, prevented livestock and poultry from functioning normally, if at all, and even to have destroyed their neighbors' crops. Occasionally, they were charged with phenomenal success in their own domestic work, but usually they were accused of keeping others from their productive activities, often making it impossible for their neighbors to prosper. Here too witches' activities were a perversion of women's traditional roles. Dairying, brewing, clothing production, and the tending of farm animals and gardens all comprised women's daily work. Witches were accused of hampering men's productive activities as well, but they specialized in damage to those domestic pursuits in which they as women had the most training, skill, and control.

The domestic tasks in which women were traditionally granted expertise soon began to shrink, however; as in medicine, men would eventually take over many of these areas of expertise, either by pushing women out altogether or by relegating them to the lowest paid and least prestigious positions in the occupational structure. In England, this process was already well underway in the seventeenth century, especially in textiles and brewing.[91] It was also underway in New England, but the primitive conditions of early settlement retarded the change. The shift in occupational spheres went furthest in coastal and river towns like Boston, Salem, Springfield, Hartford, and New Haven—towns where commercial agriculture, manufacturing, and trade were more developed, and where witchcraft accusations were most common.[92]

To flesh out the connection between women's work in a developing economy and the propensity of witches to thwart domestic processes, consider the witches (at least nineteen) who were castigated for their unusual success in "domestic" pursuits. These were women who turned their food and textile production, brewing, and other domestic work into profitable business enterprises, the "works of Men" in colonial New

England.[93] Elinor Hollingworth ran a tavern in Salem.[94] Widow Mary Hale, tried as a witch in 1680, kept a boardinghouse in Boston.[95] Mary Bradbury's butter business in Salisbury was so successful that she was able to supply outgoing ships; she was accused of witchcraft after two firkins of butter went bad on a ship several days out to sea, confirming rumors the crew had heard that she was a witch.[96]

Katherine Harrison, who along with her husband had profited greatly from the Connecticut River trade in the 1650s and 1660s, put her energies into diverse ventures. Figuring prominently in testimony against her after her husband's death were (besides her medical practice) her many acres on the river, her numerous cattle, her extraordinary spinning skills, and her beekeeping. The thirty "poles" of hops she said her neighbors destroyed suggests that she was also a brewer. Charged with calling on the Devil to aid her in these pursuits, she was also suspected of hindering the work of others. Thomas Bracy accused her of bewitching him to impede his own trade as a weaver.[97] Like midwives, healers, and female religious leaders, women who turned their traditional skills to profit placed themselves in competition with men—and in positions of vulnerability to witchcraft accusations.

Women whose husbands were disabled or temporarily absent from home were also suspect figures. Like widows, these women were compelled to act on their own or on their families' behalf—running farms and business enterprises, hiring people to perform specific tasks, dealing with legal matters, and in general engaging their neighbors as household heads. Edith Crawford of Salem was accused of witchcraft after acting as her husband's attorney in a protracted court case that lost the family their house and land in 1667. When the house burned shortly after the property had been seized, the new occupant accused Crawford of causing the fire, allegedly saying "that hee would have Her Hanged If ther were no more wimen In the world, for shee was A witch and If shee were nott A witch allreddy shee would bee won, and therefore It

was as good to Hang her at first as Last."[98] Though less
obviously vindictive, Elizabeth How's Topsfield and Ipswich
neighbors harbored a similar resentment of her economic
activities. Testimony presented against her in 1692 reveals that
she had become involved in disputes that arose because she
had been acting for many years in her blind husband's stead.[99]
At least a dozen other witches were in positions similar to that
of Crawford and How.

Two sins of a general character permeate the entire continuum of witches' behavior: the sin of lying and the sin of
pride. Both were transgressions with profound implications
within the Puritan world view, for pride was Satan's most
grievous sin, and deception was the means by which he first
inflicted his foulness upon Paradise.

All witches were presumed to lie, their alliance with the
"Prince of Liars" providing sufficient evidence of the fact. When
Anne Hutchinson claimed knowledge of God's word, she was
charged with deception by opponents who declared themselves "fully persuaded that [she was] deluded by the devil,
because the spirit of God speaks truth in all his servants."[100]
Roger Ludlow may also have found witchcraft a plausible
explanation for his differences with Mary Staplies: his charge
of witchcraft followed closely upon his debate with her in the
Fairfield church, where he apparently charged her publicly
with going on "in a tract of lying."[101] Accusations of this sin
preceded witchcraft charges in other cases as well. Most frequently, however, witches were called liars simply for denying
their worship of the Devil or for disclaiming malice, theft, or
other sins associated with witchcraft. Confessions of witchcraft
made by women after initial denials were cited as proof that
witches never told the truth. (On the other hand, men who
confessed to demonic activities, as we have seen, were usually
dismissed as liars for claiming witches' powers.)

While some witchcraft charges were the result of principled disagreements between accusers and women whom they considered liars and thus allied with Satan, some witches actually may have been guilty of lying prior to their accusation. Like heresy or theft or adultery, this sin may have aroused suspicion in the first place. Other women may have lied during the proceedings, fearful that the truth—even assertions of innocence—would cost them their lives. Confessions, however, seem generally to have emerged from a real, if momentary, belief on the part of the accused that they were, or probably were, witches. During the Salem outbreak, this belief was no doubt encouraged by knowledge of the outcome if they maintained their innocence, and by the responses of family members and neighbors to the accusation.[102] In a culture where female dissatisfaction and anger were linked with witchcraft, and where women were pressured to search their consciences for evidence of their own evil, not surprisingly some women were persuaded—albeit temporarily—that the Devil was in them.

Some accusers also admitted to lying. During the Salem outbreak Mary Warren informed the court that she and others of the possessed "did but dissemble," and Sarah Churchill pointed out how very hard it was to tell the community what it did not want to hear.[103] But these stories only demonstrate more clearly the very real power of witchcraft belief and the difficulty of separating false accusations from actual lying. When put under pressure to maintain the community's truth, both women fell back into possessed states or confessed themselves witches.

Even during periods when only one or two witches were accused and the appearance of personal motive for the accusations is strongest, it seems a mistake to consider the accusations mere lies. When George Walton said that "he believed in his heart and conscience that Grandma Jones was a witch," he may have been self-serving, but as likely as not he was telling the truth. For Hannah Jones—an aging widow, a daughter in a family without surviving sons, the female progeny of a mother who had three times faced witchcraft charges, and a woman clearly angry that her land had been "unjustly taken" by Walton—was as likely a New England witch as we will find.[104]

The one remaining sin attributed to witches was perhaps the most evil of all. This was pride, defined by minister Samuel Willard as "an overweening opinion of ones self, which makes [a person] think himself too good for his duty, and so puts him upon scornfully neglecting it."[105] Rarely was pride mentioned directly in a witchcraft accusation, but ministers assured their congregations that this sin was what made witches' alliances with Satan so obvious. More than just a single sin, it was both the source and embodiment of all sins identified with witchcraft. Pride was inextricably linked in Puritan thought to insubordination—indeed, to outright rebellion. Knowing their duty to live according to God's rules, Cotton Mather said, but discontented with those rules, witches refused to obey them, and in the process they rose up against God. "Rebellion is," Mather insisted, "as the sin of witchcraft."[106]

In its most obvious form, pride became manifest through witches' challenges to the authority of ministers, magistrates, and masters. Yet some women who questioned the authority of their husbands were also considered witches. What made William Good afraid in 1692 that his wife Sarah "either was a witch or would be one very quickly" was "her bad carriage to him."[107] Daniel Ela had similar thoughts about his own wife Elizabeth ten years earlier because she refused to humble herself before him and acknowledge that "shee was but his servantt. . . ," he being a "gentellman borne . . ." and she "butt a poore widdow" when he married her.[108] Evidence of this kind of pride is easily overlooked because husbands who suspected that their wives were witches were seldom taken seriously by the courts. Colonial culture strongly discouraged the use of witchcraft accusations as a way of severing marital bonds. Nevertheless, a wife's insubordination to her husband is implicit in many of the sins that New Englanders saw as witchcraft, from adultery to the murder of one's own spouse and children to the pursuit of independent economic activities. Even when a husband allowed or encouraged his wife's evil, other people viewed these women's actions as evidence of witchcraft.

Witchcraft in colonial New England meant more than women's refusal to subordinate themselves to men with institutional authority over them: it suggested their refusal to subordinate themselves to all persons whom God had placed above them in the social hierarchy. In some cases, women came under suspicion for acting as if they were above other women whom society had defined as their betters. Most often, though, suspicion originated in women's interactions with men, whom society implicitly held to be superior to all women. While Puritans surely would have denied the principle that *all* women were subject to *all* men, the record shows the lack of deference for male neighbors to be a common thread running through the many sins of witches. It was not just pride that most fundamentally distinguished witches from other people; it was female pride in particular.

The records do not allow us fully to see a woman becoming a witch. We have enough detail on the life of Ann Hibbens, however, to see the outlines of the process. None of the evidence presented against Hibbens in her 1656 witchcraft trial has survived,[109] but sixteen years earlier other charges had been brought against her—accusations not at the time designated as witchcraft.

Dissatisfied with the quality of work done for her by Boston joiners (carpenters) in 1640—and with what she considered their excessive rates—Hibbens took her grievances to her minister, the governor, and several other men, some of whom were joiners themselves. Initially, Hibbens found support for her complaint because some of these men shared her dissatisfaction.[110] But it was not long before her superiors united in opposition against her. Her refusal to "rest satisfied" with their judgment, rather than her grievance, became the issue.[111]

When brought before the ministers and deacons of the church for trial, Hibbens was first cited for discontent and contentiousness, then for other sins. Governor Winthrop intimated that she was guilty of seduction, arguing that she carried on the dispute with "skill and patience, laboring to draw sometimes one and sometimes another to her own judgment." Minister John Wilson and several other men charged her with making a "wisp" and a "cipher of her husband . . , usurping authority over him whom God hath made her head" as well as over God himself. John Cotton said her charges against the joiners were lies and accused her both of envy and of "thrust[ing] herself] into God's throne and seat, to know the hearts of men." Blasphemy was implied by Cotton and several others. "Indeed," claimed one of her adversaries near the end of her trial, "I do not know of what sin she is not guilty of." But the sin that led to and embodied all the others, in her opponents' view, was her "great pride of spirit." She not only refused to acknowledge her duty to obey God and man, but she persisted in seeing the "sin in this business" as the actions of the joiners. Comparing her to the biblical Miriam, who "rose up against Moses and Aaron," Deacon Thomas Oliver found her "leprous"; "she ought to be pronounced unclean," he said, and "cast out of the church" before her disease spread to others, adding that "already . . . there is danger that many hath been infected by the church's delay." Not long after, she was excommunicated.[112]

No one mentioned witchcraft directly in Hibbens's 1640 trial, but there was more than enough in her words and actions to suggest to her adversaries that she was an instrument of Satan. All that was needed was the crucial ingredient: evidence of supernatural activities. Someone may have provided it at the time, but if so it was ignored. She was, after all, the wife of a magistrate and highly respected by many people in the community. She was said to have been "counted a saint" by some.[113] In 1656, two years after her husband's death, the supernatural element was formally added and, despite opposition, her fate sealed by "the popular clamour" that "prevailed against her."[114] Though one minister, as previously noted, is rumored to have said that she was executed as a witch "only for having more wit than her neighbors,"[115] more likely it was because she displayed more of what her neighbors called "pride of spirit," or what we might consider simply as spirit. If in 1640 her husband had not been able to subdue her, and her brothers in the church had not been able to break her, how much more dangerous she must have appeared by 1656, when she was an economically independent woman alone.

In other New England witchcraft cases, the process by which a woman was transformed into a witch is harder to trace. We know that most witches, like Ann Hibbens, were inheriting or potentially inheriting women. We know too what distinguishes these women from other women in similar economic positions and what unites them with other accused witches: the community's view of them as discontented, angry, envious, malicious, seductive, lying, and proud women. Most witches did express dissatisfaction, however indirectly, with the power arrangements of their society, and in doing so they raised the specter of witchcraft, of female rebellion against God and man. The community's apprehension that they would seduce their neighbors—that their disease would spread like a plague to the innocent people around them—was so palpable that their lies had to be exposed and the danger they embodied cast out.

FIVE

Handmaidens
of the Lord

*T*HERE IS A curious paradox that students of New England witchcraft encounter. The characteristics of the New England witch—demographic, economic, religious, and sexual—emerge from *patterns* found in accusations and in the life histories of the accused; they are not visible in the content of individual accusations or in the ministerial literature. No colonist ever explicitly said why he or she saw witches as women, or particularly as older women. No one explained why some older women were suspect while others were not, why certain sins were signs of witchcraft when committed by women but not when committed by men, or why specific behaviors associated with women aroused witchcraft fears while specific behaviors associated with men did not. Indeed, New Englanders did not openly discuss most of their widely shared assumptions about women-as-witches.

This cultural silence becomes even more puzzling when we consider that many of these assumptions had once been quite openly talked about in the European witchcraft tradition. In the late fifteenth and early sixteenth centuries especially, defenders of the Christian faith spelled out in elaborate detail why they believed women rather than men were likely to join Satan's forces. The reasons they gave are not very different from those evident in the patterns the New England sources reveal. This presses upon us a question of some consequence: why had once-explicit beliefs about women's proclivity to witchcraft become implicit in their New England setting?

We can probe this question by following the lead of the anthropologist Mary Douglas and other scholars who have explored the social construction of knowledge. In Douglas's analysis, human societies relegate certain information to the category of self-evident truths. Ideas that are treated as self-evident, "as too true to warrant discussion," constitute a society's implicit knowledge. At one time explicit, implicit ideas have not simply been forgotten, but have been "actively thrust out of the way" because they conflict with ideas deemed more suitable to the social order. But the conflict is more apparent than real. In the "elusive exchange" between implicit and explicit knowledge, the implicit is "obliquely affirmed" and the society is shielded from challenges to its world view. The implicit resides in a society's symbols, rituals, and myths, which simultaneously describe, reflect, and mask that world view. To understand these processes, implicit and explicit knowledge must be examined together and in the context of their social environment.[1]

In colonial New England, the many connections between "women" and "witchcraft" were implicitly understood. In Europe, several generations before, the connections had still been explicit. Over time, these established "truths" about women's sinfulness had increasingly come into conflict with other ideas about women—ideas latent in Christian thought but brought to the fore by the Reformation and the political, economic, and social transformations that accompanied it. For the Puritans who emigrated to New England in the early seventeenth century, once-explicit assumptions about why witches were women were already self-evident.

original sin?

Perhaps NE society was characterized by a lack of self or societal introspection, no analysis - intellect stifled, etc

The swiftly changing conditions of early settlement left it uncertain at first whether, or how, witchcraft would serve the goals of New England society. Though men in positions of authority believed that certain women were working against the new colonies' interests, others did not see these women as witches. By the late 1640s, however, New Englanders embraced a witchcraft belief system as integral to their social order. Over the course of the seventeenth century, Puritan rituals, symbols, and myths perpetuated the belief that women posed ever-present dangers to human society, but the newer, post-Reformation ideas about women forced colonists to shrink from explicitly justifying this belief. They therefore continued to assume the complex of ideas about women-as-witches as self-evident truths.

Two works stand out for stating the wisdom of the older European tradition on why women were more prone than men to witchcraft. These are the influential *Malleus Maleficarum* (1486) by Heinrich Institoris and Jakob Sprenger of Germany and the less well-known *Tratado de las Supersticiones y Hechicerias* (1529) by Spain's Fray Martin de Castanega. Each of these works explained and justified the Church's view that most witches were women.

"More women than men are ministers of the devil," these three clergymen agreed, because women were by nature more evil than men: in their wickedness, they imitated the first woman, Eve. Created intellectually, morally, and physically weaker than men, the argument continued, women were subject to deeper affections and passions, harbored more uncontrollable appetites, and were more susceptible to deception. Unwilling to accept their deficiencies and unable to satisfy their inordinate desires, they more readily turned to Satan to fulfill their needs and to provide them with the power to avenge themselves on those in more fortunate positions. Women were never satisfied, these authors added, were more given to anger, jealousy, and greed, and did not hesitate to seek demonic power to deceive others, to entice them to evil, and to destroy their souls, their bodies, and their possessions. In sum, women became witches because they were born female, not male, because they were dissatisfied with their natural inadequacies and limitations, and because they wanted revenge and retribution badly enough to sell their souls for it.[3]

In elaborating on these themes, the three authors dwelt specifically on religious, sexual, and to a lesser extent economic issues. Institoris and Sprenger pointed out that lacking "understanding of spiritual things" and being "intellectually like children," women were quicker than men "to abjure the faith, which is the root of witchcraft." Heresy, then, was to be expected of women. De Castanega stressed the denial of religious authority to women as a prime reason women became witches, arguing that "because Christ did not permit women to administer his sacraments, . . . they are given more authority than men in the administration of the devil's execrations." Speaking apparently of both religious and secular knowledge, de Castanega also noted that women became witches "because they more eagerly seek out the knowledge of hidden matters, and want to be the first to know things, something their natural condition does not permit, . . . [and] because they gossip more than men, and can keep no secret, and so they teach one another, which men do not do so much." In the *Malleus,* women's tendency to share knowledge forbidden to them with their "fellow-women" was also cited as a source of their witchcraft.[4]

Institoris and Sprenger examined sexual themes more thoroughly than they did religious ones. "All witchcraft comes from carnal lust, which is in women insatiable," they argued, and it is "for the sake of fulfilling their lusts [that women] consort even with devils." Stipulating the kinds of women who practiced witchcraft, the authors placed adulterers, fornicators, and concubines at the head of their list. De Castanega noted that witches were more likely to be old women rather than young women "because once they are old, and men pay no attention to them, the women have recourse to the devil to satisfy their appetites." According to Institoris and Sprenger, witchcraft was frequently practiced through the generative act, for it was here that women asserted their greatest power over men—by "inclining the minds of men to inordinate passion, . . . obstructing their generative force, . . . removing the members accommodated to that act, . . . [and] changing men into beasts." If a man could not consummate his marriage, if his wife refused to lie with him, or if for any other reason he was unable to have sexual intercourse, then witchcraft was a likely cause—if not his partner's, then probably some other woman's. Men were seldom witches, the authors of the *Malleus* maintained, because men were less carnal: Christ "was willing to be born and to suffer" to preserve "the male sex from so great a crime."[5]

In the *Malleus,* witches also interfered with the generative force of women, using herbs and other means to prevent conceptions and to procure abortions. Devils carried out these evils, the authors said, but "through the medium of women, and not men." If a woman did not keep a man from begetting a child, then she might either kill or "devour" it once it was born, "or offer it to a devil." Though all women were capable of subverting the procreative process through witchcraft, midwives, "who surpass all others in wickedness," were the most dangerous women in this regard. In fact, the authors claimed, "no one does more harm to the Catholic Faith than midwives."[6]

Women's greed for sexual power, Institoris and Sprenger warned their male readers, was especially noticeable in the perverted desire of married women to dominate their husbands. "It is a natural vice" in women, they said, and unless men "take counsel," their wives would become witches. By way of advice, they repeated rhetorically the question posed by Cicero in his *Paradoxes:* "Can he be called a free man whose wife governs him, imposes laws on him, orders him, and forbids him to do what he wishes," or must he be called "not only a slave, but the vilest of slaves?" Since a woman "will not be governed, but will follow her own impulse even to her own destruction," a man could only expect insubordination and vengeance from his wife. Like "the accursed Jezebel," she wanted to "reign herself" and was willing to kill her own husband—even her own sons—to gain power. As if the dangers uncontrolled women posed were not already sufficiently clear, Institoris and Sprenger concluded this discussion with the warning "that nearly all the kingdoms of the world have been overthrown by women."

De Castanega was less immediately concerned with the rebellion of women against the sexual order, and he directly mentioned this type of female resentment only in ecclesiastical terms. But he deemed that a main reason more women than men were witches was that "they are more given to anger and more vengeful, and since they have less power with which to avenge themselves against those persons with whom they are angry, they seek and obtain favor and revenge from the devil." Because they were denied power in their social relations, then, women resorted to mystical power.[7]

The emphasis that Institoris and Sprenger placed on married women should not suggest that they were only concerned with the rebellion of wives. Their repeated conflation of "woman" and "wife" in their discussion of female domination suggests that they saw as witches all women who were potential or actual threats to a social hierarchy favoring men. In addition, they singled out the widow as someone who "takes it upon herself everywhere to look down on everybody, and is inflamed to all boldness by the spirit of pride." Nevertheless, they seem to have been more interested in problems married women caused men—a concern that de Castanega evidently did not share. The Spanish priest mentioned marital status only when making the observation that unmarried women, if young and rich, were rarely witches. Because men were only too willing to satisfy their desires, he intimated, these women had little need to resort to the Devil.[8]

Compared to religious and sexual themes, these three authors paid only minimal attention to gender-based economic issues. Significantly, however, de Castanega argued that poor women who were also old were likely witches for the same reason that other old women were—because men had no interest in them. Alone, without men to support them, they became dissatisfied and turned to the Devil to provide their material needs. Like other vices, he added, "poverty is often the source of many evils in persons who do not choose it voluntarily or endure it patiently." Institoris and Sprenger made no distinction between poor witches and other witches but simply declared that the "root of all woman's vices is avarice."[9]

Only once did issues of inheritance figure in these writings about witchcraft. In their elaboration of the meaning for men of women's envy, greed, and malice, Institoris and Sprenger presented their readers with men's centuries-old dilemma regarding women. Citing St. John Chrysostom and Socrates, they argued that women were "a necessary evil." If a man did not marry, he was not only lonely, but his "family dies out, and a stranger inherits." On the other hand, if a man did marry, he was subject among other abuses to a woman's discontent and anger—including her "reproaches concerning the marriage portion." Furthermore, there was "no certain arrival of an heir." Despite their greed and malice, women were essential to the orderly transmission of property from father to son. Yet their pivotal position allowed women to disrupt this process so central to male conceptions of social continuity.[10]

Although particular cultures within the European tradition emphasized different elements within this body of belief, the *Malleus* and the *Tratado* reveal that some of New England's submerged assumptions about women-as-witches had previously been quite openly expressed. Moreover, the root of those assumptions—that women threatened the sexual order—had been clearly identified. Seventeenth-century Puritan writings on women and family life reveal that the sexual hierarchy was at stake for them also, but with this difference: knowledge that detailed, explained, and justified the denigration of women had come into conflict with newer views of women. Though still vital, the old truths had been thrust from sight by the new.

The fundamental tenet of European witchcraft—that women were innately more evil than men—did not fit with other ideas Puritans brought with them to their new world. This tenet was still as necessary to Puritans as it had been for their Catholic predecessors, but it was incompatible with the emphasis Puritanism placed on the priesthood of all believers, on the importance of marriage and family relations, and on the status of women within those relations.

Puritanism took shape in late sixteenth- and early seventeenth-century England amidst a heated controversy over the nature of women, the value of marriage, and the propriety of women's social roles.[11] The dominant attitude toward women in the popular press and on stage did not differ very much from the views of Catholic witch-hunters except that overall it was less virulent, delivered as often in the form of mockery as invective. According to this opinion, women were evil, whorish, deceitful, extravagant, angry, vengeful, and, of course, insubordinate and proud. Women "are altogether a lumpe of pride," one author maintained in 1609—"a masse of pride, even altogether made of pride, and nothing else but pride, pride."[12] Considering the nature of women, marriage was at best man's folly; at worst, it was the cause of his destruction.

The problem, as some writers of this school had it, was women's increasing independence, impudence, "masculine" dress, and "masculine" ways. The presence of women in the streets and shops of the new commercial centers was merely symptomatic of their newly found "forwardness" and desire for "liberties."[13] But more than likely it was not so much women's increasing independence in the wake of commercial development that troubled these commentators; rather it was the increasing visibility of women within their traditional but increasingly commercialized occupations. Solutions to the problem, when offered, echoed a 1547 London proclamation that enjoined husbands to "keep their wives in their houses."[14]

Other writers argued that women were equal if not superior to men, called for recognition of the abuse women suffered under men's tyranny, and intimated that society would be better served if economic power resided in women's hands— but their voices were few and barely heard. More often, defenders of women simply took exception to the worst of the misogynists' charges and recounted the contributions women made to the welfare of their families and their society. The most serious challenge to prevailing opinion, however, came from a group of men who shared some of the concerns and goals of women's most avid detractors. Most of these men were Protestant ministers, and they entered the debate indirectly, through their sermons and publications on domestic relations. Though not primarily interested in bettering women's position in society, they found certain transformations in attitudes toward women essential to their own social vision. Among them, it was the Puritan divines—in both old and New England—who mounted the most cogent, most sustained, and most enduring attack on the contemporary wisdom concerning women's inherent evil.[15]

From the publication of Robert Cleaver's *A Godly Form of Householde Governement* in 1598 until at least the appearance of John Cotton's *A Meet Help* in 1699, a number of Puritan ministers did battle with "Misogynists, such as cry out against all women." If they were not unanimous on every point, most of them agreed with John Cotton that women were not "a necessary Evil," but "a necessary good." For justification of this belief, they turned to the Scriptures, to the story of the Creation. God in his infinite wisdom, John Robinson contended, had created woman from man and for man, when he "could find none fit and good enough for the man . . . amongst all the good creatures which he had made." He had made woman *from* man's rib, Samuel Willard noted, "Partly that all might derive Originally from One; Partly that she might be the more Dear and Precious to him, and Beloved by him as a piece of himself." He had made her *for* "man's conveniency and comfort," Cotton said, to be a helpmeet in all his spiritual and secular endeavors and "a most sweet and intimate companion." It followed from both the means and purposes of God's Creation that women and men were "joynt Heirs of salvation," that marriage was an honorable, even ideal state, and that women who fulfilled the purposes of their creation deserved to be praised, not vilified by godly men. In 1598, Cleaver called men foolish who detested women and marriage. For Cotton, a century later, such men were "a sort of Blasphemers."[16]

What had happened? Why did Puritans (along with their reforming brethren[17]) insist on a shift in attitude that would by the nineteenth century result in a full reversal of a number of sixteenth-century notions about the "innate" qualities of men and women?[18] We can begin to answer this question by considering a few elements critical in bringing about the transformation.

The Puritan challenge to the authority of church and state covered many issues, but one point not in dispute was the necessity of authority itself. Puritans were as disturbed by the lack of order in their society as were their enemies and were as fully committed to the principle of hierarchy. Though Puritanism developed during the period of upheaval that followed the breakup of the feudal order, Puritans were nevertheless determined to smother the sources of upheaval. Like other propertied Englishmen, Puritan men worried especially about masterlessness—insubordination in women, children, servants, vagabonds, beggars, and even in themselves.[19]

Where they differed with other men of property was in their belief that existing authority was both ineffective and misplaced. "Faced with the ineffectuality of authorities in everyday life," one historian has argued, "the Puritans dramatically and emphatically denied the chain of authority in the church and enthroned conscience in its place. . . . The radical solution to social deterioration was not the strengthening of external authority. It was, rather, the internalization of authority itself."[20] Foremost among the lessons Puritans taught was God's insistence on complete submission to divine will as expressed in the Bible and interpreted by ministers and magistrates. Outward compliance was not enough. Individuals who were fully committed to following the laws of God were *self*-controlled, needing only the Scriptures and an educated ministry to guide them on the path of right behavior. Submission to God's will had to be not only complete but voluntary. External discipline was still necessary to control the ungodly, but even they could be taught a measure of self-discipline.

The internal commitment to God's laws was to be inculcated primarily within the family, under the guidance and watchful eye of the head of the household, who conducted family prayer and instilled moral values in his dependents. It was not easy for family heads to ensure willing submission in their dependents, Puritans readily admitted. Minister John Robinson was talking specifically about children when he said that the "stubbornness, and stoutness of mind arising from natural pride . . . must . . . be broken and beaten down, . . . [the] root of actual rebellion both against God and man . . . destroyed," but his remarks reflect the larger Puritan belief in the difficulty of curbing human willfulness.[21] For subordinates to accept their places in the hierarchical order, they must first be disciplined to accept the *sin* in their very tendency to rebel. From there, it was possible to develop enlightened consciences.

The family was also crucial as a symbol of a hierarchical society. Functioning as both "a little Church" and "a little Commonwealth," it served as a model of relationships between God and his creatures and as a model for all social relations.[22] As husband, father, and master to wife, children, and servants, the head of the household stood in the same relationship to them as the minister did to his congregants and as the magistrate did to his subjects. Also, his relationship to them mirrored God's to him. Indeed, the authority of God was vested in him as household head, and his relationship to God was immediate: he served God directly. There was therefore no need for a priesthood to mediate between God and family heads. Other household members had immortal souls and could pray to God directly, but they served God indirectly by serving their superiors within the domestic frame. This model enhanced the position of all male heads of household and made any challenge to their authority a challenge to God's authority. It thereby more firmly tied other family members into positions of subordination.[23]

The relationship of household heads to other family members fit within a larger Puritan world view. God had created the world, Puritans maintained, in the form of a great "Chain of Being" in which man was both above other creatures and subordinate to the Deity. God had ordained that human relationships were to be similarly patterned, with husbands superior to wives, parents to children, masters to servants, ministers to congregants, and magistrates to subjects. All, however, were subordinate to God. In each of these relations, inferiors served God by serving their superiors. While Puritans viewed the parent-child relation as a natural one, all other unequal relationships were described as voluntary, based on a covenant between the individuals concerned. God also required that family heads enter into another contractual relationship, called a "family covenant." Under this agreement, men promised to ensure obedience in all their dependents, in return for God's promise of prosperity.[24]

Finally, the family also guided children in the right selection of their "particular callings." For the English divine William Perkins, particular callings were of two types. The first was God's call to individuals to enter into one or more of the several kinds of unequal social relations (husband/wife, parent/child, master/servant, and so on), relations that were "the essence and foundation of any society, without which the society cannot be." The second was God's call to specific kinds of employment by which individuals earned their livelihoods. In each case, God did the calling, but children had to endeavor to know what God had in mind for them, and parents were responsible to see that their charges made appropriate choices. Once chosen, callings were to be attended to conscientiously, not for honor or material reward but in the service of God.[25] What Perkins did not say was that for Puritans the second sort of calling did not apply to females. Woman was called for only one employment, the work of a wife.

The elevation of household heads to a godlike position within the family, and the importance of the family in maintaining a hierarchical social order, clarify the Puritans' insistence on the worth and dignity of women. For Puritan ministers were less interested in a new valuation of the female sex than in serving the needs of the godly men they counted on to bring order out of chaos. These were men like themselves who would pursue their callings with diligence, could be entrusted with responsibility, and would control their own immoral impulses for the sake of their salvation and the good of society. Godly men needed helpmeets, not hindrances; companions, not competitors; alter egos, not autonomous mates. They needed wives who were faithful and loyal; who assisted them in their piety, in their vocations, and in the government of their families; who revered them and acknowledged them as "Lord."[26] There was no place in this vision for the belief that women were *incapable* of fulfilling such a role. Nor was there a place in the ideal Puritan society for women who refused to fill it. A new conception of "woman" was essential—one that simultaneously denied her special proclivity for evil and enjoined "voluntary subjection . . . for conscience sake."[27]

As Puritan ministers set about the task of reeducating their congregations on issues of womanhood, their emphases varied. Some placed greater stress on the mutuality and "near equality" of the marriage relation, on the praises due virtuous women, and on the limitations of husbands' authority. Others dwelled more pointedly on the superior position of the male, the absolute requirement of female subjection, and the dire consequences of disobedience. But all spoke to both aspects of women's position. By the early eighteenth century, the former approach would take precedence over the latter, indicating more the extent of the clergy's success than any alteration in their goals.[28] Until that time, however, the work of *converting* women to subjection—and men to enlightened rule—was a central Puritan concern. From the beginning the message was clear: women who failed to serve men failed to serve God. To be numbered among God's elect, women had to acknowledge this service as their calling and *believe* they were created for this purpose.

What kinds of service did this belief entail? John Cotton held that such service "answeres natural, oeconomical and theological ends." Women answered natural ends in two ways, ministers agreed. First, they provided men with the intimacy, companionship, and solace they needed in their lives. Unlike "eyther maide servant or man-servant, the which doo serve men for feare, or else for wages . . . ," Robert Cleaver told the male reader, "thy wife will be led onely by love, and therefore shee doth every thing better then all other." She was, moreover, "the fellow and comforter of all cares and thoughts, . . . the last that leaveth thee at thy departing, and the first that receyveth thee at thy returning: thou departest from her with . . . sweete kisses and imbracements, she receyveth thee at thy returne home: unto her thou disclosest thy joy and thy heaviness."[29] In the increasingly competitive and individualistic society of England and early New England, in which men were more regularly leaving and returning to the household, and in which adult emotional relationships outside the nuclear unit

an early example of cult of domesticity
—with the focus on men rather than woman

were becoming more truncated,[30] wives would provide husbands with the intimacy and support they might not find elsewhere.

Though Puritans expected wives to confine themselves to domestic life and therefore not to require an emotional buffer against the world, they insisted that conjugal affection was also a duty of husbands. The feelings appropriate to husbands and wives were to correspond to their respective positions. The duty of a husband "as superior . . . is called Love," Samuel Willard explained; a husband should love his wife as "his second self" and as "the weaker Vessel." The feelings of a wife, on the other hand, were to spring from submission, reverence, and fear—not a "slavish Fear," he warned, "which is nourished with hatred or aversion: but a noble and generous Fear, which proceeds from Love."[31]

Women answered "natural ends" as well by assisting their husbands in the propagation of the species, which John Cotton referred to as "help[ing] build the House." Man's convenience required that his helpmeet be a woman, Willard noted, because "no other could have answered all the Ends of Human Society."[32] Beyond this, Puritans had little else to say about the practical side of the sexual union.

On women as mothers rather than men's companions, Puritans were relatively silent. This difference becomes especially significant when we consider the frequency with which ministers referred to the Creation story in Genesis, with its symbolic denial of women as childbearers. In a curious inversion of women's procreative power, the story portrays Eve as born from the body of Adam.[33] It attributes to a male god the primary role in creating both man and woman and makes no mention of prelapsarian Eve as a mother. In this connection the Puritan reluctance to explore the issues of female generativity appears to be part of the larger Protestant effort to eliminate the female principle from their account of human origins.[34] Women's life-giving and life-sustaining functions were still essential to society, but by seldom alluding to them, except

Key

as punishments for Eve's sin, Puritans, like other Protestants, deprived them of much of their symbolic power.

Puritans also said little about sexual expression within marriage. They did, however, elevate it, as they elevated woman within marriage, to a positive good. This was a sharp departure from the Catholic ideal of a lifelong commitment to virginity, which in some Protestant minds merely led to illicit sex, abortion, and infanticide. But the Puritans were not rejecting Catholicism's assumptions about the base nature of sexual impulses, nor about the greater inability of women to control those impulses. They were simply taking another approach to the maintenance of sexual order. Just as Catholics had honored celibacy, the Puritans drew their own lines of demarcation. Because it was "of God," sexual intercourse, like other worldly pleasures, was to be enjoyed, but only within its proper context—marriage.[35]

The Puritan acceptance of sexual expression within marriage had as its converse a strong emphasis on marital fidelity. Marriage was "a medicine against uncleanness" and fidelity, they insisted, was an equal responsibility of both husband and wife.[36] Nevertheless, Puritans believed that a wife's unfaithfulness was more abominable than her husband's. They defined adultery exclusively as sexual intercourse "with a married, or espoused wife."[37] A husband who had intercourse with a married woman other than his wife was considered an adulterer, but a husband who lay with a single woman was guilty only of the much less serious sin of fornication. A wife was adulterous for any sexual relationship outside of her marriage—regardless of the marital status of her partner.

At issue here, as this definition of adultery makes clear, was not sexual incontinence in general but the specific threat posed by female incontinence. Two concerns seem to have been at work. The first was that adultery expressed a woman's insubordination to her husband and therefore a challenge to the husband's right of property *in* his wife. And second, by diverting a man's legacy from his legitimate heirs, adultery could disrupt the orderly transmission of the social estate to the next generation.[38] When William Perkins said that adultery was a sin worse than theft, which was then a capital crime in England, he was speaking to the seriousness with which Puritans looked upon a wife's special duty to be loyal to the marriage bed.[39] But his comparison also revealed how important property rights—both in women and in real property—had become in England. When Puritans came to power, both in old and New England, they made adultery, as they defined it, a crime punishable by death.[40] The other services a wife performed for her husband were binding by the terms of the marriage covenant, but fidelity was the only bond whose breach explicitly jeopardized her life.

A woman answered economic ends, John Cotton wrote, when she acted as her husband's assistant in family affairs and in the government of the household. Indeed, Puritans defined the relation of husband and wife (like that of master and servant) as an economic one, distinguishing it from the natural bond between parent and child. A wife's duties in the household were encompassed under the rubric of "ordering things within doors," by which was meant the day-to-day maintenance of the family and the supervision of young children, older daughters, and female servants. "The house is [woman's] Center," Cotton said, whereas a man took part in the world of relations beyond the domestic realm, even if much of his work was done in or near the household.[41] The actual division of labor was rarely spelled out in the domestic literature, but the praise Puritans lavished on those ministers' wives who handled all routine matters with industry, diligence, and thrift—thereby freeing their husbands for matters of greater weight—suggests the ideal.[42]

The clergy took pains to encourage extensive female activity within the household and broad female authority over children and servants. According to Samuel Willard, a woman had "a joint Interest in governing the rest of their Family" and in that sense is "an Head of the Family." In his description of the virtuous wife, Cotton Mather told his readers that a husband "finds it his Advantage" to let such a wife "keep the Keys of all," because she will "so Regulate all the Domestick Expenses" that he shall have little reason to "complain of Any Thing embezzled."[43]

But a woman who took charge of domestic affairs might easily overstep the bounds of her authority by transgressing the line between female and male worlds. To guard against this possibility, ministers were also careful to delimit the wife's powers. Cotton Mather expressed the sentiments of his ministerial colleagues when he warned the wife that "though she be . . . a Mistress, yet she owns that she has a Master," whom she had to obey in every matter, great or small: "she will not so much as take in, or cast out a servant, without Consulting Him; nor . . . receive any Guests or Goods into the House" without his approbation. While she was to assist him in his prosperity, she had to be ever mindful of the inequality in the degree of familial authority.[44] Within the Puritan household, then, women were to be the workers, providing the daily labor and making the mundane decisions that kept the little commonwealth intact—yet never presuming themselves at its head.

For this arrangement to work, ideal Puritan women were to become "keeper[s] at home . . . keeping and improving what is got by the industry of the man."[45] For this reason they had to restrict themselves to a single calling in a society which offered men an expanding array of vocations. Indeed, the very diversity available to men seems to have brought constrictions for women.

The image of the ideal Puritan woman may have emerged in part as a response to the fear of female promiscuity, which was always considered a threat when women encountered the larger world independent of close male guidance. As Cotton Mather reminded women, by not being "too much from Home" the wife protected herself from her husband's suspicions of infidelity. Perhaps as important, this new ideal was meant to ensure that the domestic unit would remain a secure repository for the rewards of the husband's efforts, and to safeguard against situations in which men and women might face each other on equal terms. Domestic literature of the time included the warning that the virtuous woman was never "a wanderer abroad" but always "a worker at home." A symbol used to describe the model wife was the snail: "that little creature, that goes no further than it can carry its house on its head." Woman served economic ends but was not an economic creature. Ministers insisted that woman's work itself had little or no remunerative value; at best "the Pennyes that she saves do add unto the heaps of the Pounds that are Got by him." His work was to provide, hers to serve and preserve. That was the nature of their covenant.[46]

A woman served "theological" ends by assisting her husband in his piety and honesty. While a wife was to acknowledge her husband as her priest and prophet, and therefore as her spiritual guide, one of her most pressing duties was to work for her husband's and children's eternal good. To be sure, Puritans were concerned with the spiritual state of women and stressed the mutual duty of husband and wife to promote one another's salvation, but Puritan literature placed an even greater emphasis on the regeneration of men. Among other advantages of the work women were to perform was that it allowed men the time to "meditate of heavenly things, without distraction of mind."[47]

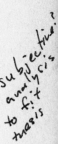

If women were to aid in their husbands' salvation, their spiritual status had to be enhanced. The tendency of men to deny that women had souls worthy of being saved had to be confronted first. Speaking to the male reader, one English minister insisted that his wife had as noble a soul as he, arguing that "souls have no sexes ... in the better part, they are both men."[48] Even after this fundamental precept was estab-

lished, there still remained the problem of convincing men
that woman—so long derided as the one who drew man into
sin—could be a helpmeet in this respect. It was doubly difficult because Puritans looked to the story of Eve's temptation
of Adam—and to women's intellectual and spiritual inferiority—to justify male rule. John Cotton did as well as anyone in
constructing the required rationale. Just because woman had
once failed to attain the ends of her creation, he said, did not
mean that she always would; to the contrary, a keen sense of
her original weakness "should make [her] the more wary for
the future."[49]

Success in changing women's religious image, like success
in advocating the domestic enterprise of virtuous wives, carried with it new problems. Excluded more and more from direct
participation in the economic world, but accorded a new recognition in the spiritual realm, some women began to act as if
they were men's spiritual equals. The activism of women on
behalf of the faith could be appreciated as long as Puritanism
stood in opposition to the established church, but once Puritans were in power, and women continued to challenge established authority, the clergy discovered their own earlier
tolerance to be misguided.[50]

There was a fine line between the belief that women had
souls equal to men's in the eyes of God and the belief that
women were men's equals in spiritual matters, but the Puritan
ministry were determined to draw it. They argued for the first
point by claiming that woman was subsumed in the concept
"man," alluding to the version of Creation in Genesis where
Eve and Adam were created simultaneously: "So God created
man in his own image, in the image of God he created him;
male and female he created them" (Gen. 1:27). They argued
against the second point—the assertion of spiritual equality—
by citing the second version of Creation in Genesis, in which
Adam was formed first from the dust of the earth and Eve
later from his rib: "It is not good that the man should be alone;
I will make him a help meet for him" (Gen. 2:18). That God

intended women to be subordinate to men in spiritual matters, as in all other things, was also shown, Puritans maintained, by his having created woman not only from and for
but also after man. The "Distance observed in the Creation of
these Two" was a distinct sign of man's "Priority, in the Covenant."[51] Contradictions in their arguments made it difficult
for ministers to countenance women who presumed a direct
relationship with God, but the Puritan position became
increasingly untenable as women began to dominate church
membership. In New England this trend became visible as early
as the 1650s.[52] By 1692, Cotton Mather reported that women
outnumbered men in his congregation by three or four to one.[53]

As the old idea of woman as a necessary evil was gradually
transformed into the idea of woman as a necessary good, the
fear and hostility that men felt toward women remained. The
old view of woman was suppressed, but it made its presence
known in the many faults and tensions that riddled Puritan
formulations on woman. Though largely unspoken, the old
assumptions modified the seemingly more enlightened
knowledge Puritans imparted. The new discourse, "first uttered
out of the pulpit,"[54] was in fact dedicated to affirming the beliefs
of the old, but in ways that would better serve male interests
in a society that was itself being transformed.

The belief that woman was evil continued to reside in the
myth at the core of Puritan culture—the biblical tale of human
origins. Really two myths in one, it is the story of Creation in
the Garden of Eden and the story of Adam and Eve's fall from
grace. Our concern is mostly with the latter, but the two tales
are nonetheless interdependent—the joys of Paradise making comprehensible the agonies of Paradise lost.

In their version of human origins, the Puritan clergy were
more ambiguous than usual about when they were discussing
"man, male and female," and when they were discussing men
only. Despite its many contradictions,[55] this creation myth

allowed the Puritans to establish their two most cherished truths: hierarchy and order.[56] Even before the Fall, they maintained, God had designated woman as both inferior to and destined to serve man—though her original inferiority was based "in innocency" and without "grief." Woman's initial identity was not—like man's—as a separate individual, but as a wife in relation to a husband. The very purpose of her creation allowed Puritans to extend the idea of her subordination *as wife* to her subordination *as woman*, in much the same manner as Anglican minister Matthew Griffiths did when he observed: "No sooner was she a Woman, but presently a Wife; so that Woman and Wife are of the same standing." So interchangeable were these terms in the minds of the clergy that they could barely conceive of woman's relationship to God except through a husband.[57]

Woman's position in the Puritan version of Eden was analogous to that of the angels and the animals. Angels were formed before Creation as morally perfect spiritual beings. Though angels were clearly above man in the hierarchy of Creation, and though man was not to have dominion over them, God would require the angels to "minister for man." Animals were even closer to the position of woman since they too were created specifically to serve man.[58]

The Puritan account of the Fall follows the standard Christian version in its general outlines.[59] Discontented with their position in the hierarchical order, Adam and Eve succumbed to the Devil's temptation to eat the forbidden fruit, thus challenging God's supremacy over them and rebelling against the order of Creation. Guilty of pride, both were punished, but Eve doubly because she gave in to the temptation first, thereby causing man's downfall.

Puritan elaborations on this tale are revealing. According to Samuel Willard, Adam and Eve were both principal causes of man's fall, but there were also three instrumental causes: the serpent, the Devil, and the woman. Exonerating the serpent as a creature lacking the ability to reason, he went on to discuss the two "blamable Causes," the Devil and Eve. The events of the Fall originated with the Devil, he said, explaining that the word "Devil" was a collective term for a group of apostate angels. Filled with pride in their positions as the most noble of God's creations, discontented that they were assigned to serve "such a peasant as man," envious of what they saw as a "greater honour conferred upon him," and consumed with malice against God and man, the apostate angels sought revenge by plotting man's downfall. What motivated them was not their displeasure at their place in the hierarchical order, Willard claimed, for only God was above them. Rather it was their "supreme contempt for their employment." United by their evil intentions, they are called "Satan" in the Scriptures as a sign that they had traded their natural subjection to God for a diabolical subjection to the "Prince of Evil." In the process of accomplishing their ends, they were the first to speak falsehoods in Eden, becoming in the process blasphemers against God and murderers of the bodies and souls of men. "They seduced them . . . and thus in procuring of man's fall, they compleated their own; in making of him miserable, they made themselves Devils."[60]

Eve's story—and her motivations—were more complex. Entering the body of the serpent, the Devil addressed himself to Eve, Willard said, suggesting to her that if she ate the fruit he offered, she would become godlike. Her senses suddenly deluded, she gave in to her lusts: "the lusts of the flesh, in giving way to carnal appetite, good for food; the lust of the eye, in entertaining the desirable aspect of the forbidden fruit, pleasant to the eyes; [and] the lusts of pride, in aspiring after more wisdom than God saw meet to endow a creature withal, to make one wise." Easily seduced, she in turn seduced Adam, thereby implicating him in her guilt. She commended the fruit, "makes offers to him, insinuates herself into him, backs all that the Serpent had said, and attracts him to joint consent with her in the great Transgression." Eve was moved not only by her sensuality but, like Satan, by pride. Her action bespoke the pride of a desire for knowledge, and by extension for God's position, rather than the resentment of her obligation to serve man.[61]

Adam and Eve were both punished for the sin of pride, for rebelling against the order of Creation, but Eve rebelled both as part of man and as man's "other." For this reason, Willard called her both a principal and an instrumental cause of man's fall. According to Willard, when God commanded man not to eat the fruit of the tree of knowledge, "though their prohibition be expresst as given to Adam in the singular [necessarily so, as Eve had yet to be created in the chapter Willard was citing] . . . yet Eve understood it as comprehending them both." Thus she shared with Adam responsibility as a principal in the matter. "Yet, looking upon her as made for the man, and by the Creators law owing a subordination to him, so she may also be looked upon as instrumental." Elaborating on this point, Willard argued that having been created as his helpmeet, she ought to have encouraged and fortified him in that obedience which God had required of them both. Instead she became a mischief, "an occasion, yea a blamable cause of his ruin." For this, the Lord placed his "special curse" upon the female sex: "Unto the woman he said, I will greatly multiply thy sorrow and thy conception: in sorrow shalt thou bring forth children: and thy desire shall be to thy husband, and he shall rule over thee."[62]

Part of woman's sin, then, was the seduction of man; another part was her failure to serve man. Though Willard never explicitly charged woman with having the same sinister motives as Satan, he did strengthen the association between these two instruments of man's fall by defining her as the Devil's willing agent: she acted "upon deliberation," he said, "and was voluntary in what she did."[63]

In contrast, Adam (as distinguished from "man") lacked any motive for his sin. His role in the Fall was essentially passive. When God confronted the pair about their sin Adam defended himself by pointing the accusatory finger at his mate:

"the woman which thou gavest to be with me, she gave me of the tree, and I did eat." Willard exonerated Adam by supporting his disclaimer and by describing him as an unwitting victim of his temptress wife: "Adam was not deceived, but the woman being deceived, was in the transgression." The burden of Adam's guilt was thereby lifted, and the blame placed on Eve. If "man's" sin in the Garden of Eden was pride, it was woman subsumed in man who committed it. Her male counterpart deserved a share of the punishment, but merely for allowing himself to be made "a servant of servants." Willard reinforced this point in his description of the sins that made human beings like devils. It is by now a familiar list: pride, discontent, envy, malice, lying, blasphemy, seduction, and murder. Some were explicitly Eve's, others implicitly hers; none were attributed to Adam.[64]

Eve was the main symbol of woman-as-evil in Puritan culture. She was, in many ways, the archetypal witch. Whatever the new beliefs affirmed about women's potential goodness, the persistence of Eve as a figure in the Puritan cosmology signals the endurance of older if more covert beliefs. Women could be taught to internalize the authority of men, Puritans thought—but they knew that the sweeping denial of self they demanded of women was "too bitter a pill to be well digested," that it had to "be sweetened" before it could "be swallowed."[65] The story of the Fall taught the lesson that female submission would not come easily—not, certainly, through a theological reformulation alone. Their continuing references to the Fall bespeak Puritan belief that the subjection of the daughters of Eve, whether religious, economic, or sexual, would have to be coerced. That was the message of Eve's punishment.

Ever fearful that women's conversion to virtuous womanhood was incomplete, ministers sometimes resorted to more vivid images of physical and psychological coercion. They warned the Puritan husband that he should not "bee satisfied that hee hath robed his wife of her virginitie, but in that hee hath possession and use of her will." Women tempted to abandon their chastity, and therefore their God, were told to resolve "that if ever these Other Lords do after this Obtain any thing from you, it shall be by the Violence of a Rape." For women who had yet to learn the necessity of subjection came the ever-present threat of additional punishment: "Christ will sorely revenge the rebellion of evill wives." Though the clergy protested again and again that the position of wives was different from that of servants, when they tried to picture what husbands' position would be like if the power relations within marriage were reversed, they envisioned men kept as vassals or enchained as slaves.[66]

Ministers described this reversal of the sexual order as a complete perversion of the laws of God and the laws of nature. The most frequently employed symbols of female usurpers were perversions of those other beings destined to serve man: angels and animals. For woman to be "a man-kinde woman or a masterly wife" conjured up images of fallen angels, demons, and monsters, distortions of nature in every respect.[67]

The tensions within the new ideology suggest that Puritans could no more resolve the ambivalence in their feelings than they could the contradictions in their thought. There was a deep and fundamental split in the Puritan psyche where women were concerned: their two conflicting sets of beliefs about women coexisted, albeit precariously, one on a conscious level, the other layers beneath. If woman was good—if she was chaste, submissive, deferential—then who was this creature whose image so frequently, if so fleetingly, passed through the mind and who so regularly controlled the night? Who was this female figure who was so clearly what woman was not? The ministers were not the only ones who lived with this tension, of course. The dual view of women affected everyone, male and female alike. Still, as the primary arbiters of culture in an age when God still reigned supreme, the clergy played the crucial role not only in creating the virtuous wife but in perpetuating belief in her malevolent predecessor.

In colonial New England, the intensity of this psychic tension is best seen in the writings of Cotton Mather—perhaps simply because he wrote so much, perhaps because his own ambivalence was so extreme.

In 1692, Mather published his lengthiest treatise on womanhood, *Ornaments for the Daughters of Zion*. His purpose, as he stated in his preface, was "to advocate virtue among those who can not forget their Ornaments and to promote a fear of God in the female sex." He was concerned both with women's behavior and with their relationship to God. He devoted much of his attention to the celebration of individual women, mostly biblical figures, whose lives were distinguished by quiet piety and godly ways. He presented them as models for New England women to emulate.

That same year, Mather completed *Wonders of the Invisible World*, his major justification for the Salem witchcraft trials and executions. Mather's focus here was on the behavior of witches and their relationships with the Devil—particularly women's complicity in Satan's attempts to overthrow the churches of New England. The book featured the witchcraft testimony presented against five of the accused at Salem, four of whom were women.

The nearly simultaneous publication of these two mirror-image works was not, it would seem, merely coincidental. Though Mather's witchcraft book does not explicitly address the reason why most of his subjects are women, his witches are nonetheless embodiments of peculiarly female forms of evil. Proud, discontented, envious, and malicious, they stood in direct contrast to the embodiments of female good in *Ornaments*, all of whom fully accepted the place God had chosen for them and regarded a willing and joyous submission to his will as the ultimate expression of their faith. Unable to ignore the profound uneasiness these two diametrically opposed views generated, Mather, like other New Englanders, relegated the still-powerful belief in women's evil to witches, on whom his fear and hatred could be unleashed. He was thereby freed to lavish praise on virtuous women—women who repressed the "witch" in themselves. Though his resolution allowed him to preserve man's superior position in the universe, Mather's heavy reliance in *Ornaments* on figures of Eve reveals how very delicate the balance was.

Mather's resolution was also his culture's. In the late sixteenth and seventeenth centuries, Puritans and other like-minded Protestants were engaged in the task of transforming an ideology, formulating beliefs that would better serve them in a world in which many of the old hierarchies and truths were no longer useful or plausible. They devised a new conception of man which, though drawn from the old, increasingly conceived him as an individual in relation to his God and his neighbors. It was a formulation that better fit the new economic order. The new man required a new woman: not an individual like himself, but a being who made possible his mobility, his accumulation of property, his sense of self-importance, and his subjection to new masters. By defining women as capable and worthy of the helpmeet role, the Puritan authorities offered a powerful inducement for women to embrace it. But they also recognized that the task they had set for themselves was a difficult one. If women were to repress their own needs, their own goals, their own interests—and identify with the needs, goals, and interests of the men in their families—then the impulse to speak and act on their own behalf had to be stifled.

As the witchcraft trials and executions show, only force could ensure such a sweeping denial of self. New England

witches were women who resisted the new truths, either symbolically or in fact. In doing so, they were visible—and profoundly disturbing—reminders of the potential resistance in
all women.

Puritans' witchcraft beliefs are finally inseparable from their
ideas about women and from their larger religious world view.
The witch was both the negative model by which the virtuous
woman was defined and the focus for Puritan explanations of
the problem of evil. In both respects, Puritan culture resembles other cultures with witchcraft beliefs: the witch image sets
off in stark relief the most cherished values of these societies.
A central element in these cosmologies, witches explain the
presence of not only illness, death, and personal misfortune,
but of attitudes and behavior antithetical to the culture's moral
universe.[68]

For Puritans, hierarchy and order were the most cherished
values. People who did not accept their place in the social order
were the very embodiments of evil. Disorderly women posed
a greater threat than disorderly men because the male/female
relation provided the very model of and for all hierarchical
relations, and because Puritans hoped that the subordination
of women to men would ensure men's stake in maintaining
those relations. Many years ago the anthropologist Monica
Hunter Wilson said that witchcraft beliefs were "the standard-
ized nightmare of a group, and . . . the comparative analysis
of such nightmares . . . one of the keys to the understanding
of society."[69] New England's nightmare was what the historian
Natalie Zemon Davis has called "women on top": women as
the willing agents of the Prince of Evil in his effort to topple
the whole hierarchical system.[70]

SIX

New England's Well-ordered Society

IT WAS NOT simply as Puritans that New Englanders drew on witchcraft beliefs in the seventeenth century. Their need for witches also grew out of their experience as settlers. New England may have been a religious commonwealth, but its people were nevertheless colonizing a land and creating a society—an enterprise as much individual and secular as collective and spiritual. It was an endeavor that generated contradictions of its own.

To locate witchcraft in its structural as well as its ideological context is to raise issues that so far we have discussed only sporadically, most notably the relationships between the witch and her accusers. For though the witch was a creation of Puritan belief, she was also the creation of the neighbors who denounced her, and the story of witchcraft is as much theirs as hers.

The relationships between accuser and accused were so complex that sorting them out completely is an impossible task. Where community consensus concerning a woman's witchcraft was strongest, as many as twenty, thirty, or forty people might come into court to explain how their suspicions had been aroused. They might relate incidents that had taken place weeks, years, even decades before, and their testimony left much that was ambiguous, often including the source of the original complaint. The impression one carries away after reading thousands of these depositions is that over the years, individuals who had been involved in minor confrontations with the accused shared their concerns with their neighbors, some of whom in turn saw her shape in their own difficulties and shared this with their neighbors, and so on until the community's leaders responded to the danger at hand. The individual who filed the official complaint, if a complaint was filed, was only one and perhaps only the most recent of many accusers. To try to identify the origin of a witchcraft accusation in such cases is to try to penetrate a web of community gossip so dense as to deter even the most dogged investigator.[1]

Moreover, to acknowledge only those people who named names as accusers overlooks the ministers, magistrates, juries, and other members of the community who validated some accusations and invalidated others. Considering the complicated social meanings of witchcraft in New England, and the consistency with which certain kinds of people were brought into court, we must recognize that the community was as much an accuser as any individual within it.

Still, society's concerns were articulated in the fears and fantasies of the few. If for the purposes of discussion we accept as New England's accusers only people who named names or testified against individual witches, 732 such persons are identifiable. Seventy-eight of these (just over 10 percent) were possessed persons, people who experienced convulsions and other manifestations of the Devil's desire to recruit more witches. Their story is well documented and in many ways quite distinct from that of other accusers. For those reasons, possessed accusers will be discussed separately, in the chapter to follow.

Of the remaining 654 accusers, very little has been written. We know that most of these non-possessed accusers (probably

90 percent) were adults and that most (roughly two-thirds) were men.[2] They encompassed a broad age range: of the 380 who can be identified by age, more were in their twenties, thirties, and forties than were older, though persons over fifty were overrepresented given their numbers in the larger population (see table 13). Like the witches they called to account, most non-possessed accusers were married: of the 424 who can be identified by marital status, 337 (about four-fifths) had spouses when they lodged their accusations (see table 14).

Apart from these demographic characteristics, non-possessed accusers were quite representative of the larger population. Most of them seem to have come from the lower and middling ranks of society, though merchants, magistrates, and others from the upper ranks expressed witchcraft suspicions often enough to suggest that they were well-represented among accusers.[3] Accusations usually emerged from everyday encounters such as visiting, sharing work, exchanging goods and services, or squabbling over wandering livestock or transgressed boundaries. Those lodged by elite accusers were more

TABLE 13. Non-possessed Accusers by Sex and Age, New England, 1620–1725

Age	Female	Male	Total
Under 10	3	1	4
10–19	19	16	35
20–29	30	46	76
30–39	24	62	86
40–49	29	59	88
50–59	16	41	57
60–69	2	17	19
70 and over	3	12	15
TOTAL	126	254	380

TABLE 14. Non-possessed Accusers by Sex and Marital Status, New England, 1620–1725

Marital Status	Female	Male	Total
Single	29	39	68
Married	124	213	337
Widowed	9	10	19
TOTAL	162	262	424

[handwritten: why more in 14 than in table 13?]

likely than others to originate in hierarchial relations, such as conflicts between master and servant. Non-possessed accusers knew their witches, often well. They were likely to live next door or just down the road from the accused, close enough to have regular contact with them. Though only occasionally members of the same family, it was not uncommon for accusers and accused to be living or have lived, at least temporarily, under the same roof.

Because we cannot easily distinguish non-possessed accusers from the rest of the New England population, we can understand the role they played in witchcraft rituals only by understanding their larger social setting. We must ask then what it was about New England's developing social arrangements that led so many New England settlers to accuse their female neighbors of witchcraft.[4] Though women regularly expressed witchcraft fears, we will consider first the social sources of witch fear in men.

The Puritans who came to New England in the early seventeenth century were transported by the vision of a more godly society than the one they had known. Nevertheless, the "city upon a hill" that they hoped to create quickly encountered the difficulties of trying to escape the past. It proved vulnerable as well to the environment in which it was set and to the idiosyncratic notions of its inhabitants, many of whom did not share the founders' beliefs and goals. For the first generation of settlers, both male and female, these diverse influences made for an ambiguous social world.

The ambiguities facing women emerge most graphically in two nearly simultaneous events of the early 1630s in the newly formed town of Salem: the granting of land, called "maid lotts," to single women, and the issuing of an order that all women had to wear veils in public, "under penalty of non-communion . . . and as a matter of duty and absolute necessity."[5] Neither of these practices had been established in England. To grant land to unmarried females in New England could eventually have created a substantial group of economically independent women, whereas to require that women wear veils in public was to underscore quite vividly women's dependence and submission. These two expressions of the unsettled nature of women's roles in early colonial New England were abandoned almost immediately, the former as an "evil" and a "bad president," the latter as an unenlightened practice.[6] But together they capture something of the uncertainty, flexibility, and sometimes outright division that distinguished the first New England efforts to specify gender arrangements.

That uncertainty may in part have been related to the unbalanced sex ratio that characterized New England throughout the lives of most of the first settlers. New England settlement has been accurately described as a movement of families, but that should not obscure its noticeably male character. On the first forty-six vessels to arrive in New England during the 1620s and 1630s, there were 157 males for every hundred females.[7] Among adults, the sex ratio was even higher: as many as 228 adult males may have migrated for every hundred adult females who did.[8] Not until the second generation would the preponderance of men in New England towns level off, and then only in the oldest communities.

The early years were the hardest, of course, on men and women alike. Death rates were high, affecting not only the very young and the very old but people of all ages. Within a short time the first generation of colonists would find New England a much healthier environment than England,[9] but not before they had suffered their losses and made their compromises.

The sex ratio imbalance, coupled with the initially high mortality rates, also affected the age at which women married. In Plymouth colony, for females born between 1600 and 1650, the average age at first marriage was between twenty and twenty-one, considerably younger than the average age at which English women married at this time.[10] Precise age-at-first-marriage figures do not exist for other New England communities during the pre-1650 years, but the evidence we have suggests a similar experience for women who migrated to other communities. For the rest of the century, moreover, the evidence indicates that the newer the settlement the younger the age at which women married.[11]

From the beginning of New England settlement, the pressure to marry was considerable on both men and women. We know that some women during this early period chose not to marry, and hence to live with the epithet of "Thornback,"[12] but they were exceptions. Unless a woman possessed inherited wealth, her options were few. The wages women could demand were too low to allow self-support, and the magistrates' insistence that everyone live under family government meant that to remain single was, for most women, to live under the authority of a father, brother, or master. In the 1630s an unmarried woman of twenty-five was referred to as an "antient maid," an expression of social pressure[13] and an indication that in New England, where women lacked economic independence and where there was an overabundance of men, most women married and they married relatively young.

We cannot be sure how many children survived to adulthood during the first couple of decades, nor how many women were widowed and did not remarry. We do know that in Plymouth colony and in the town of Andover, Massachusetts, parents of the first-generation families may have had, on the average, as many as seven or eight children who lived until at least age twenty-one.[14] If so, these towns had unusually low infant and child mortality rates as compared to Europe: for Plymouth these mortality rates were no more than 25 percent and for Andover less than 16 percent. But these figures do not include children born before settlement, nor can they tell us much about larger towns like Boston and Salem, where infant mortality rates were higher.[15] Furthermore, these rates may not reflect the general under-recording of child and infant deaths, especially during the first years of settlement.[16] So although many of their children survived to adulthood, New England parents of the first generation often saw their siblings and offspring die. We know less about the number of women who were widowed during this period.[17] Literary sources, however, suggest that widows could and did marry quickly and easily.[18]

Child mortality and the incidence of widowhood are especially important for their economic implications. If many children did not live to adulthood in the 1630s and 1640s and adult death rates were high, we might expect inheritance patterns to reflect these demographic conditions, as they did in the southern colonies at this time.[19] Although we cannot say that this was the case throughout New England, the probate records for one community, Salem, are revealing.

These records suggest that for Salem in the 1630s and 1640s, people who died during the period of initial settlement had many fewer surviving children than would those just beginning their families at this time. These records mention forty-one children (twenty-six sons and fifteen daughters), many of them underage at the time the probate record was filed. In only two families were there as many as seven children, and on the average there were 2.4 children per family. Roughly one-third of these families had no surviving children at all.[20]

The Salem probate records also disclose patterns of inheritance that were unusual when compared to either England or to New England in later decades. We have seen that one of the most widely accepted principles of inheritance during the seventeenth century was the widow's entitlement to dower— the *use* of one-third of her husband's real property for the duration of her life only. Yet one-third of these probate cases were records of women's estates, and all of these women had property of their own to devise to their heirs. Moreover, half of the men who wrote wills during this period left their widows ownership rather than mere use of some (if not all) of their estates. This pattern of widow inheritance does not seem to have resulted from prenuptial contracts, arrangements found in later decades by which women, usually former widows, retained the right to dispose of property they had brought to the marriage. Nor did the magistrates encourage this manner of disposing property: the several intestate records among the early probate documents suggest that when the magistrates made the decision, and when there were children as potential heirs, the widow received only her "thirds," as was customary in England at this time.[21]

Rather, these patterns suggest that there may have been some margin for flexibility in New England inheritance practices during the first two or three decades. This flexibility would have been promoted by the youthfulness of surviving children, by the considerable chance that they might not reach adulthood, and by the precariousness of adult survival. Perhaps it was encouraged as well by the abundance of land and the scarcity of women. It was at least allowed by statute: the first body of laws compiled in Massachusetts in 1641 held concerning the treatment of widows only that all persons over twenty-one had the right to leave wills or otherwise dispose of their property as they pleased, and that if "any man at his death shall not leave his wife a competent portion of his estate," then upon complaint to the General Court "she shall be relieved."[22]

The widow's right to inherit property outright did not become the custom in Salem or in New England as a whole.

In Salem, the proportion of inheriting widows was largest during the early decades of settlement; with each succeeding decade, the proportion dropped, reaching a low of 21 percent by the 1680s.[23] The harbinger of change came much earlier, in 1647, when Massachusetts magistrates spelled out the law of dower in intestate cases. Confirming that a widow's right to one-third of the real property was for life only, they at first included a passage stating that she was also entitled to one-third of the movable property. Not long after, the magistrates deleted the additional passage.[24]

Salem had at least for a time sanctioned a type of female who stood at odds with the conscientious helpmeet celebrated in Puritan visions of ideal gender relations. This type of woman could hold and dispose of property as independently as the males in her family. She occupied a relatively autonomous position in the structure of society. Indeed, despite assumptions that widows remarried quickly in the early and mid-seventeenth century, some of the widows who benefited from inheritances in early Salem remained widows despite opportunities to remarry. Such women strained the delicate balance of conflicting beliefs at the core of Puritan attitudes toward women.

The relation of women to religious doctrine and institutions was similarly ambiguous during the early years of settlement. In the religious sphere, however, it was social rather than demographic conditions that brought to the surface the contradictory elements in the larger Puritan world view. And the religious activism of women helped expose those contradictions.

The women of early New England were used to an active religious role. As Puritans, many of the first settlers had been schooled since childhood in opposition to established authority. During the years of religious ferment that preceded Puritan political victories in England, ministers may have expressed misgivings about openly encouraging women to disobey Anglican rule.[25] But after the Puritans came to power in England, the implications of women's training in issues of religious doctrine became clear. [And in New England, Puritan rule obtained from the very first.] ?

Even before Anne Hutchinson challenged the Puritan authorities in the mid-1630s, there were signs of an ensuing battle between women and their religious and secular leaders. Like their male companions, most of the first female settlers had risked the dangerous ocean voyage to New England specifically to participate in setting up God's kingdom. They shared no single vision of what that kingdom would be like, but they were not easily deterred. Anne Hutchinson's excommunication and banishment sent a clear and emphatic message to her female followers and to other religiously aggressive women who might, like Hutchinson, assert their own spiritual authority.

The message was not immediately heeded by women in Boston or in other communities. Mary Dyer, Jane Hawkins, and at least four other women were prosecuted for religious defiance in Boston in the wake of Hutchinson's expulsion: Judith Smith in 1638, for "obstinate persisting" in "sundry Errors"; Katherine Finch that same year, for "speaking against the magistrates, against the Churches, and against the Elders"; Widow Hammond in 1639 for saying "that Mrs. Hutchinson neyther deserved the Censure which was putt upon her in the Church, nor in the Common Weale"; and Sarah Keayne in 1646, for "irregular prophesying in mixed assemblies."[26]

New Haven experienced a similar pattern of female recalcitrance in the mid-1640s. Anne Eaton, wife of the governor of the colony, was excommunicated in 1644 for "her disavowal of infant baptism" and for other offences that mounted after she refused to admit her error. Two years later, Lucy Brewster was accused of "sympathizing with Eaton and of saying [the minister John] Davenport made her 'sermon sick.' " During the same court, a Mrs. Moore and her daughter, Mrs.

Leach, were prosecuted for their outspoken denigration of ministerial authority.[27]

In Salem, the authorities found female dissent an even greater problem. At least seven women were called before church or court officials for disorderly religious behavior in the late 1630s and the 1640s. Several men committed religious crimes in Salem during these years, but in all but one of their cases the charges were minor ("fowling" on the Sabbath, for example).[28] The religious crimes of the women, on the other hand, were interpreted as heresy. Elinor Truslar, who was said to have "question[ed] the government ever since she came," was accused of declaring that the town's minister and its principal magistrate were unfaithful to the church and that the minister "taught the people lies." Mary Oliver, who simply insisted on her right "as a Christian" to church membership, was eventually charged with "disturbing the peace of the church," reproaching the elders and the magistrates, and propounding dangerous opinions.[29] To John Winthrop, Oliver was "far before Mrs. Hutchinson . . . for ability of speech, and appearance of zeal and devotion" and therefore was "the fitter instrument to have done hurt, but that she was poor and had little acquaintance."[30]

A few dissenting women recanted their positions and were simply admonished or fined. But most persisted in their "errors" until excommunicated, officially banished, or driven from the colony. According to their opponents they bore their punishments with what Winthrop described as a "masculine spirit."[31] This display of female obstinacy was part of an energetic debate that covered a whole range of women's religious behavior: whether a woman could prophesy; whether she could publicly relate the religious experience marking her acceptance of grace (which was necessary, some argued, if church members were to judge her fitness for membership); whether she should be considered an individual, as opposed to a wife, with regard to church membership or dismissal; whether St. Paul's injunction that women be silent in the churches extended to pro-pounding questions to the minister after the sermon, voting in church meetings, or participating in decisions about mem-bership in the church; and even whether the sound of wom-en's voices in the singing of psalms would offend God's ear.[32]

This debate—like women's religious activism itself—grew as much out of the diverse experiences of settlement as it did out of the contradictions in Puritan doctrine. In early New England, the minister and the laity had considerable power to decide the practices of their own churches.[33] Some congrega-tions emphasized the view that women enjoyed spiritual equality with men. In those churches women could prophesy, or relate their conversion experiences as men did, publicly to the whole congregation rather than privately to their husbands or their ministers. Although we do not know how most churches arranged their gender relations, in the wake of the Antinom-ian controversy liberal readings of Puritan doctrine regarding women were increasingly frowned upon by the established clergy.

The debate over women's position within the church, then, was occasioned both by the latitude earlier afforded women in some congregations and by women's own vocal assertions of spiritual equality. This debate may have been stimulated also by the growing visibility of women as church members: despite the disproportionate numbers of men in the larger population, in the 1640s women already composed majorities of the elect in some congregations, and by the 1650s in most.

By the late 1640s, however, the outcome of the conflict over women's spiritual status was foreshadowed by the abrupt decline in Puritan women's opposition to their male leaders, and by the growing numbers of women who were called to account for their behavior in both the church and the com-monwealth. As the historian Mary Maples Dunn has noted, not only were women disciplined within the church "in num-bers out of proportion to their share of congregational populations," but "their offenses were increasingly connected with social behavior, not with heresy."[34] Much of this aberrant social behavior was sexual.

During the early years of settlement, Puritans in Massachusetts Bay were also uncertain about how to translate their sexual beliefs into public policy. As early as 1631, Massachusetts passed its first adultery law, stating "that if any man shall have carnall copulation with another mans wife, they both shal be punished by death."[35] The act was originally provoked by John Dawe's adultery with an unnamed Indian woman. The magistrates decided not to hang either of the offending parties, possibly because the woman involved was not the wife of a colonist or perhaps, as later cases would suggest, because Puritan magistrates were reluctant to administer in full measure the punishment that legally fit the crime. In this case, they simply ordered Dawe "severely whipped for intiseing an Indian woman to lye with him." No charges were filed against the woman.[36]

In the ensuing several years the Massachusetts magistrates attempted to articulate more precisely the forms and degree of punishment appropriate to the different varieties of sexual offenses. In 1632, they ordered that Robert Huitt and Mary Ridge be "whipt for committing fornication togeather."[37] Here the Court of Assistants set out what was to become a common punishment for sexual misdemeanors among the unmarried, or among married men and single women. In 1635 the authorities turned their attention to the problem of fornication between persons who later married. They fined two men, Edward Gyles and John Galley, for "knoweing" their wives "carnally before marriage," but they did not punish either of the two wives.[38] In 1638, they ordered John Hathaway, Robert Allen, and Margaret Seale whipped and banished for adultery but simultaneously confirmed their 1631 law stipulating that the punishment for adultery was death.[39]

In at least three of these cases, the magistrates did not hold the woman responsible for her sexual misbehavior. This was not unusual. In Massachusetts in the 1630s and early 1640s, many more men than women were prosecuted for sexual offenses. Although a few of these cases involved forced sexual acts, legal actions against men predominated largely because the most common sexual offense was premarital intercourse resulting in pregnancy and the courts did not prosecute the woman involved if she subsequently married the father of the child. Between 1630 and 1639, seventeen men were charged with fornication-related crimes in Massachusetts' two highest courts, while only two women were so charged.[40]

Even considering the inconsistencies in Puritan sexual beliefs, this differential treatment of men and women is surprising. We might expect the courts either to hold men and women equally responsible for their sexual behavior or, considering the place of Eve in the Puritan world view, to place the greater blame on women. Perhaps the legal response spoke to the scarcity of women during these years and the magistrates' desire to ensure the colony's survival. By marrying and legitimizing the children of their illicit unions, women who committed the sin of fornication may have sufficiently redeemed themselves in the eyes of the authorities. In any event, the courts' leniency with women was short-lived.

For the period 1640–44, eighteen men and ten women were charged with fornication-related offenses in the two highest Massachusetts courts.[41] The ratio of male to female offenders had changed since the 1630s from roughly 4:1 to just less than 2:1. After 1644 the higher courts no longer handled any but the most serious sexual crimes, but in Essex County, Massachusetts, the direction of the change was even more evident. Between 1636 and 1650, the Essex courts adjudicated fifty-six sexual offense cases: thirty of the offenders (54 percent) were women. The tendency to hold women more responsible than men for violations of sexual norms, which would become more obvious over the rest of the century, dates from the mid-1640s.[42]

The increased proportion of women among those charged with sexual offenses in Essex County arose in part from the magistrates' new willingness, first evidenced in Essex in 1643, to hold women equally responsible with men for incontinence before marriage. But the courts also displayed a growing reluctance to prosecute men for some sexual crimes and a growing inclination, present even during the early years, to conceive of certain crimes in images of female sexuality. In a 1650 letter to Connecticut governor John Winthrop, Jr., minister Roger Williams condemned adultery as "that filthy devill of whorish practices."[43] Williams's words suggest that the idea that women led men to sexual sin was too deeply embedded to be eradicated easily by the Puritans' more enlightened ideas about women. Yet there was no theologically consistent way to punish only women for men's and women's assertion of sexual independence. The resolution to this problem, like the resolution to the problem of women's religious and economic independence, was never openly acknowledged, but a resolution was found.

Witchcraft accusations, trials, and executions began in earnest in New England in 1647. As we have seen, the accused were from the start primarily women who had violated gender norms—norms that had not always been clearly articulated or agreed upon during the early years of settlement but which by the mid-1640s were being enforced. Most of the accused were women who had no brothers or sons, women who either had inherited or were likely to inherit property. Many of these same women had committed or were thought to have committed fornication, infanticide, or other sexual or sexually related offenses. A few others were women who stubbornly maintained their own versions of religious truth. Except for this last group, witches were not normally accused by the religious or secular authorities but by their own neighbors. This suggests that by the mid-1640s, signs of female independence had also become objectionable to the larger community.

During the second and third generation of New England settlement, witchcraft accusations had little to do with women's challenge to the religious system. Quakers were the exception, and the authorities continued to use innuendo rather than formal accusations in most of the Quaker cases. Other women were accused of refusing to attend church or otherwise displaying their disrespect for the Puritan faith, but this testimony was offered simply as confirmation of their witchcraft and not as the principal evidence of it. None of the few remaining non-Quaker women who were prosecuted for religious crimes in this period appears on lists of suspected witches.

The explanation for this change may lie in the success of official actions against Puritan women who challenged the religious system. By treating female dissent as evidence of witchcraft as well as heresy, the authorities may have effectively silenced Puritan women's opposition. Indeed, by 1660 the debate over women's participation in the church had all but ended—and women had lost many of the gains of the early years.[44] After 1660 Puritan ministers increasingly found reasons to celebrate rather than vilify their most active female congregants, but women's religious activity had taken on a decidedly submissive character. Women continued to join the church in proportionately larger numbers than men for the rest of the century, but if the ministers can be believed, female congregants now listened more than they spoke—and when they spoke, it was not in church.[45]

Ironically, the clergy's success in bringing women to God may have fostered witchcraft accusations in other areas. The growing visibility of women in the church did not go unnoticed: by 1692, with no more than a quarter of his congregation male, even Cotton Mather was forced to speculate that women might be more religious than men.[46] As women's religious commitment became more obvious over the second half of the seventeenth century, the contradictions in Puritan beliefs about women intensified, encouraging those who lived with those contradictions to associate some women with the evil of Satan. The new religious submission of women might have quieted fears about certain kinds of female independence but aroused fears about other kinds.

If religious tensions became submerged in other issues, the sexual tensions evident in the first outburst of witchcraft accusations continued to grow. Fornication and adultery aroused greater and greater concern in New England as the century wore on. This may have reflected an increase in the incidence of these crimes or a greater community sensitivity to sexual activity outside of marriage. In any case, the evidence from Essex County shows a growing number of sexual offenders: the county courts, which had adjudicated fifty-six cases in the fifteen-year period between 1636 and 1650, handled 237 cases during the decade of the 1670s.[47]

For the period 1650–1700, charges of sexual misconduct in Essex County show a new focus on illicit conceptions and, especially, illegitimate births, rather than on sexual misbehavior *per se*.[48] This new concern made women, as the bearers of children, more vulnerable to special public scrutiny. Although any inferences are complicated by the difficulty of distinguishing some male sexual-abuse cases from cases involving mutual consent, the evidence shows that by the 1680s at least 60 percent of the prosecutions were against women.[49] The trend toward holding women responsible for the more general failure to adhere to community sexual norms, visible in Essex County as early as the late 1640s, had by the 1680s become fully realized.

There were important exceptions. In Essex County, for example, men were still regularly prosecuted and punished on sexual charges. Some of these men were charged with rape or less extreme forms of sexual coercion, but most were in court, along with their wives, for having had a child too soon after their marriage. In these latter cases men and women continued to be punished equally, until at least the 1680s, increasingly with fines if they could pay them and with whippings if they could not. The other significant group of male sexual offenders dealt with by the court were poor and transient men who were charged with fornication or adultery. In Essex County, and possibly in other parts of New England, men of the middling or upper ranks of society were less frequently prosecuted for sexual offenses, and when they were they often escaped punishment.[50]

While this is the larger picture in Essex County, many nuances and outright contradictions are visible within it, as we might expect of a region going through a profound shift in its conceptions of sexuality. As early as the 1650s, illegitimacy had become the principal community concern with regard to sexual behavior.[51] Pressure on errant couples to marry solved many of the cases, but in those involving young women made pregnant by their masters, by their masters' sons, or by men generally of a higher rank than the women, such measures simply would not do. One response was to deter young women from making such charges—true or untrue—by severely punishing and publicly humiliating those who did. In 1654, for example, Elizabeth Drew was whipped twelve stripes (a punishment comparable to that for rape of a single woman) for naming her master's son as the father of her child. When Drew persisted in her story she was whipped an additional twenty stripes and forced to stand in public on lecture day with a paper on her forehead proclaiming herself "A SLANDERER OF MR ZEROBABELL ENDICOTT."[52]

But this approach was not entirely satisfactory. Someone had to be named the father in such cases, because a single woman could rarely support herself, let alone a child, and the community often was left with part of the burden. Holding the father equally responsible with the mother would have conflicted with the prevailing values of hierarchy and men's sexual independence. The response to male sexual offenses, then, was inconsistent: a combination of public outrage and the legal fiction of harsh treatment with the practice of increasing public acceptance and indulgence.[53]

In 1658, the Massachusetts General Court reaffirmed a law originally passed in 1642 that stated that any man convicted of fornication with a single woman would be punished by the court's "enjoyning marriage, or fine, or corporal punishment, or all or any of these."[54] In 1665, the magistrates added the threat of disenfranchisement.[55] These statutes seem to indicate that the community had determined to hold men as responsible for their actions as it held women. But in practice magistrates themselves opposed this, and they disposed of many male sexual offenders with leniency. The disenfranchisement clause was apparently never carried out; nor were forced marriages.[56] As we have seen, the courts did subject some men convicted of fornication (most of them poor or without influence) to whippings and other punishments, but the numbers of women punished for acts of mutual consent were larger.

Despite these inconsistencies, the magistrates continued their public stance, passing a law in 1668 that required that "any man . . . legally convicted to be the Father of a Bastard childe . . . be at the care and charge to maintaine and bring up the same, by such Assistance of the Mother as nature requireth." They added that in the absence of other proof, if a woman persevered in her identification of the father throughout the labor of childbirth, then that man would be held responsible "notwithstanding his denial."[57]

But the magistrates persisted in their refusal to enforce this policy consistently. During the third quarter of the seventeenth century, increasing numbers of men who were charged with sexual abuse—such as the "cruel and lascivious beating" of Ann Thorndike by Job Swinerton—continued to receive mild treatment.[58] More and more men denied paternity, bringing in witnesses to testify to the disreputable character of their female accusers. Poor men resorted to fleeing the colony to escape the legal retribution they could expect. But most male sexual offenders were not cowed by the court's threats.

By the 1680s and 1690s, some men in Essex County who denied paternity were being released from responsibility for child support in cases in which they charged the mother with sexual promiscuity or themselves pleaded hardship, or both.[59] The magistrates were becoming more inclined to base their decisions on the reputation of the woman. In a related development during the latter decades of the century, the court at times agreed to relieve fathers from maintenance charges if they placed the child in service: mothers' objections, when made, were overruled in these cases, and the court warned these women that if they refused to agree to the arrangements they could take full financial responsibility themselves.[60]

After 1680, except for the poor, Essex County men were only infrequently whipped or fined for fornication with women they did not subsequently marry, or for what we would call adultery with a single woman. Adultery with a married woman continued to bring harsh penalties, except in some cases where the woman's husband was without influence. Women, however, continued to be held responsible for both the illicit sexual act and its consequences. Women were liable for the child's care and sometimes for his or her maintenance—in some cases even when the child was put out to service. Beyond that, women were still whipped or sometimes fined for fornication and were punished more often and more severely—by public humiliation as well as beatings—for adultery of any kind.[61] By the late seventeenth century, the stigma of having an illegitimate child and the difficulty of caring for and maintaining that child were, along with the fines and public degradations, the principal deterrents to sexual misbehavior: all were burdens borne primarily if not exclusively by women.[62]

The combination of economic concerns and the increasing incidence of illegitimacy go a long way toward explaining

New England's double standard of sexual accountability—and its witchcraft accusations and trials. As the seventeenth century wore on, more and more men were refusing to marry the mothers of their children. Illegitimate children and their mothers were becoming a greater financial burden not only to the community but also to these women's parents and siblings.[63] The visibility of unwed mothers and their offspring highlighted one of the most fundamental contradictions in the sexual beliefs of men: to condone sexual license in men was to condone it implicitly in women.

Yet the tolerance shown male sexual indiscretion almost never extended to other men's liaisons with one's own wife and daughters. Even to acknowledge such a possibility meant that a man could never know for sure if his wife were faithful or if her children were also his. Men's property, in both senses of the word, was at stake.[64] The cost of male sexual independence was female sexual independence and the uncertainty about whether men's estates would pass on to their own progeny. During the second half of the seventeenth century, both concerns were sources of considerable tension, and the two were almost impossible to separate. If one source of this tension was the problem of illegitimacy, another was simply the growing numbers of women.

It is not clear exactly when the sex ratio in New England began to even out. The first firm figures we have are for the latter part of the eighteenth century, by which time the early preponderance of men had been replaced by the preponderance of women in most settled communities. In 1765 Hingham, for instance, the adult sex ratio was 79.05 (males per hundred females); in 1765 Concord it was 88.[65] But the shift had begun long before. Ipswich, Massachusetts, seems to have had more female than male settlers as early as the late 1650s; and in parts of Plymouth Colony, this was the case by the mid-1660s.[66] Although the preponderance of males continued into the eighteenth century in some established communities, a declining and in some cases a reversed sex ratio characterized the last half of the seventeenth century in most older communities.[67]

Several factors contributed to this change in the sexual makeup of early New England towns. Most obviously, children born in these communities would have been about equally males and females; barring unusual circumstances, the sex ratio would have begun to balance out with the second generation. Although most immigrants continued to be male, later arrivals tended to settle in new communities where the opportunities to benefit from land divisions were better; their numbers would not have significantly affected the sex ratio in the older towns. In addition, as the century wore on, the longevity of women seems to have increased in relation to men in some communities, thereby compensating statistically for deaths during childbirth.[68] Further, King Philip's War (1675–76) took the lives of many more New England men than women.[69]

Fathers in the oldest communities at this time were having difficulty settling all their sons on town lands, and this too affected the sexual composition of New England. Child and adult mortality rates dropped significantly after the initial years of settlement, meaning not only that more sons survived to adulthood but also that the parent generation lived longer. Relatively less land was available per son, and in some cases fathers deferred its transmission. For these sons—especially those whose fathers had themselves been latecomers or were poor—opportunities were often better in outlying areas. Therefore some of these older communities experienced an out-migration of men, many of whom left before marrying.[70]

The declining sex ratio affected women in many ways. Most notably, the age at first marriage rose for women. In Plymouth, for example, it increased from a little over twenty early in the century to 22.3 by the end of the 1600s. In Andover, first-generation women married, on the average, at nineteen; the second generation at 22.3, and the third at 24.5. Prior to

1691, the average age at first marriage for Hingham women was twenty-two; for the next generation it was up to 24.7. For males, the average age at first marriage over this same period either dropped somewhat or rose less sharply than it did for women.[71]

Such changes in the age at first marriage for women marked an important social phenomenon. With women as a group marrying older, even the youngest brides were older than their counterparts in earlier generations, and the oldest brides married considerably later than the majority of women had earlier.[72] This was both a sign and a cause of social transformation. In seventeenth-century New England, where economic factors as well as demography played a major role in determining when and whom one married, the increase in the average age of first marriage for women in settled communities reflected a constriction of economic opportunities. Sons were having a harder time accumulating a material base on which to start a family, and as we will see daughters were becoming less significant to potential husbands as means of economic accumulation.[73] This latter effect worked to the disadvantage of some groups of women more than others. Poor women, always only marginally "marriageable" on these grounds, would have found it harder to locate husbands. Daughters of the middling ranks, however, probably experienced greater relative change in marriageability, since the decline in the middling group's economic position more dramatically affected the marriage portions going to sons and daughters.

But the rising age of first marriage for females was a cause as well as an effect of larger social dislocations. It directly affected, for instance, the numbers of children born to families: simply, a woman who marries late has fewer fertile years in marriage than a woman who marries early. In Ipswich a delay of six years in the average age of first marriage resulted in an average decrease of up to three children per family.[74] This meant, among other things, a decrease in the number of sons born—at least to families in which the mother had mar-

ried late—and so an increase in the incidence of families with
no male heirs. While this phenomenon might have eased the
economic straits increasingly faced by second and third generation sons, it was not strong enough to free them from those
straits.[75]

The changing sex ratio also had an effect on the numbers
of spinsters in established communities. Permanent spinsterhood increased in late seventeenth-century Hingham, Andover,
and Plymouth, and doubtless in other towns. In Hingham,
women who remained single throughout their lives constituted 5.5 percent of the adult female population at the end of
the seventeenth century. Though most of Andover's third
generation reached adulthood after 1700, some of them came
of marriage age earlier, and among the women of this generation who lived to age twenty-six, 7.4 percent remained single.
Although we do not have precise information for Plymouth,
the numbers of women who never married in this colony were
"noticeable" by 1700.[76]

The numbers of widows grew as well. In Ipswich, for
instance, fifty women and sixty-nine men were widowed
between 1633 and 1750. But the widowers remarried in greater
proportions and more quickly than the widows. Widowers had
an excellent chance of remarrying up to age sixty, while widows' chances of remarriage deteriorated rapidly after age forty.
In Wethersfield, Connecticut, at the turn of the century, women
tended to outlive men by about six years. Widowers there
remarried twice as often as widows (66 percent of the men as
compared to 30.8 percent of the women) and three times faster
(within twelve months, as compared to three years). In
Hingham, the chances of a widow's remarrying decreased over
time, and those widows who did marry again faced a lengthier
interval between the death of a spouse and the remarriage.[77]

Two reasons appear to explain the low remarriage rates of
colonial New England widows. One historian suggests that in
Wethersfield the wealthier the widower, the greater the likelihood that he would remarry, while the wealthier the widow,

the less the likelihood that she would remarry. For those with the economic option, widowers appear to have looked for another wife, while widows often opted to remain alone. Another historian attributes the larger number of women who remained widows in Hingham to their age: women past menopause had outlived much of their usefulness to colonial men.[78] Among widows who did not remarry surely a combination of these two experiences obtained: some were able to support themselves and so to elect to remain alone, while for others age excluded them from the marriage market, regardless of their material circumstances. The second experience may have been the more common: since the chances of a woman's losing her spouse were greatest after forty—while for men they were greatest before thirty—women were generally older than men when their spouses died, enough older for men to have deemed them unserviceable.[79]

The problem of "overcrowding" in settled New England communities was not only demographic. It was economic as well, and this dimension also affected the lives of second and third generation women. It seems a paradox to find constricting local conditions in a region that in comparison to England offered apparently boundless economic opportunity.[80] Nevertheless this process was real, and it influenced inheritance patterns, mobility, and the polarization of rich and poor, especially in seaport and river towns.

Salem was one of these seaport communities. The areas surrounding Salem had been settled early, and most of the lands within its borders had been taken by the first generation of settlers. Beginning in the 1650s there were continual boundary disputes between Salem's residents and those of surrounding towns. Most second and third generation Salem children lived as adults on subdivided lands or moved on. Those sons and daughters who continued to farm within Salem found themselves less well off than their parents, if not poor in absolute terms. The resulting tensions were heightened by the concentration of land ownership in the hands of a relative few and by the spread of commercial farming for local and foreign markets. Trade networks expanded so rapidly that by 1650 Salem was already a thriving mercantile center. Distinctions had always existed between the prosperous and the not-so-prosperous, but they became even more visible as the seventeenth century progressed, particularly as merchants became the most economically and politically powerful group in the community.[81]

Springfield, Massachusetts, experienced extensive commercial development and economic inequality even earlier. From its founding in 1636 as a Connecticut River fur-trading post, Springfield was oriented toward an international as well as a New England market. A single family, the Pynchons, dominated the direction of the economy from the beginning and controlled most of its resources. For other townspeople, most of whom depended on the Pynchons' good will for their livelihoods, access to these resources came hard. Even after the town shifted its economic base from furs to agricultural products in the 1650s and 1660s, land ownership continued to be restricted and individual holdings remained small. Few families could prosper easily, let alone provide all their sons with land, even in their wills. Parents and children who remained in Springfield faced the ongoing frustration of their economic goals.[82]

Land problems also afflicted towns without a mercantile orientation. Andover, for instance, was one of those farming communities in which a high birth rate combined with low child and adult mortality rates to constrict the process of land transmission. Though most second and third generation Andover sons were settled on lands by the late seventeenth century, they commonly had to wait for many years to gain ownership of their inheritance, because their fathers were unwilling to relinquish full control. Even in Andover's unusually healthy economic environment, fathers had to maintain their continuing prosperity and economic independence at the expense of their sons. In a society in which land ownership determined men's political and economic status, most Andover men could not secure autonomy until long after they had come of age, many of them until their fathers' deaths.[83]

We know little about the impact of these material conditions on women or on the relations between men and women. In Salem, however, the probate records disclose that some men responded to the plight of second and third generation sons by adjusting the portions of their estates that went to their wives and daughters.[84]

These Salem records show that at least until 1681, magistrates disposed of intestate property much as they had done during the early years of settlement. They upheld the widow's right to dower, usually leaving her about one-third of the estate for her use during her life. They divided the rest of the estate among the children. The eldest son received a double share, the daughters and younger sons equal shares. When there were no sons, daughters inherited equally. The exceptions were almost always in cases where the estate was quite small and the children young. In these cases the widow was likely to be awarded most if not all of the estate to help her raise the children.[85] Early in the century, we find several intestate records of widows' estates, since women were still inheriting property in significant numbers. After 1670, so few women were in that position that only one intestate record shows the disposition of a woman's property.

Wills written in Salem followed fairly closely the principle of leaving the eldest son a double portion of the estate, but there were many exceptions. These wills deviated in other ways too from the intestate cases. Before 1650, there were too few inheritance cases involving families with both sons and daughters surviving to warrant any conclusions, but after that time the records show that most fathers were not conforming to the intestate pattern of allotting equal shares of estates to daughters and younger sons (see table 15). Although it is con-

TABLE 15. Relative Inheritances of Daughters and Younger Sons as Revealed in Wills, Salem, Massachusetts, 1651–1700

Period	Number of Cases	Dispositions in Favor of Younger Sons	Equal Dispositions among Younger Sons and Daughters
1651–1660	9	6 (67%)	3 (33%)
1661–1670	9	7 (78%)	2 (22%)
1671–1680	21	19 (91%)	2 (9%)
1681–1690*	11	10 (90%)	1 (9%)
1691–1700*	10	9 (90%)	1 (10%)

*incomplete data

ceivable that these fathers gave their daughters part of their portions earlier as dowries while withholding their sons' full shares, this does not seem to have been the case: even when a man's children were still quite young at the time he wrote his will, the pattern held. The pattern also became more obvious over the course of the century. Whereas a quarter to a third of the fathers who left wills in Salem in the 1650s and 1660s treated their younger sons and their daughters equally, only about 10 percent did so in the last three decades of the century.[86] If fathers in Salem and other settled communities were responding to the difficulty of settling their sons on land in this manner, their actions may account for the increasing numbers of spinsters, even in towns such as Andover or Hingham where the sex ratios were still favorable to men. In Hingham, for instance, rather than marry downward economically men tended to marry women from other towns.[87]

The treatment of wives in wills also changed in Salem during the seventeenth century. Though half of the men who wrote wills prior to 1650 left their widows ownership of property rather than merely its use, less than one-third of them did so after mid-century (see table 16). This suggests that the earlier deviation from the pattern of dower established in intestate law and practice was only a temporary expedient to deal with the special conditions of those years. As men lived longer and more of their sons survived to inherit, fewer men were inclined to leave their widows economically independent. The number of women leaving wills also decreased— from 35 percent of the total in the years prior to 1650 to 8 percent in the 1690s—indicating the gradual decline of a group of women who inherited property despite the presence of sons (see table 17).

The declining frequency with which men left women property of their own coincided with other important changes in Salem's inheritance practices. As we have seen, most men left their widows the use of one-third of their real property. Sometimes a man stipulated that his widow was to have more than one-third, but only rarely less. But whereas women's dower rights were interpreted in intestate cases as the use of this property for life, as often as not Salem men limited its use to their wives' widowhood. As a result, many widows who remar-

TABLE 16.   Patterns of Widow Inheritance, Salem, Massachusetts, 1638–1700

Period	Number of Cases	Ownership of Property	Property Use Only
1638–1650	10	5 (50%)	5 (50%)
1651–1660	13	4 (31%)	9 (69%)
1661–1670	16	5 (31%)	11 (69%)
1671–1680	26	8 (31%)	18 (69%)
1681–1690*	19	4 (21%)	15 (79%)
1691–1700*	24	6 (25%)	18 (75%)

*incomplete data

TABLE 17.　Wills and Intestate Cases by Sex of Estate Holder, Salem, Massachusetts, 1638–1700

Period	Number of Cases	Female		Male	
1638–1650	17	6	(35%)	11	(65%)
1651–1660	32	6	(19%)	26	(81%)
1661–1670	53	7	(13%)	46	(87%)
1671–1680	80	6	(7.5%)	74	(92.5%)
1681–1690*	20	2	(10%)	18	(90%)
1691–1700*	24	2	(8%)	22	(92%)

*incomplete data

ried did not bring their dower right to the new marriage. Instead, their "thirds" were immediately passed on to their husbands' heirs. This practice eliminated any economic advantage widows may have had over single women as potential marriage partners.

In making decisions that would benefit their children at their wives' expense, men were not necessarily acting out of callous disregard for their wives. As Salem widows faced an increasingly narrow access to estates, elaborately worded protection clauses appeared in Salem men's wills. Virtually absent prior to 1650, and only occasionally present during the 1650s, by the 1660s and 1670s these clauses had become an established pattern. They spelled out in painstaking detail the exact rights of the widow in what had become her son's house— from the rooms she could use to the number of cords of wood she could burn to the amount of space she could cultivate in the garden plot, even to her right of access to the house. While these clauses expressed men's genuine concern for their widows' well-being, they also reveal men's fears that their sons would not provide even the most fundamental necessities for their aging mothers and stepmothers.

A related development, first evident in Salem in the 1650s but more common later in the century, was the post-mortem agreement. These contracts took several forms, but most often the agreement was arranged by a widow and her deceased husband's surviving children—who more times than not were her own—in cases where the husband had not left a will. The agreement usually provided for the widow's renunciation of her dower rights in exchange for a cash settlement or direct ownership of a smaller portion of the estate or elaborate forms of protection. Though the chief material beneficiary was usually the eldest son, most women seem to have signed these agreements willingly. The main purpose of these contracts was to transfer all but a small portion of the estate to the children so that they did not have to wait until their mother's death for the bulk of their inheritances. Other post-mortem agreements were made by young widows and their fathers-in-law; in these cases, the women's husbands had died without producing male heirs. Most common during and just after King Philip's War, these agreements usually provided a cash settlement for the young woman, and for her daughters if she had any, in exchange for the return of the landed estate to her father-in-law.

The decisions embodied in the wills of Salem men expressed most acutely the difficulty fathers were having providing their sons with enough property to live comfortably. But especially in the protection clauses men devised, and in widows' renunciations of their own dower rights, fathers and mothers spoke poignantly to the conflict of economic interests within families. Hard to avoid in any community where land ownership is the basis of adult autonomy, this clash of interests was magnified in early New England towns by the number of sons—and daughters—to be provided for and by the longevity of both mothers and fathers. Whatever decisions parents made, the situation was ripe for open friction or smoldering resentment.

Litigation over inheritances was not a regular feature of

estate settlement. Where sons were the principal or sole heirs, open dispute was rare: in these cases overt conflict erupted only when the mother had remarried and children of the first marriage believed their rights had been usurped by children of the second. As this exception suggests, litigation usually resulted when men felt that their right to inherit had been obstructed by the actions of women or by other men's actions in favor of women. Some of the women involved in these court battles were single, some were widowed, and some were married to second or third husbands. These last cases usually pitted the conflicting interests of sons and stepfathers against each other, but their origin lay as well in women's longevity, or more precisely in the resulting delay in the transfer of property to the next generation. When the property interests of two men were in contention, the court might come down on either side. When men were disputing women directly, the court usually decided against women's right to property ownership, even when that right had been spelled out in their husbands' or fathers' wills.[88]

Clashes of economic interests within families, as well as the larger community conflicts that intensified them, carried the greatest implications for witchcraft accusations, for they exposed the fear of independent women that lay at the heart of New England's nightmare.

The connections between economic conflict and witchcraft represent well-trod ground for historians. Paul Boyer and Stephen Nissenbaum argued in an influential book that the 1692 Salem outbreak was the outgrowth of deep-seated conflicts between the rising mercantile class and the people who were tied to a land-based economy. In this view, the wealth, status, and political power of the merchants in Salem were achieved at the expense of the farmers. The 1692 witchcraft accusations were a continuation on a psychological level of a power struggle between the two groups that had been going on in the economic, political, and ecclesiastical arenas for at least two generations. The accusers were persons with a stake in maintaining the traditional social order of a farming community, while the accused were persons who were identified with the values and material benefits of mercantile capitalism.[89]

Similarly, Steven Innes has linked the witchcraft accusations in Springfield in the late 1640s and early 1650s to the tensions created by the economic dependency of the majority of men in that town. Lending support to Boyer and Nissenbaum's interpretation, Innes ascribes at least one of these accusations to widespread resentment against the town's founder, William Pynchon. Because Pynchon's power over their lives made it difficult for townsmen to retaliate against him, they deflected their dissatisfaction onto the witch Hugh Parsons, a man whose economic behavior and goals parodied their own.[90]

Neither Boyer and Nissenbaum nor Innes tells us very much about why witches were primarily women. But in their careful reconstructions of the histories of Salem and Springfield, they—along with Philip Greven for Andover—have identified the economic concerns at the core of men's lives. But women too were profoundly affected by these concerns.

The main issues that split these communities were: when and how men would pass on their property, an issue that divided fathers and sons; whether power and authority would continue to reside in a religious and landed elite or be grasped by a newly risen, religiously diverse mercantile elite; and finally to what degree economic and to some extent political power was to be shared between the lower-and-middling ranks and the middling-and-upper ranks of men.

Conflict between elites could be acted out within the structure of established institutions, but conflict between sons and fathers, or between social ranks, could not. Even after Puritan authority was challenged by the emerging power of the merchants, the social hierarchy the Puritans had established in

New England was not fundamentally questioned. Relations among men, like relations between men and women, were prescribed by the hierarchical order of Creation and God's carefully ordered society. Fathers were defined as above sons, and although less overtly, all men were ranked by wealth. Deference was required of subordinates in all hierarchical male relations.

The most pervasive tension between men was probably that which pitted one social rank against another, but the most potentially explosive tension existed in the father/son relationship. Even without the special difficulties sons had gaining access to land in settled communities, all men depended on their fathers' goodwill and generosity for their own prosperity. If a father decided to maintain control of his land until his death, for instance, the son had no legal recourse. The superiority of fathers was difficult for sons to confront, in part because the laws requiring the subordination of children to parents were so strict, but more because the father/son relation was cemented by both affective bonds and the threat of disinheritance.

Men occasionally expressed their discontent with their place in the hierarchical social order, but when they did they always invited the reprisals of their superiors. Further, their own belief that the social system was divinely ordained and that pride was the Devil's own sin impeded rebellion. Short of revolt, they lived daily with the tension created by their own internal conflicts and resentment of their economic plight.

Though women, as we will see, shared similar tensions, men had much more at stake in their social system, for within it economic power was a male prerogative. Even those sons who resented their fathers' superior position knew that someday that position would be theirs. Puritan belief also allowed that every man—no matter how impoverished his condition, no matter how limited his horizons—had an exalted position in the social structure. In law as in belief, men were held to be women's superiors, and through marriage every man could expect to be served by a woman. By providing men with help-meets, the gender hierarchy encouraged men's commitment to all hierarchical relations—even when some of those relations worked to their decided disadvantage.

If men found it hard to acknowledge, let alone express, their resentment against other men, they encountered less difficulty in expressing their resentment against women. Even mothers were vulnerable. By the early eighteenth century, ministers found scorn and neglect of mothers so common that they felt compelled to denounce what Increase Mather described as adult children's tendency to "despise an Aged Mother" and what Cotton Mather called the "Barbarity of Ingratitude."[91] By that time the economic plight of widows was so extreme that ministers wrote as if widowhood were synonymous with poverty. The clergy said little about why so many women had to be entirely supported by their offspring, but they were appalled that so many adult children did not willingly provide for their mothers and implied that some actually wished their mothers dead.[92]

The roots of sons' resentment are clear. No matter what decisions father and mothers made about their own or their sons' economic futures, simply by living long lives mothers, like fathers, threatened their sons' economic interests. Whether a woman remained a widow or remarried, whether she held on to her means of support or relinquished them, she competed with her sons for precious resources.

The Puritan emphasis on the respect due both mother and father may have strengthened the bonds of affection, preventing most seventeenth-century sons from expressing hostility toward their mothers. But this may have made the frustrations of sons even more explosive, especially since they knew that their mothers' predicament was inescapable. Fathers who maintained full control over their property until their deaths, or who provided well for their widows and daughters, would have heightened the animosity of their sons—not only toward themselves but toward the women who continued to stand in the way of inheritances long denied.

These resentments came out, but they were not directed at the men who were their principal sources. Rather they were expressed as witchcraft accusations, primarily aimed at older women, who like accusers' own mothers vied with men for land and other scarce material resources. Whether as actual or potential inheritors of property, as healers or tavern-keepers or merchants, most accused witches were women who symbolized the obstacles to property and prosperity. This was as apparent in Springfield at mid-century as it was in Salem and Andover near the century's close. My research does not support the idea (as Boyer and Nissenbaum's argument about Salem suggests) that these women were beneficiaries of the new economic order. Some witches clearly were, but most were not. And in a more fundamental way, all witches stood symbolically opposed to—and were therefore subversive of—that order, in that they did not accept their assigned place within it.[93]

Puritan belief made it easy to hold women responsible for the failures of the emerging economic system. Discontent, anger, envy, malice, and pride were understandable responses to the stresses of social and economic change. Yet the clergy's repeated descriptions of these responses as sins against the hierarchical order of Creation, and their association of women with these sins and with the Devil, encouraged the conviction among men that if anyone were to blame for their troubles it was the daughters of Eve.

Sexual tensions also fostered witchcraft accusations, and these too were endemic to the social arrangements of colonial New England. In allowing for their own sexual freedom, men had to live with the fear, and the reality, of women's interference with the orderly transfer of property from father to son. In requiring women's sexual and economic dependence, they were compelled to support women in that dependence. In claiming for themselves the privilege of deciding how property would be transmitted, they had to live with other men's decisions about who would inherit and when. It was a formula that invited the Devil.

We already know the stories of many of the women who were New England's witches—women like Katherine Harrison and Ann Hibbens, who maintained their economic independence until the end, and women like Rachel Clinton and Sarah Good, who were forced into dependency. Only rarely, though, do we have enough information on the relationships of individual women with their neighbors to see the day-to-day dynamics that generated the fear that these women were practicing witchcraft. For the most part the connections between New England's social structure and its witchcraft beliefs emerge only when we look generally at land scarcity, sexual and economic tension, and demographic change. Yet elusive as they were, we can catch glimpses of these connections, even in the history of one of New England's most unlikely witches.

Early in 1675, Edmund Faulkner settled his eldest son, twenty-four-year-old Francis Faulkner, on land he had purchased from the town of Andover several years before.[94] Later that year, Francis took advantage of the opportunity his father provided and married Abigail Dane, the daughter of Andover's minister, the Reverend Francis Dane. A year and a half after that, Edmund Faulkner deeded his son roughly half of his own accumulated estate, thereby making him one of the youngest landowners in town.

In both his decisions, the elder Faulkner stood out as an exception among his peers. Most Andover men could not easily afford to purchase land for their sons, and they gave up control of their estates only with their own deaths. Most of Francis's contemporaries would wait until their late twenties or their thirties to marry, and usually much longer for economic independence. Francis's good fortune came at the expense of his brother and sisters. His brother was not able to marry until he was twenty-eight, and his portion was small.

His sisters' portions may have been smaller still: when Edmund Faulkner wrote his will in 1684, he bequeathed his daughters very little of his £388 estate. To one of his sons-in-law he left a pillow, "being willing," he said, "would my Estate have reacht it, to have manifested my love towards him in a larger manner."[95]

Abigail Faulkner's story, like that of most witches, comes to us largely from the records of her witchcraft trial.[96] At first glance, her personal history would never lead us to suspect her for one of Satan's allies. Her age is unknown, but she probably married young, and she was still bearing children when she was accused. Between her marriage and her imprisonment seventeen years later, she had given birth to two sons (both of whom were still alive in 1692) and four daughters (one of whom had died), and she was pregnant at the time of her incarceration. She also had brothers, and by all accounts the Dane and Faulkner families were unusual in both their prosperity and social status. No sexual misconduct or other witchlike behavior is discernible in her past—at least not before 1687. The same cannot be said for several of Abigail's female relatives. Her sister, widow Elizabeth Johnson, had many years before been prosecuted for fornication. Her sister-in-law, Deliverance Dane, was still married but had no surviving sons. Her stepmother, Hannah Dane, exerted almost full control of a £587 estate left to her by her first husband.[97]

In 1687, Abigail herself began to resemble a witch. In that year, her father-in-law died and her husband came into the rest of his sizeable inheritance. More significantly, her husband became too ill to manage his own affairs. The exact nature of his illness is unclear, but he suffered from convulsions, and his memory and understanding were impaired. He was unable to do anything for himself. With no adult sons to assume responsibility, Abigail took charge of the family estate.

We can only speculate about the response of the men of Abigail's generation, most of whom were still waiting for the kind of privilege her husband had been accorded, when that privilege devolved to a woman. In 1692, in the midst of the Salem outbreak, Abigail Faulkner was "cried down" as a witch. Accused with her were two of her daughters, her sister, her sister-in-law, and two nieces and a nephew. Apparently even her father was suspected, though he was never formally accused.[98]

The origin of the complaint against her is obscure, but it was evidently filed by one of several neighbors, all of whom had children who testified that she afflicted them. Abigail initially denied any witchcraft, but later she acknowledged that the Devil might have taken advantage of the malice in her heart. She owned that "she was angry at what folk said" when one of her nieces was accused and at their laughter when they suggested that her sister would be next. She also admitted that in her anger she "did look with an evil eye on the afflicted persons and did consent that they should be afflicted, becaus they were the caus of bringing her kindred out."[99] To her judges, this may have been evidence enough, for they convicted her and sentenced her to die. Her pregnancy, however, delayed her execution—and ultimately saved her life.

In 1703, a decade after the end of the Salem outbreak, Abigail Faulkner submitted a petition to the Massachusetts magistrates that captures the full force of witchcraft beliefs in seventeenth-century New England and their relentless, awesome presence in women's lives. It was not the first petition Abigail and her family had filed since she was released from prison in 1693, but the others were concerned with the effect of her conviction on the Faulkner estate. This one spoke more plaintively of its effect on her state of mind. In it, she asked the court for an official purging of the record and the full vindication of her name. "I am yet suffred to live," she said,

> but this only as a Malefactor, Convict[ed] upon record of the most heinous Crimes that mankind Can be supposed to be guilty of, which besides its utter Ruining and Defac-

ing my Reputation, will Certainly Expose my selfe to Iminent Danger by New accusations, which will thereby be the more redily believed, [and] will Remaine as a perpetuall brand of Infamy upon my family. . . .[100]

Abigail could not know, of course, what only time would reveal: that the witchcraft prosecutions were at last over, that the accusations were virtually over, and that the image of woman-as-evil was even then passing into its more purely secular form, to be played out in the class and racial dynamics of a modern industrial economy.[101]

SEVEN

Brands Plucked Out
of the Burning

*P*URITAN BELIEFS WERE articulated primarily by men, and most accusations of witchcraft were lodged by men. Thus our search for the ideological and socio-economic origins of witchcraft has focused on men. Yet women themselves harbored witchcraft beliefs and were present among the ranks of accusers. Most New England women in fact seem to have shared with their fathers, husbands, brothers, and sons a pervasive fear of the witches in their midst and to have supported the efforts of their ministers and magistrates to purge God's "city upon a hill" of its female evildoers. Since witches were usually women, women's own adherence to those beliefs remains puzzling.

Besides accused witches, only two other groups of females left any substantive evidence of their feelings about witchcraft or their stake in prosecutions. Both groups were composed of accusers. Those in one group, like most male accusers, described themselves as targets of witches' malicious attacks on their own or their families' health and prosperity. Those in the other group described themselves as possessed by witches, as special victims of witches' frustrated attempts to augment their own ranks by seducing other females to Satan's cause.

Non-possessed female accusers seem quite similar to their male counterparts. Their age and marital status, and the economic position of their families, suggest that they were as representative of the larger adult population as were non-possessed male accusers.[1] The testimony of non-possessed accusers seems not to be gender-specific, though in their testimony non-possessed females talked more often about harm done to their children, while their male counterparts spoke more often of nocturnal attacks on their own bodies and harm done to cattle. Moreover, the sex of non-possessed accusers did not affect the type of people they named as the source of their troubles. The evidence we have would suggest that most female accusers experienced and responded to the demographic, economic, religious, and sexual tensions of their society much as the male accusers in their communities did.

Possessed accusers present quite a different picture. Since sixty-seven of New England's seventy-eight possessed accusers (86 percent) were female, and since possessed males played only minor roles in witchcraft events, we can for the purposes of discussion treat the possessed as a distinctly female group.[2] Their demographic characteristics clearly distinguish them from non-possessed accusers, male and female alike, and their experience of social and economic tensions strongly suggests their subordinate position in the social structure. In their collective histories, possessed accusers left us considerable evidence of the process by which New England women learned to fear and reject the potential for witchcraft, in themselves and in other women.

Like non-possessed accusers, possessed females ranged widely in age: the youngest was about seven, the eldest over eighty. But whereas most non-possessed accusers were between twenty and sixty when they lodged witchcraft accusations,[3] most of the fifty-nine possessed females whose ages are known were under thirty, with a highly concentrated cluster in the range of sixteen to twenty-five (see table 18). More than just numer-

TABLE 18.   Possessed Accusers by Sex and Age,
New England, 1620–1725

Age	Female	Male	Total
Under 10	3	1	4
10–19	27	5	32
20–29	13	1	14
30–39	8	1	9
40–49	3	0	3
50–59	1	0	1
60–69	3	0	3
70 and over	1	0	1
TOTAL	59	8	67

TABLE 19.   Possessed Accusers by Sex and Marital Status,
New England, 1620–1725

Marital Status	Female	Male	Total
Single	42	9	51
Married	20	1	21
Widowed	3	0	3
TOTAL	65	10	75

ically significant, females in the sixteen to twenty-five age group
(along with three girls between eleven and fifteen) were among
New England's most active accusers. Considerable attention
was given them, and they thus provide the most extensive
documentation of possession. Though non-possessed accusers tended to be married, the majority of the possessed were
single (see table 19), as were virtually all possessed females
who were between sixteen and twenty-five. Among older possessed females, however, married women predominated, out-

numbering widows by more than six to one. Possession does not seem to have occurred at all in single women over thirty or in divorced or deserted women.[4]

The age differences between possessed and non-possessed accusers account for another striking contrast between them. While non-possessed accusers, both male and female, were likely to have had established (if antagonistic) relationships with the women they accused as witches, prior relationships between the possessed and their witches were much less common. Often the possessed barely knew the women they named as their tormentors or had had only minimal contact with them. In many cases, accuser and accused had never even met. Despite many exceptions, especially among older possessed women, this pattern suggests that while we can justifiably look to the well-documented conflicts between witches and their non-possessed accusers for the origin of most witchcraft accusations, we must look elsewhere to account for accusations lodged by the possessed.

The possessed, then, were not typical accusers, or even typical female accusers. They accounted for only about 10 percent of all accusers and no more than 25 percent of all female accusers. Their youthfulness and their tendency to name as the cause of their difficulties women with established witchcraft reputations encourages us to see them simply as mouthpieces for larger community concerns.[5] Yet because they were unusually articulate about witch behavior and because they usually pointed accusations at more than just one or two women, they were crucial figures in New England's three witchcraft outbreaks. Most importantly, their possession experiences expressed vividly one of the central paradoxes of New England witchcraft: accusers denounced witches for behaviors and emotions that were widespread among the colonists, not least of all among the accusers themselves. More than any other group, possessed accusers brought this contradiction closer to the surface of community recognition. The possessed by definition embodied the characteristics of their possessors—and were themselves, like the people they accused, in most cases female.

Finally, the history of woman-as-witch in New England is incomplete without the story of the impact of the witch image on women other than the accused. All New England women, no doubt, lived their lives in its shadow—their thought, their behavior, their sense of themselves and other women profoundly shaped by its power. But for some females—those their society called possessed—the witch was as intensely attractive a figure as she was fearful. In the experience of these particular accusers lies the answer to one of the most baffling questions about witchcraft: in a culture in which witches were the most powerful symbols of human evil, and where most witches were female, why was it sometimes other females who most vociferously cried them down?

Since possession took on its greatest importance in New England during the Salem outbreak, our attention goes first to a particular group of women who succumbed to possession during this episode—those twenty-four young female accusers who were over sixteen but still single at this time. Of the twenty-one of these for whom information is available, seventeen had lost one or both of their parents. At least thirteen had lost their fathers. We might expect this demographic characteristic to have been common among middle-aged accusers, but it was unusual for young people in late seventeenth-century New England. Indeed, it distinguished these possessed women from other relatively young accusers, even from other single females over sixteen who were possessed prior to the 1692–93 outbreaks. Among all other groups of young accusers, the proportion of persons with one or both parents deceased never went beyond the 25 or 30 percent we might expect for early New England.

These parental deaths had resulted largely from war-related Indian attacks. The young females in this group had lived with their parents in several small settlements along the Maine frontier that had been destroyed by Indians (and sometimes their French allies) between 1675 and 1691. Some of these young women had even witnessed one or both of their parents' violent deaths. As orphans, they had accompanied hundreds of other refugees to Salem, Boston, and other long-settled eastern Massachusetts towns in the years prior to the Salem outbreak.[6] Some moved in with relatives or family friends, most with strangers, but all were relative newcomers to their communities. As a group, these young orphans played *the* most dramatic roles in the events of 1692–93, naming as the cause of their plight not only the people their neighbors already assumed were witches but others never before suspected in these towns. Some of these previously unknown witches were people the possessed had known, seen, or heard of in their former Maine communities.[7]

Like other young possessed females, just about all of these women, even those who lived with relatives, were servants. Living with another family as a servant was a common experience for young, unmarried women in early New England. For these women, however, it was unclear when, if ever, their condition and status would change. The frontier wars that had taken the lives of their parents had left their fathers' estates considerably diminished, if not virtually destroyed. Little if anything remained for their dowries.[8] With few men interested in women without dowries, the marriage prospects of these women, and thus their long-term material well-being, looked especially grim.

We cannot be sure what their marriage possibilities would have been had their parents lived, but certainly they would have been more varied. Sarah Churchill, whose Saco, Maine, family had considerably property and an English gentry heritage (as well as a history of irreverence for community values), might have expected to marry quite well.[9] Mercy Lewis, originally from Falmouth, Maine, seems to have come from a family at the other end of the economic scale and therefore might never have been able to anticipate genuine prosperity.[10] Mary Watkins, whose family lived near the mouth of the Kennebec River in Maine, probably fell between these two economic extremes; for Watkins, as perhaps for most of these orphans, the prospects for prosperity would have been ambiguous.[11] Though some of the possessed orphans had been quite young when they lost their parents, they must have been keenly aware of the discrepancy between their own positions and those of the women in the families they served.

That their prospects were indeed dismal is at least suggested by the little we know of their subsequent lives. In 1709, at the age of thirty-seven, Sarah Churchill married a Berwick, Maine, weaver and claimed at least some of her inheritance; in 1720, she and her husband sold for £50 a piece of Saco property which her maternal grandfather had given to her mother.[12] She did not, however, live at or near the level of prosperity that her original family enjoyed. Few others of these possessed refugees did as well as Churchill. Like most of the former possessed who married at all, Mercy Lewis married late, at about age twenty-eight, and then only after giving birth to her first child.[13] Mary Watkins's circumstances were even more tenuous. Accusing *herself* of witchcraft after being threatened with punishment if she did not withdraw her accusation against her wealthy mistress, she spent several months in the Boston jail. The surviving members of her family refused to help secure her release, despite her inheritance of some property from the estates of both her father and brother. When the magistrates put her inheritance in the hands of her brother-in-law, who lived in the same town as Watkins, she could not get at it to pay her own jail fees and was forced to stay there. In desperation, she eventually filed a formal appeal to the jailer, in which she asked to be sold to Virginia as a servant, citing as the reason that her "friends, relations, and kindred, [were] slighting [her] to extremity." The jailer apparently arranged for her indenture, after which the records are silent about her life.[14]

Mary Watkins's experience may have been the most extreme of any of the possessed, and the plight of the Maine refugees more acute than that of other young possessed women. But Mary Watkins's difficulty in gaining access to her inheritance was not unusual, since the courts were reluctant to allow women, especially single women, control over their own economic resources. And these resources were dwindling, as we have seen. Many young single women suffered from the economic and demographic changes of the seventeenth century, which affected young women even more than they did young men. In Salem, where land shortages and declining death rates altered inheritance patterns over the course of the century, young women faced the likelihood that their shares of their fathers' estates (some to be given in the form of dowries) would be reduced in favor of their brothers. Combined with shifting sex ratios, these economic constrictions led not only to an increase in women's age at first marriage but also to a larger number of women who never married. As times got hard, these conditions were exacerbated by the decisions of some young men simply to move on and of others to seek better material prospects by marrying women outside their communities. Poor women were by no means the only ones affected: most young females coming of age in these towns faced a more uncertain future than that faced by their brothers—or that faced years before by their mothers and grandmothers.[15]

A law passed by the Massachusetts General Court in its 1692–93 session indicates the extent of this crisis. Reaffirming the necessity for single people to live "under some orderly family government," it also affirmed that single women "of good repute" should be able to practice "any lawful trade or employment for a livelihood . . . any law, usage or custom to the contrary notwithstanding."[16] This statute does not seem to have been an attempt to relieve the growing financial hardships on single women themselves, since service remained the main occupation open to them and no woman could support herself on the £5 or £10 a year female servants earned. More likely, the law was passed to relieve the economic pressure on their families, who were expected to make up the difference between single women's earnings and the cost of their maintenance.

Young women's economic difficulties would have been compounded by "mistakes" in their sexual behavior. At a point in their lives when sexual interests were especially strong, young women were regularly if subtly reminded of their special vulnerability to sexual misconduct. A woman who had sexual relations with a man who was not her husband was held responsible for both the sin and the possible consequences.[17] Young women had the dual burden of repressing their own sexual desires as well as those of their partners.

Some women may have hoped that pregnancy would ensure marriage, but such desperate measures were probably rare. Women in the late seventeenth century knew that marriage did not follow pregnancy as a matter of course, as it so often had for women of their mothers' and especially their grandmothers' generation. They knew too that if they bore a child out of wedlock, their marriage prospects would deteriorate. Young women were no doubt aware of other women faced with that problem and the stigma with which they lived. They also knew firsthand the special vulnerability of female servants, who were the most common objects not only of sexual advances but of sexual harassment and coercion. Young women's dilemmas would have intensified when the men responsible occupied higher social positions, especially in cases in which the sexual interest was mutual.[18]

If single possessed women were of an age when sexual issues were paramount, no evidence suggests that they were sexually active before or during their possession.[19] Their religious training and faith may have precluded sexual activity. In fact, religious training seems to have been unusually thorough among young possessed females, who were particularly well-versed in the ways of the Lord—and in the ways of the Devil.

All young people in Puritan New England were expected

to know and embrace the principles of religion. Parents were required by law to hold regular family prayer, to teach their children, servants, and apprentices the word of God and the capital laws of the colony, and to see to it that their young charges learned to read the Bible and spent most of their Sabbath in church. But these laws were by no means followed by everyone, or even with equal fervor among committed Puritans. In some households young people were catechized more thoroughly than in others, and it was in just such godly environments that possession was most likely to occur. Several of the possessed were either daughters of ministers or female relatives who lived with ministers. Others were or had recently been servants in ministers' households. Still others, observers commented, had been raised by some of New England's most pious and conscientious parents.[20] On the surface, at least, these possessed females should have been the least likely objects of Satan's desire for new witches and the most able to resist Satan's wiles. Yet the opposite was the case.

Possession, whether in colonial New England or in other societies in which it still occurs, is a collective as well as an individual phenomenon.[21] It affects women primarily, and frequently spreads among groups of women, as it did in Connecticut in 1662–63 and Massachusetts in 1692–93. Individual females undergo the experience, and events in their personal histories help explain it, but the larger meaning of possession is cultural. There are patterns in the behavior of the possessed: the words and actions are learned, and they vary in only minor ways from one individual to another. To explain New England possession, then, we must consider it first as a cultural performance, a symbolic religious ritual through which a series of shared meanings were communicated—by the possessed women themselves, by the ministers who interpreted their words and behavior, and by the community audience for the dramatic events.[22]

The possessed themselves left no descriptions of what they were going through. What we know of their thoughts and feelings comes from the clergy, with their attendant biases. Sometimes the ministers simply recorded and commented on what had been related to them by court reporters and other observers; more often they wrote from firsthand experience of the exorcisms to which they sometimes subjected the possessed. The records, then, are most useful for explaining Puritan interpretations of the spiritual and social significance of possession. They can also tell us something about the emotional lives of the possessed, but only if we acknowledge their implicit biases.

The first signs of possession, the ministers tell us, were sometimes ambiguous, as when sixteen-year-old Elizabeth Knapp of Groton, who became possessed in 1672, began "to carry herself in a strange and unwonted manner," giving occasional shrieks and then breaking into peals of laughter.[23] More often, compelling physical evidence was present from the start. This typically included strange fits, with violent, contorted body movements; prolonged trances and paralyzed limbs; difficulty in eating, breathing, seeing, hearing, and speaking; sensations of being beaten, pricked with pins, strangled, or stabbed; grotesque screams and pitiful weeping, punctuated by a strange but equally unsettling calm between convulsions, when little if anything was remembered and nothing seemed amiss.

During the early weeks of the Salem outbreak, the possessed apparently said little about what was troubling them, and observers seemed reluctant to call their unusual behavior possession. But in other cases the possessed or those around them made plain what was happening. Within three weeks of the initial signs of her distress, Elizabeth Knapp indicated that the Devil had appeared to her and that either a particular woman in the neighborhood or "the Devil in her likeness and habit" had caused her first fit a few days before.[24] According to Cotton Mather, thirteen-year-old Martha Godwin's fits in

1688 followed immediately after widow Glover had "bestowed very bad Language upon the Girl," and seventeen-year-old Mercy Short's fits in 1693 began right after witch Sarah Good "bestowed some ill words upon her."[25] These examples suggest that possession was sometimes the direct result of an altercation with a reputed witch (both Glover and Good were responding to the younger women's insults); at other times possession occurred seemingly out of the blue, setting off a search for the woman responsible. In either case, once the fits manifested themselves in females, suspicion of supernatural activity quickly followed.

Other explanations were occasionally offered for these afflictions. Epilepsy was suspected in a few cases and then discarded for not explaining enough of the symptoms. Hysteria, also called "suffocation of the mother," seemed more promising.[26] Confessing that he "never yet learned the Name of the Natural Distemper, whereto these odd symptoms do belong," Cotton Mather discussed hysteria as a possible explanation of the fits of seventeen-year-old Margaret Rule in Boston in 1693. But Mather, like his New England contemporaries, found it impossible to believe that the Devil was not directly involved. "I do believe," he said,

> that the Evil Angels do often take Advantage from Natural Distempers in the Children of Men to annoy them with such further Mischiefs as we call preternatural. The Malignant Vapours and Humours of our Diseased Bodies may be used by Devils, thereinto insinuating as engine of the Execution of their Malice upon those Bodies; and perhaps for this reason one Sex may suffer more Troubles of some kinds from the Invisible World than the other, as well as for that reason for which the Old Serpent made where he did his first Address.[27]

As his reference to the Devil's seduction of Eve implies, whatever other explanations he entertained Mather finally could not conceive of the fits and other behaviors of the young women he observed as anything but possession.

Mather was not alone in this view, and neither were the Puritans of New England. For as long as medical history has been recorded in the Western world, behaviors like those exhibited among New England's possessed have been observed, particularly in women. For just as long, two explanations of their causes have competed for acceptance—one natural, the other supernatural. During the European witch-hunts of the sixteenth and seventeenth centuries, the demonic explanation dominated Western thinking, with witches designated the precipitating agents in most cases.[28] Even doctors discussed these behaviors as having both natural and supernatural origins. Dr. Thomas Browne testified in a 1664 witchcraft trial in England that the fits of some young females "were natural and nothing else but what they call the mother, but only heightened to a great excess by the subtilty of the Devil, co-operating with the Malice of these which we term Witches, at whose Instance he doth these Villanies."[29]

By the time Mather wrote, a quarter of a century later, views such as Browne's were part of a long and accepted tradition. Whatever else these young women were experiencing (and that is a separate issue), they and the people around them understood their behavior in terms of their religious beliefs. Witches, acting as Satan's agents, were tempting young females to join Satan's forces. When these females resisted, they were physically attacked, and possession was the visible sign of both that resistance and that attack. When a witch (or the Devil) stuck pins into the body of one of the possessed, she was "miserably hurt with Pins which were found stuck into her Neck, Back and Arms."[30] When a witch (or the Devil) pinched one of the possessed, "black and blew marks of the pinches became immediately visible unto the standers by."[31] When a witch (or the Devil) would "Flash upon [a possessed person] the Flames of a Fire," observers "saw not the Flames" but the "Blisters thereby Raised upon her" and smelled the brimstone.[32] Neither the ministers who confirmed these tortures nor the other witnesses actually saw witches or the Devil, but they did see the afflictions that resulted and that left them little if any doubt as to their cause. Equally convinced were the possessed themselves, who not only saw their tormentors but felt the excruciating pain.

This is not to say that the possessed were "mentally ill." To consider possession a sign of individual psychopathology implies the existence of a mass psychopathology.[33] As some anthropologists and medical historians have long maintained, if a culture's belief system incorporates the concept of demonic possession, it is rational for people within that culture to become possessed, to experience the torments their spiritual leaders say they will, and in much the same way their spiritual leaders say they will experience them.[34] The possessed of early New England did not step beyond the bounds of their social world; they stood firmly within it, articulating vital aspects of their culture.

Possessed females did experience profound conflict,[35] but their ministers defined this conflict as a theological one—the result of a struggle between God and the Devil for the souls of the possessed. Possession revealed this as the conflict between good and evil: were the possessed going to lead virtuous lives, obeying God in all that he commanded, or were they going to rebel against God, become witches, and work with Satan to overthrow God's kingdom on earth? The ministers undertook to ensure that the possessed opted for God and virtuous womanhood. Fearing that the possessed were perilously close to choosing lives of wickedness, the clergy set out to rescue their volatile young charges from the fires of Hell: as Cotton Mather put it, to pluck these brands out of the burning.[36] To do so, the witch within these women had to be exorcized.

Were it simply a theological issue for the females involved, they never would have become possessed: they accepted the tenets of their faith as much as anyone around them. But the issues were more complicated for them, and their conflicts more immediate and more personal. Witness Elizabeth Knapp's struggle in 1672, described in detail by her pastor, Groton's Samuel Willard.

Elizabeth Knapp was forced to work out her conflicts with the Devil himself. According to Willard, in one of her early fits, "in which she was violent in bodily motions . . . in roarings and screamings, representing a dark resemblance of hellish torments," she frequently cried out " 'money, money,' sometimes 'sin and misery' " along with other, unrecorded words. She tried to blame her condition on an older woman in town, but because Willard did not think the woman a witch, he did not heed Knapp's accusation. Under pressure to reveal the "true and real occasion" of her fits, she declared that the Devil had appeared to her many times over the previous three years, that he offered to make her a witch, and that he proffered to her "money, silks, fine clothes, ease from labor, to show her the whole world, etc." She admitted that the Devil came because of her discontent, and that he came more frequently once she started to work as a servant in the Willard household—a household much more prosperous than her own. She further confessed that she was tempted to murder her own parents, her neighbors, the Willard children, "especially the youngest," and herself. She vehemently denied, at least at first, having signed a covenant with Satan.[37]

As the weeks went by, Knapp's fits became more intense and her sense of what was happening more confused. She alternated between violent convulsive states and trancelike stupors, between denying that she had given in to the Devil's temptations to become a witch and admitting that she had. She believed at times that her great discontent made her a witch: "It is too late for me," she murmured plaintively at one point; at another, with little affect, she revealed that the Devil told her what she had long feared, that "she had done it already . . . ," that "she was his sure enough." Other times, she struggled against this particular Puritan truth: she condemned herself as a sinner, admitted that she was tempted to sign the Devil's book, but "utterly disclaimed" having done so. Throughout her possession, there were frequent periods when she could not speak at all, when her breath or speech was "stopped" by her invisible adversary. At one point, Willard noted, "her tongue was for many hours together drawn into a semicircle up to the roof of her mouth" and could not be dislodged, despite the efforts of some people to do so.[38]

In the second month of her possession, after an unsuccessful attempt to hold a second woman accountable for her anguish, which was followed by her fullest confession to date, she called Willard to her. In tears, she admitted "that she had belied the Devil in saying she had given him of her blood, etc., [and] professed that the most of the apparitions she had spoken of [during this confession] were but fancies, as images represented in a dream, [and] earnestly entreated [Willard] to believe her." He did not believe her. When he pushed her again to tell the truth, she returned, in greater detail, to the next closest thing to the truth that she knew—her original story:

> She . . . declared . . . that the Devil had sometimes appeared to her; that the occasion of it was her discontent; that her condition displeased her, her labor was burdensome to her, [and] she was neither content to be at home nor abroad; and [that she] had oftentimes strong persuasions to practice in witchcraft, had often wished the Devil would come to her at such and such times, and [had] resolved that if he would she would give herself up to him soul and body. But though he had oft times appeared to her, yet at such times he had not discovered himself, and therefore she had been preserved from such a thing.[39]

But for Knapp to say that she was simply possessed was not enough for Willard, who as her minister was expected to do more—chiefly, to get her to rest contented with the condition that so displeased her. His response to her at this time was equivocal: he told her "that she had used preposterous courses, and therefore it was no marvel that she had been led into such contradictions," but he "tendered her all the help [he] could, if she would make use of [him] and more privately relate any weighty and serious case of conscience to [him]." This response precipitated a crisis. At first she just told him that she knew nothing more than she had related to him, but afterward her fits became more extreme and her emotions more volatile. She tried to kill herself and began to lash out at others, "striking" those who tried to hold her, "spitting in their faces," and then laughing. A few days later, Willard said, the Devil in Elizabeth Knapp took over completely.[40]

The Devil made his presence known, Willard continued, "by drawing her tongue out of her mouth most frightfully to an extraordinary length and greatness, and [making] many amazing postures of her body." He then began to speak "vocally in her," railing at her father and another person, "calling them rogues, charging them for folly in going to hear a black rogue who told them nothing but a parcel of lies and deceived them, and many like expressions." Once Willard himself entered the scene, Satan turned his rage on him directly, calling him "a great rogue," then "a great black rogue," and telling Willard that he told the people "a company of lies." Amazed and apparently visibly shaken, Willard fought back, challenging the Devil to prove his charges and calling *him* "a liar and a deceiver." Then the Devil denied he was Satan, saying he was a "pretty black boy" and Knapp his "pretty girl," adding that he had no love for Willard. When Willard retorted that he, "Through God's grace," hated him as well, the Devil answered with "you had better love me." Once other people in the room also began to converse with the Devil, Willard tried to put a stop to the discourse and pray, but the Devil afterwards resumed his heckling of his godly adversary, even claiming that he "was stronger than God."[41]

Two days later, Knapp confessed that the Devil "entered into her the second night after her first taking, that when she was going to bed he entered in (as she conceived) at her mouth, and had been in her ever since." She also said that "if there were ever a devil in the world there was one in her." After the aid of an "assembly of ministers" was precluded by inclement weather, the Devil continued occasionally to speak within her, but within a few weeks he was "physically" gone—apparently for good. She continued "for the most part speechless," feeling "as if a string was tied about the roots of her tongue and reached down into her vitals and pulled her tongue down—and then most when she strove to speak." Her fits became less intense, although she was observed "always to fall into fits when any strangers go to visit her—and the more go, the more violent are her fits." By the beginning of the third month of her possession, Knapp had again disowned having signed the covenant, had denied knowing whether or how the Devil entered her, and had reaffirmed that the cause of her fits was her discontent and that she was still tempted to murder. When Willard brought his lengthy account to a close, she was still possessed. She acknowledged that the Devil yet had "power of her body" but expressed a fervent hope that "he should not of her soul."[42]

In his final remarks, Willard cast Knapp's behavior in terms of the Puritan view of possession. Although reluctant to pass authoritative judgement on what he had witnessed for the preceding two and a half months, he clearly believed that Knapp's "distemper" was both real and diabolical and that the Devil was actually present within her. To support his belief, he pointed out that the enormous strength of Knapp's fits was "beyond the force of dissimulation"; that the healthiness of her body when she was not having convulsions argued against any "natural" explanation; and that when "the voice spoke" within her, her mouth and vocal chords did not move and her throat was swelled to the size of a fist. As further evidence that Satan spoke through her, he told his readers that Knapp had never expressed such hostility to him. On the contrary, both before and after "being thus taken" she had always been "observed to speak respectfully concerning [him]." He also

noted that the words uttered to him were aspersions Knapp
said the Devil had suggested to her during his temptation of
her, and that Knapp "had freely acknowledged that the Devil
was wont to appear to her in the house of God, and divert her
mind, and charge her [that] she should not give ear to what
that black-coated rogue spoke." Willard and other Puritans
knew this to be typical of Satan's behavior.[43]

Because Knapp was still ostensibly possessed, Willard could
not finally say whether or not she had become a witch. Either
way, like Knapp, he had not given up completely. "Charity
would hope the best," he said, "love would fear the worst, but
thus much is clear: she is an object of pity, and I desire that
all that hear of her would compassionate her forlorn state.
She is (I question not) a subject of hope, and therefore all
means ought to be used for her recovery." Witch or not, however, Knapp was not simply an innocent victim. Her dissatisfaction had brought the Devil to her, and that moral ultimately
had to be communicated. "She is a monument of divine sever-
ity," Willard concluded, "and the Lord grant that all that see
or hear may fear and tremble."[44]

From the Puritan perspective, Elizabeth Knapp's possession was the result of her ambivalence about the kind of woman
she wanted to be. Had she been willing to rest satisfied with
her lack of financial resources, with her work as a servant, and
with her limited horizons, she would not have become possessed. The sin that brought the Devil to her was discontent
with her condition, with her place in the divinely planned social
order. It was the same sin that defined other, older women as
witches and therefore, not surprisingly, the one that led Knapp
at times to see herself as a witch. But for Puritans, possession
was not itself witchcraft, only the potential for witchcraft.
Ministers could prevent the onset of witchcraft by helping the
possessed adjust to their place in society. In Knapp's case the
Devil was able to take advantage of her discontent by attract-
ing her with the things she most desired and leading her to
commit (or to the brink of committing) other sins identified

with witches, but he was not able to win her completely. Despite Willard's fears, Knapp never became a witch; she married and lived out her life as befitted a good Puritan wife and mother. So successfully did she obliterate her discontent and internalize her culture's model of virtuous womanhood that she almost completely disappears from the public records after 1673.[45]

None of the other descriptions of New England possession are as revealing as Willard's account of the Elizabeth Knapp's struggle, but they do disclose the parallels between Knapp's experience and the possession of other young women. For instance, other possessed females and their ministers obviously shared with Knapp and Willard the belief that witches and the Devil focused their appeals on women's discontents and that in their fits the possessed were tempted to become witches.[46] Yet Knapp was exceptional in acknowledging her discontents openly. Only occasionally did possessed females reveal the specific temptations laid before them. Most often, they portrayed themselves simply as hapless victims, referring vaguely to how they were tempted with "fine things," "comforts," or "the world." Nineteen-year-old Mercy Lewis could only report that her former master George Burroughs "caried me up to an exceeding high mountain and shewed me all the kingdoms of the earth and tould me that he would give them all to me if I would writ in his book. . . ."[47] Mercy Short provided as detailed a description as Knapp's about what was offered to her if she would become a witch—a husband and fine clothes, among other things—but she never explained why she was singled out to be offered these things.[48]

In other ways, however, either the possessed themselves or other colonists alluded to female dissatisfactions. Although describing it as a "vain curiosity," minister John Hale noted that in 1692 several young possessed females in Salem were unhappy with their marriage prospects and just before their first fits had resorted to divination to find out their future husbands' occupations.[49] Similarly, Ann Cole of Hartford revealed that her mind was on her marital status when she became possessed in 1662; she was concerned, she said, not only that witches were afflicting her body but that they were trying "to spoil her name, hinder her marriage, etc."[50] Martha Godwin and her younger brothers and sister were unhappy with the tasks required of them in their household; during their possessions, Cotton Mather observed, "whatever Work they were bid to do," the specific limbs necessary to do it became so paralyzed that it was impossible for them to proceed.[51] Nearly all of the possessed registered their discontent with their religious training. Once possessed, they shared Elizabeth Knapp's deep aversion to the word of God—and to the ministers who revealed the word to them.[52]

The reluctance of the possessed to admit their discontent is not surprising in light of the disapprobation female dissatisfaction drew in Puritan culture. To acknowledge those feelings could, as it did with Elizabeth Knapp, convert the fear into the certainty that one was a witch. Possession rituals were supposed to do just the opposite: to convince young women that the danger lay outside them, not within.[53] The line between the two conceptions was a thin one, however, and many people, both possessed and not, could not always draw this distinction. Once the danger was identified as discontent *within* the possessed, they became vulnerable to witchcraft accusations, either from others or from themselves.

This was especially true during outbreaks, when the fear of witchcraft was most intense and when many "unlikely" witches were named. During the 1692–93 witch-hunts, colonists frequently registered this cultural confusion. Elderly George Jacobs, who could get little or no work out of his possessed servant Sarah Churchill, expressed his annoyance by calling her a "bitch witch" and may have been the person she said threatened to throw her into the dungeon with the other witches if she continued her possession. Extremely frightened and disconcerted, Churchill first concurred with Jacobs that she was a witch and then, privately to a woman she had known years before in Maine, denied that her confession was true. When asked why she did not publicly explain what had happened, she said that she had stood on her confession too long, adding "that If she told Mr [minister Nicholas] Noys but once she had sat hur hand to the Book he would beleve her but if she told the truth and saied she had not seat her hand to the Book a hundred times he would not beleve hur."[54]

The same kind of pressure was put on Mary Warren by her master John Proctor, who despite her possession kept her at his spinning wheel, threatened to beat her, and expressed publicly his desire to see all the possessed hang. Warren on separate occasions proclaimed that the possessed "did but dissemble," confessed herself a witch, and retreated into possession.[55] Not incidentally, both Churchill and Warren accused their masters of witchcraft after the men's initial angry responses to their possessions. All told, at least nine of the Salem possessed were publicly accused of witchcraft during the trials, although most of them were accused by others, not themselves.

The ambiguous connection between witchcraft and possession is also suggested by several accused witches who, like the slave Tituba, fell into states of possession after they were accused of witchcraft.[56] It was expressed as well by the response of Sarah Osborne to the accusation made against her. When confronted the morning of her trial by several young women who said she afflicted them, her bewildered response was that "shee was more like to be bewitched than that she was a witch." Like other people in Puritan New England, Osborne feared witches and demons, and she once "saw or dreamed" that they wanted to harm her, but she was not likely to be taken seriously as a possessed person.[57] Sixty years old, involved in a property dispute with her sons, known for sexual misconduct in her more youthful years, and recognized as an irregular church attender, Osborne better fit her society's conception of a witch than one possesed by a witch.

Possession, then, was a dramatic religious ritual through which young females publicly enacted their struggle to avoid internalizing the evil of witchcraft. The many reenactments of this performance not only lent Puritan doctrine a symbolic sanction, it also affirmed the social hierarchy of colonial New England. By employing the language of possession in their sermons and writings—complete with witches and demons— ministers doubtless hoped to save their young charges from damnation. At the same time, they ensured that the desire of some females to escape their subordination was never clearly articulated, and their many dissatisfactions never specifically addressed.

If possession is most easily understood as a ritual expression of Puritan belief and New England's gender arrangements, it was also an oblique challenge to both religious and social norms. However difficult it was for the possessed to speak of their plight without employing the language available to them, they shaped the possession ritual to voice feelings that were proscribed by their faith.

Possession expressed an underlying power struggle between the possessed and the authorities who were culturally sanctioned to interpret their experience. One area of potential conflict was in the designation of responsibility for possession. In some cases there was little or no disagreement. When Martha Godwin named the impoverished and outspoken widow Glover as her possessor, no one with any say in the matter objected, least of all Godwin's minister, Cotton Mather. Glover was hanged.[58] But commonly there was disagreement, as when Elizabeth Knapp accused two women whom Samuel Willard was apparently unwilling to consider witches. Whatever his reasons, Willard had the power to dismiss Knapp's version of what she was experiencing. Sometimes the possessed were able to claim more authority in this regard, or at least fought much harder than Knapp to do so.

The Salem episode is a case in point. When the Salem events began, the possesed were at first unable to tell who was responsible for their torments. Probably with some outside encouragement, they eventually came up with the names of three people—Tituba, Sarah Good, and Sarah Osborne—all of whom fit closely enough their community's beliefs about witches to arouse little surprise or opposition. But when they began to name additional people—Martha Corey, Dorcas Good, Rebecca Nurse, Sarah Cloyce, Elizabeth Proctor, and John Proctor—all "respectable" matrons, small children, or men— some members of the community balked. They began to question and resist the possessed's right to their visions—and to turn the accusations back on the accusers.[59]

The possessed were able to carry the day. Some men and some married women from prosperous families were hanged, in part because of the deep and long-festering division within the community and in part because those convicted had in some way affirmed the prevailing witchcraft beliefs.[60] Indeed, the special insight Puritans attributed to the possessed was utterly disregarded only when they named people, or the close relatives of people, with substantial power in the colony. Among these were: Samuel Willard; John and Dudley Bradstreet, sons of a former Massachusetts governor; Mary Phips, wife of Massachusetts's then governor; Sarah Hale, wife of minister John Hale; and Margaret Thatcher, widow of a prominent minister and mother-in-law of one of the Salem judges.

Salem's possessed had named not only the women the community might have expected to seduce and torment younger women into becoming witches, but also persons the possessed themselves considered seducers or tormentors. Among the accused were several people, including George Jacobs, John Proctor, and George Burroughs, who had been masters of the possessed. Also accused were John Alden, John Flood, Nicholas Frost, and Thomas Hardy—all of whom were soldiers or traders who, along with George Burroughs, had taken part in but survived the Maine wars that had orphaned

so many of the possessed.[61] Among other charges, George
Jacobs was accused of beating female servants with his staff,
George Burroughs of abusing and killing his first two wives,
and John Alden of living with Indian women, having children
by them, and selling ammunition to both Indian and French
men.[62]

The power struggle enacted through possession had
another dimension. The possessed and their ministers were
engaged in a fierce negotiation, initiated by the possessed, about
the legitimacy of female discontent, resentment, and anger. It
was a legitimacy the clergy never conceded. If the clergy had
God on their side, the possessed had a formidable ally in the
Devil. If the outcome of the ensuing battle was pre-ordained
in Puritan New England, the possessed did not lose it without
a sustained struggle.

We can see this dimension best in Elizabeth Knapp's relationship with Samuel Willard. When not possessed, Knapp
was in every way respectful of the man who was both her minister and master. When the demons were in her, however, she
expressed an intense hostility toward him. She railed at him
and called him a liar. She castigated her father and others for
listening to him. She challenged his authority in the community and his power over her. Among those she wanted to kill
were Williard and his children.

Willard's account reveals the sources of this deep, painful
ambivalence. Elizabeth Knapp was a young woman who had
accepted the Puritan explanation for her troubles, who deeply
appreciated Willard's concern for her plight and his dedica-
tion to freeing her from the demons that held her in their
power. But she had cause to resent him. He was a young, well-
off, Harvard-educated minister whose life was full of promise;
she was a young woman with little schooling and little pros-
pect of anything but service to others, whether as a servant,
daughter, or wife. He spent most of his time reading, writing,
and traveling; she had never been taught to write, seldom left
Groton, and spent her time sweeping his house, caring for his

children, carrying in his wood, keeping his fires burning—all so he could continue his work in peace and comfort.[63]

These were the surface resentments, and Knapp found ways to talk about these openly, even as she agreed that they were signs of her deplorable sinfulness. But the intensity of her fits and the violence of her response to Willard spoke of a deeper resentment that was so fundamentally a part of her being that she could not acknowledge it, even to herself. Only when taken over by the Prince of Evil could she express the full force of her feelings—her *desire for* the independence and power embodied in the symbol of the witch and her rage at the man who taught her that independence and power were the ultimate female evils. When possessed, she could assert the witch within, she could rebel against the many restrictions placed upon her, she could dismiss the kind man in the black robe who himself symbolized her longed-for independence and power and tell him what a rogue she thought he was. For the moment, she could be as powerful as he.

Other possessed females indicated a similar ambivalence toward both their ministers and their faith and struggled as vigorously to assert what their culture deemed unacceptable in women. When not possessed, they too treated their ministers with the respect due God's representatives. But when possessed, they stopped their ears when their ministers preached or mocked them in their pulpits. They were blinded when the Puritan Bible was placed in front of them or deafened when people prayed for their souls. Martha Godwin had no trouble reading Catholic or Quaker books, Cotton Mather explained, or books that argued that witches did not exist. But she could not get near the Bible, books that argued for the existence of witches, or Puritan catechisms for children without falling into what he described as "hideous Convulsions."[64] Ministers were not surprised that witches and demons would afflict the possessed in these ways—after all, they were trying to draw these young women away from their faith—but they were taken aback, they said, because the possessed were for the most part

pious and godly young women who up until the time of their
possessions were model young Christians. As astonishing to
ministers was how often the possessed lashed out at them in
their fits, and how articulate these diatribes were. They described
the possessed as more intelligent than they had previously
thought, more knowledgeable about religion, and exceptionally witty in attacking it.[65] With the restraints temporarily
broken, the possessed were, like Elizabeth Knapp, barely
recognizable to their ministers—and impossible to control.

We must remember, however, that the possessed did not
deliberately confront, let alone substantially alter, the cultural
values or hierarchical relations of their society. To the contrary, possession was acceptable, if not actively encouraged,
because it ultimately affirmed existing gender and class
arrangements, specifically the subordinate position of the possessed and, finally, all women.[66] If during their possessions
these women obliquely challenged Puritan beliefs and social
arrangements, it was only their residual support of religious
and social norms that was finally allowed recognition. Indeed,
during their brief respite from powerlessness, the possessed
continued to blame both themselves and other (older, seemingly more independent and powerful) women for their condition. In their fits, most of their anger was directed inward,
on themselves, and, more overtly, outward on women their
culture designated as their arch-enemies. While their accusations of "unlikely" witches helped to bring witchcraft prosecutions to an end and contributed to the dramatic alteration
of witchcraft beliefs,[67] colonial society did not change in fundamental ways. New ways would be found in the eighteenth
century to keep most women in their place.[68]

One remaining dimension of possession is revealed by
removing it from the context of colonial New England. Taking away the language of witches and the Devil, we are still
left with the convulsions, the trances, the inability to talk, the

paralyzed limbs, and the several other physical manifestations of possession. We can attribute them simply to the possessed's fear of witches, both within and without, but these physical responses might have existed even if New Englanders and their ancestors had never created witches. They have manifested themselves in women in most cultures of the world, many of which employed no concept of witchcraft.

Anthropologists have begun to decipher the mysterious physical behaviors of possession. They suggest that the possessed disengage themselves from "the socially constructed world of everyday life" and enter a state in which what is deemed socially dangerous within their psyche is allowed freer reign. Here their discontent, anger, resentment, and other unacceptable feelings can be expressed without the usual reprisals. From this perspective, possession appears to be a special, altered state of consciousness which some women enter as an involuntary reaction to profound emotional conflict. This conflict emerges from the need simultaneously to embrace social norms and to rebel against them—to live out more autonomous, self-directed lives. With no legitimate way to express this conflict directly, the unbearable psychic tensions are expressed physically—through women's bodies.[69]

The New England possessed were frequently unable to speak: their tongues curled upward toward the roofs of their mouths or curled downward and outward to extraordinary lengths; their throats were constricted or swelled to many times their normal sizes; their words would not come, however hard they tried to speak, and their breath simply would not catch. They strove to communicate through these many physical disabilities what they so much wanted but so much feared to say: that their situations enraged them. Their fits expressed that rage, but not in a way that brought to the surface of normal consciousness the enormous psychic pain that they were experiencing. Their "socially constructed selves" had not been—and could not be—totally obliterated.

The same kind of symbolic expression is apparent in the

other physical manifestations of possession. Their hearing impaired, or lost in a trance, the possessed simply could not hear the accustomed call to duty. Their arms, legs, or hands paralyzed, they simply could not do the spinning, sweeping, hauling, and serving customarily required of them. When pinched, bitten, and beaten by forces others could not see or touch, they expressed both their sense of victimization and their own desire to attack the sometimes barely visible and equally untouchable sources of their frustrations. In their complaints of being starved, and in their inability to eat for days on end, they spoke to the depths of their emotional hunger and deprivation, perhaps as well to the denial of their sexual appetites. Both the emotional and the sexual seem to be represented in their overpowering convulsions, the symbolic release of their many pent-up tensions.

This physical response to their plight would have been most common in women raised in particularly religious households. They were the ones who were most pressured to internalize their society's values, who most frequently heard their parents and ministers warning them of the dangers of rebelling against God's laws. And they had the most to lose by overt rebellion. If these women allowed their conflicts to surface in any other manner, they risked not only society's vengeance but also the loss of approval and love of the people closest to them—most particularly their own fathers or the godly men whom many of the possessed identified as fathers.[70] Elizabeth Knapp was probably not alone in her fear that her extraordinary anger would alienate the man who seemed both to care the most and to insist most strongly on her self-renunciation.

Witchcraft possession in early New England, then, was an interpretation placed upon on a physical and emotional response to a set of social conditions that had no intrinsic relationship to witches or the Devil. These conditions were in some respect specific to Puritan New England, but they are also evident in other societies. Like women in other times and places, the New England possessed were rebelling against pressures to internalize stifling gender and class hierarchies.[71] Puritans understood that reaction as "witchcraft possession" or "diabolical possession"; other historical and contemporary cultures call it "spirit possession." In modern Western cultures, it is called "hysteria" or some other form of individual psychopathology. The specific label, however, only tells us how certain cultures resist the knowledge of female dissatisfaction and anger with their condition.

Like women in other societies, the New England possessed were able, through this culturally sanctioned physical and emotional response, to affect some of these hierarchical arrangements, if only temporarily. They were also able to focus the community's concern on their difficulties. For once, they were the main actors in the social drama. And the more attention they received, the more they dramatized their socially generated anguish and their internally generated desire to rebel. As the community looked on, their bodies expressed what they otherwise could not: that the enormous pressures put upon them to accept a religiously based, male-centered social order was more than they could bear. To accept the community's truth was to deny the self. To assert the self was to suffer the response of a threatened community. Given this choice, they chose a world of their own.

This world, though, offered no real escape. Their religious beliefs led the possessed finally to confirm the only reality their culture allowed, the reality articulated by their ministers and affirmed by most men and women in their communities. There were only two kinds of women: godly women and witches. If witches symbolized female resistance to this dualism, so too did the possessed. But the possessed also represented female capitulation.

Epilogue

WHEN ANDOVER'S ABIGAIL FAULKNER petitioned the Massachusetts authorities in 1703 to remove the stigma of witchcraft from her name, she spoke to the continuing anguish of living with a witch's reputation. Other women in the early eighteenth century no doubt shared her concerns and her plight, since at least some accusations and extralegal reprisals continued long after official support for witchcraft accusations came to an end.[1] But after the Salem and Fairfield outbreaks, witchcraft beliefs and prosecutions were no longer sanctioned in the larger culture.

Ironically, much of the credit for this sudden and dramatic change of events goes to the possessed. Perhaps imperfectly understanding their culture's unspoken witchcraft assumptions, the possessed had never limited their accusations to people their society designated as likely witches. Although the evidence in no way suggests that the possessed intended to defy New England's established codes, not long into the Salem outbreak it became clear to many of New England's elite that the possessed had usurped a power they were never meant to claim. Only the considered efforts of an Increase Mather could undo what he and his contemporaries had worked so hard to do—to convince their New England congregations that the Devil worked in knowable ways to undermine the Puritan way.

Though others have noted that the possessed were no respecters of status distinctions,[2] historians have generally ignored their role in the demise of New England's witchcraft beliefs and prosecutions. That credit has gone to the elite, not only of New England but of Europe. Following the lead of students of European witchcraft, historians of New England have cited "Enlightenment" thinking as the cause of the change, arguing that the ruling classes of Europe and, later, America underwent a profound shift in their ideas about witches in the wake of the development of "scientific" or "rational" modes of thought. From a few men described as ahead of their time, skepticism about the role of the Devil and his minions in human affairs spread among the educated. By the time of the Salem outbreak, according to this view, several of New England's most prominent men had already joined the forces of reason. Others followed soon after.[3]

This argument overlooks the way the possessed (and other often uneducated and low-ranking individuals) enlightened the intellectuals, not only in New England but in Europe as well. A minor phenomenon prior to the late sixteenth century, by the seventeenth century possession had become a regular feature of European witchcraft trials. At least in part because Europe's possessed shared their New England counterparts' tendency to ignore gender and class distinctions when lodging witchcraft complaints, possession often led to large-scale witch-hunts, with increasing numbers of men and prosperous women found among Satan's allies. Some evidence suggests that European possession was also likely to occur in deeply religious environments;[4] if so, this sheds light on why doubts about the reality of witchcraft often went hand in hand with criticism of the established clergy.

This is not to say that the power the possessed assumed completely accounts for the decline of witchcraft in either setting. On the contrary, like its emergence, witchcraft's demise surely had other structural as well as ideological causes. Unfortunately, we know little about New England women's lives and the relations between men and women in the early and mid-eighteenth century and only a little more about religious and secular views of womanhood. Yet here, not in the Enlightenment, I suspect, lies the rest of witchcraft's history.

Although we cannot complete that history, we find in subsequent developments in New England some hints as to its outcome. By the end of the seventeenth century, the power of the Puritan ministry—and indeed Puritanism itself—was in question. The Great Awakening of the late 1730s and early 1740s led to a brief if intense revival of religious fervor among New England's population, but Puritans never fully regained hegemony in the region. Because witchcraft's power in New England was tied to that of Puritanism, their simultaneous demise is understandable.[5] Interestingly, the Awakening produced physical responses in its (mostly young or female) adherents that resembled those of the possessed,[6] but the Awakening's leaders plucked these brands out of the burning without the intermediate step of exorcizing their demons. Resistance to the Lord rather than resistance to the Devil distinguished the agonies of the unconverted from those of the possessed. Not incidentally, the demographic and economic tensions that underlay the Awakening in the town of its orgin closely resembled those that sparked many an earlier witchcraft accusation.[7]

The sexual tensions that characterized the seventeenth century also remained, but New Englanders may have found ways to reduce them. In New Haven, at least, men could expect to escape the consequences of their sexual offenses after the early eighteenth century. From then on, women and their families shouldered virtually the whole burden of illegitimacy. Only by suing the father of a child born out of wedlock could a woman hope to receive child support, and even then her chances were slim.[8] New Haven, and apparently other

New England towns, had decided to resolve some of the problem of women's sexual independence by giving up the pre-
tense of a single sexual standard.[9]

At the same time, images of Eve gradually disappeared
from ministerial sermons and women were increasingly pro-
trayed as passive, dependent, chaste, powerless, and content.[10] Secular literature written for the middle and upper
classes in both England and New England told women that it
was their nature to be passionless, signaling what one historian had called "a pivotal point in the transformation from
external to internal controls of sexual behavior."[11] Simultaneously, the witch figure herself took on a less intimidating
shape in the minds of the larger population. Ideologically, both
the virtuous woman and the witch had been desexed and
domesticated.

The old fear of female sexual power had not disappeared.
Indeed, the increasing emphasis on women's lack of sexual
power was simply a new way of diminishing it, part of a larger
eighteenth-century reconstruction of womanhood.[12] The celebration of the Puritan helpmeet of the seventeenth century
had not, as the witchcraft trials attest, converted women to
submission. The elaboration of a more diffident, self-sacrific-
ing, innately spiritual but more secularly based female ideal
would have greater success.

By the early nineteenth century, the new formulation of
womanhood was fully developed, and it expressed the fears
and goals of the emerging industrial society. The ideology of
domesticity proclaimed that "woman" embodied a moral purity
that distinguished her from man and that required women to
spread their moral influence as the "mothers of civilization."[13]
Created to serve the needs of the new middle class, this ideology gained widespread acceptance in part because it explicitly asserted that all women shared the same nature, but it
implicitly excluded from "womanhood" those who could not
or would not aspire to the ideal. Woman-as-evil had gradually
taken on not a single but a dual shape—one formed by race,

the other by class. By the nineteenth century, black women and poor white women were viewed as embodying many of the characteristics of the witch: they were increasingly portrayed as seductive, sexually uncontrolled, and threatening to the social and moral order.[14] To be a "woman" was to eschew the powers once identified with the witch and to use one's newly celebrated "influence" in defense of domesticity. Acceptance of the ideology's explicit and implicit truths assured white women of the middle and upper classes that the evil was not in them.

Appendix

List of Accused Witches
Whose Names Recur Frequently in this Text

BRIDGET BISHOP (*formerly* BRIDGET OLIVER). A Salem woman who was accused and apparently tried and acquitted of witch-craft in the winter of 1679–80 when she was the widow Oliver; retried and convicted during the Salem outbreak, after her marriage to Edward Bishop; the first woman executed during this outbreak.

ELIZABETH BLACKLEACH.   A Hartford woman who was accused of witchcraft, along with her husband John, during the 1662–63 Hartford outbreak; never arrested; John Blackleach sued their accuser for molestation and defamation of character.

RACHEL CLINTON (*also called* RACHEL HAFFIELD).   Divorced from her husband in 1681, she was accused of witchcraft twice, once by her Ipswich, Massachusetts, neighbors in about 1687, again during the Salem outbreak; imprisoned early in 1692;

eventually tried and convicted, but freed early in 1693, after the governor issued his general pardon of the remaining Salem accused.

EUNICE COLE. From Hampton, Massachusetts (now New Hampshire). Complained against as a witch at least three times, the first time in 1656, when she seems to have been convicted but not executed, the last time in 1680; spent many of the intervening years in the Boston jail.

MARTHA COREY. A Salem woman who was accused of witchcraft, along with her husband Giles and Alice Parker, who may have been her stepdaughter, early in the Salem outbreak; Giles Corey was pressed to death with rocks after he refused to enter a plea; Martha Corey and Alice Parker were tried, convicted, and executed in September 1692.

MERCY DESBOROUGH. From Fairfield, Connecticut; the only woman to be found guilty of witchcraft during the Fairfield outbreak in 1692–93; reprieved by Connecticut authorities after the Massachusetts governor pardoned the remaining Salem accused in 1693.

MARY DYER. One of Anne Hutchinson's supporters in Boston during the Antinomian controversy of the 1630s; never formally accused of witchcraft, but the target of innuendo; executed in 1660 for her Quaker activism.

(MARY?) GLOVER. A Boston widow accused of possessing four children in the Godwin family in 1688; was tried, convicted, and executed after she allegedly confessed to witchcraft.

ELIZABETH GODMAN. Lived in New Haven in the house of the colony's deputy governor; suspected of witchcraft in the 1650s; tried but not convicted, despite extensive testimony presented against her.

DORCAS GOOD. The four-year-old daughter of Salem witch Sarah Good; accused of witchcraft during the Salem outbreak, shortly after her mother was named; imprisoned in the Boston jail for seven or eight months and then released.

SARAH GOOD. Daughter of a prosperous Wenham, Massachusetts, innkeeper; reduced to poverty by the time of the Salem outbreak; was living in Salem when the accusations began and was one of the first persons named in this episode; also one of the first to be tried, convicted, and executed.

REBECCA GREENSMITH. A Hartford woman who was executed as a witch along with her husband Nathaniel during the 1662–63 Hartford outbreak; she was accused by several of her neighbors and, according to one of the town's ministers, confessed to a lengthy list of witchcraft crimes.

KATHERINE HARRISON. Living in Wethersfield, Connecticut, since the early 1650s, this newly widowed and financially independent woman was complained against by dozens of her neighbors in the late 1660s; found guilty in 1669, but the authorities disagreed about her punishment; banished from the colony in 1670.

JANE HAWKINS. A Boston midwife and one of Anne Hutchinson's followers in the 1630s; never formally accused of witchcraft, but suspected of it; was banished from Massachusetts and, despite her several petitions to the authorities, was not allowed to return.

ANN HIBBENS. A Boston widow who was hanged as a witch in 1656; accusers unknown; her husband William had been a magistrate and her execution seems to have evoked considerable controversy in the community.

ANNE HUTCHINSON. A central figure in Boston's Antinomian controversy in the 1630s; suspected but never formally accused of witchcraft; banished from Massachusetts Bay as a heretic.

MARY JOHNSON.   A Wethersfield servant who is most well-known as one of New England's first confessing witches; was found guilty and hanged in Hartford in 1648.

HANNAH JONES.   Accused of witchcraft in 1682 by one of her Portsmouth, New Hampshire, neighbors; though required to post bond, she was never tried; her mother, Jane Walford, had lived with witchcraft suspicion most of her adult life, and it passed on to Hannah and the other Walford daughters.

MARGARET JONES.   Massachusetts's first witch, executed in Boston in 1648; her husband Thomas was suspected as well, but he was never prosecuted.

SUSANNA MARTIN.   From Salisbury and Amesbury, Massachusetts; was accused of witchcraft twice, once in 1669, when she seems to have been tried and acquitted, and the second time in Salem in 1692; found guilty and hanged early in the Salem outbreak.

REBECCA NURSE.   Elderly wife of prosperous Salem Village farmer, Samuel Nurse; along with her two sisters, Sarah Cloyce and Mary Easty, she was one of the first "unlikely" witches named during the Salem outbreak; public outrage at her conviction and execution has often been credited with generating the first vocal opposition to the 1692–93 trials.

BRIDGET OLIVER.   (*see* BRIDGET BISHOP)

SARAH OSBORNE.   A Salem Village resident and one of the first three women accused of witchcraft in the Salem outbreak; rumor had it that she cohabited with her much younger second husband before she married him and that the couple conspired to deny the two sons of her former marriage their rightful inheritances; she died in prison before she could be tried.

ELIZABETH PROCTOR.   A granddaughter of Lynn, Massachusetts, witch Ann Burt; lived in Salem in 1692; named as a witch, along with her husband, sister, sister-in-law, and several of her children during the Salem outbreak; tried and convicted, but her pregnancy delayed her execution and thus saved her life; released from prison in 1693; her husband John had already been executed.

MARY STAPLIES.   A New Haven woman who was accused of witchcraft in 1653 by one of her most prominent neighbors; officially cleared of suspicion after Thomas Staplies initiated a slander suit against her detractor, she was named as a witch again during the Fairfield outbreak; escaped prosecution in 1692 as well, as did her daughter and grandaughter, who were named with her.

TITUBA (INDIAN?).   A Carib Indian woman who along with her husband, John Indian, was a slave in the household of Salem's minister in 1692; one of the first women complained against during the Salem outbreak; escaped hanging by confessing to diverse witchcraft crimes.

Notes

PREFACE

1. See esp. Cotton Mather, *The Wonders of the Invisible World* (1693; facsimile of the 1862 London edition, Ann Arbor, Mich., 1974); Thomas Hutchinson, *The History of the Colony and Province of Massachusetts Bay*, 2 vols. (London, 1765–68), 2:15–62 (hereafter cited as Hutchinson, *History of Massachusetts Bay*); Nathaniel Hawthorne, "Young Goodman Brown," in *Hawthorne: Selected Tales and Sketches*, 3d ed. (New York, 1970), 149–63; L. Frank Baum, *The Wonderful Wizard of Oz*, in *The Wizard of Oz*, ed. Michael Patrick Hearn (New York, 1983), 1–132; Arthur Miller, *The Crucible*, in *Arthur Miller's Collected Plays* (New York, 1957), 223–330; John Updike, *The Witches of Eastwick* (New York, 1984).

2. Paul Boyer and Stephen Nissenbaum, *Salem Possessed: The Social Origins of Witchcraft* (Cambridge, Mass., 1974); John Putnam Demos, *Entertaining Satan: Witchcraft and the Culture of Early New England* (New York, 1982); Richard Weisman, *Witchcraft, Magic, and Religion in 17th-Century Massachusetts* (Amherst, Mass., 1984).

3. Mary Daly, *Gyn/Ecology: The Metaethics of Radical Feminism* (Boston, 1978), chap. 6; Erica Jong, *Witches* (New York, 1981); Starhawk, *The Spiral Dance: The Rebirth of the Ancient Religion of the Great Goddess* (New York, 1979).

4. Estimates of the number of people executed as witches during the witch-hunting years are only guesses; too many records have been lost or destroyed and too little work has been done on particular regions and time periods. Responsible scholars disagree about what constitutes a reasonable guess. Most agree, however, that the deaths reached holocaust proportions in many areas of Europe and that in the sparsely populated American colonies, which were settled relatively late in the history of Western witchcraft, at least 36 persons were executed. For discussions of the figures for Europe, see, for instance, Norman Cohn, *Europe's Inner Demons: An Enquiry Inspired by the Great Witch-Hunt* (New York, 1975), 253–54; Rosemary Radford Ruether, *New Woman, New Earth: Sexist Ideologies and Human Liberation* (New York, 1983), 89 and 111 n. For a comparative analysis of the sex ratio of accused witches in 16th- and 17th-c. Europe, see E. William Monter, *Witchcraft in France and Switzerland: The Borderlands during the Reformation* (Ithaca, N.Y., 1976), 118–21. Monter's figures (based on 5302 accusations) put the proportion of females among the accused at just about 80 percent. The proportion of females among convicted and executed witches would be higher, if Alan Macfarlane's findings for England and my own for New England are representative. See Macfarlane, *Witchcraft in Tudor and Stuart England: A Regional and Comparative Study* (New York, 1970), 160; and below, 47–51.

5. See, for example, Macfarlane, *Witchcraft in Tudor and Stuart England;* Boyer and Nissenbaum, *Salem Possessed.*

6. See Monter, *Witchcraft in France and Switzerland,* esp. chap. 5; "The Pedestal and the Stake: Courtly Love and Witchcraft," in *Becoming Visible: Women in European History,* ed. Renate Bridenthal and Claudia Koonz (Boston, 1977), 121–36; H. C. Erik Midelfort, *Witch Hunting in Southwestern Germany, 1562–1684* (Stanford, Calif., 1972), chap. 7; Demos, *Entertaining Satan,* chaps. 3, 6. Feminist analyses of witchcraft have offered important insights as well, but most of this work is based on secondary sources. Most useful are Jong, *Witches;* Daly, *Gyn/Ecology,* chap. 6; Ruether, *New Woman, New Earth,* chap. 4; Andrea Dworkin, *Woman Hating* (New York, 1974), chap. 7; Barbara Ehrenreich and Deirdre English, *Witches, Midwives, and Nurses: A History of Women Healers* (Old Westbury, N.Y., 1973); Sylvia Bovenschen, "The Contemporary Witch, the Historical Witch and the Witch Myth: The Witch, Subject of the Appropriation of Nature and Object of the Domination of Nature," *New German Critique* 15 (Fall 1978):83–119.

CHAPTER ONE
New England's Witchcraft Beliefs

1. *Records of the Governor and Company of the Massachusetts Bay in New England*, 6 vols., ed. Nathaniel B. Shurtleff (Boston, 1853–54), 4 (pt. 1):269 (hereafter cited as *Mass. Records*). Criminal trial procedure varied over time and from colony to colony in New England, but in Massachusetts, witchcraft trials usually took place in the Court of Assistants, with a jury of trials, or occasionally in the General Court, where all of the colony's elected representatives voted to convict or acquit. In either case, the magistrates (the elected Assistants) acted as judges. If, as in Ann Hibbens's trial, the magistrates did not agree with the jury's verdict in the Court of Assistants, they referred the case to the General Court. In each of the colonies, though, local courts initially gathered the evidence, examined the accused, and decided whether the case was serious enough to be turned over to one of the higher courts for trial. See also below, 13–14.

2. *Mass. Records* 4 (pt. 1):269; William Hubbard, *A General History of New England, Collections of the Massachusetts Historical Society*, 2d ser., 5–6 (1815), 574.

3. It is not possible to ascertain the exact number of witchcraft trials, convictions, or executions in this or any decade of early New England history. Nor can we determine exactly how many persons were accused of witchcraft. Too many trial records have been lost and too many accusations were not formalized by complaint to the authorities. The figures given here, and all other figures on accused witches presented in this study, have been compiled from both existing court records and other public and private colonial documents that mention additional individuals or cases. In gathering this information, I have benefited considerably from several lists of witches compiled by other scholars. For the most comprehensive of these, see Demos, *Entertaining Satan*, 401–9; *The Salem Witchcraft Papers: Verbatim Transcripts of the Legal Documents of the Salem Witchcraft Outbreak of 1692*, 3 vols., ed. Paul Boyer and Stephen Nissenbaum (New York, 1977), esp. the contents section at the beginning of each volume (hereafter cited as *Witchcraft Papers*); Lyle Koehler, *A Search for Power: The "Weaker Sex" in Seventeenth-Century New England* (Urbana, Ill,. 1980), 474–91; and Weisman, *Witchcraft, Magic, and Religion*, 191–221. Since some of these lists include only persons accused of witchcraft at particular times or places, or only persons involved in legal actions concerning witchcraft, I have found that they are best used

in conjunction with one another. This method has also made it possible to correct for errors of omission or inclusion on my own and other scholars' lists.

4. Keith Thomas, *Religion and the Decline of Magic* (New York, 1971), 441–52, 520; Macfarlane, *Witchcraft in Tudor and Stuart England*, 160.

5. Hubbard, *General History of New England*, 574; *New England Historical and Genealogical Register*, 6 (1852), 287–88. Scholars have sometimes assumed that Hibbens had few economic resources at the time of her trial, primarily because her husband had once suffered a financial loss of £500. When she died, however, she left £344 to her heirs, a substantial estate for anyone in 1656, and particularly for a woman.

6. Thomas, *Religion and the Decline of Magic*, 520; Macfarlane, *Witchcraft in Tudor and Stuart England*, 150–51.

7. The best study of the witchcraft beliefs the colonists brought with them from England is Thomas, *Religion and the Decline of Magic*, esp. chaps. 2–9 and 14–18.

8. For actual figures on the proportions of women, men, and children among the accused, see below, 47–51, 64–66.

9. Samuel Wyllys Papers, Supplement: Depositions on Cases of Witchcraft Tried in Connecticut, 1662–1693, photostat copies of original documents from the Wyllys Papers, Annmary Brown Memorial, Brown University Library, Providence, R.I. (manuscript volume, Archives, History and Genealogy Unit, Connecticut State Library, Hartford, Conn.), 1 (hereafter cited as Wyllys Papers Supplement). This list closely resembles the one drawn up in the late 16th or early 17th c. by the English Puritan minister William Perkins. See "A Discourse of the Damned Art of Witchcraft," in *The Work of William Perkins*, ed. Ian Breward (Abington, England, 1970), 602–3.

10. On the relationship between these two sets of concerns in England, see Clive Holmes, "Popular Culture? Witches, Magistrates, and Divines in Early Modern England," in *Understanding Popular Culture: Europe from the Middle Ages to the Nineteenth Century*, ed. Steven L. Kaplan (New York, 1984), 85–111. For an interpretation of this relationship in New England different from the one developed in this chapter, see Weisman, *Witchcraft, Magic, and Religion*. Debate on this issue has been stimulated by Thomas, *Religion and the Decline of Magic* and Demos, *Entertaining Satan;* both authors suggest that the fears and anxieties of the religious and secular elites were less significant in the development of witchcraft beliefs and prosecutions than the fears and anxieties of the rest of the population. For more on

this controversy in its European context, see Cohn, *Europe's Inner Demons*, esp. chaps. 8–12; Richard Kieckhefer, *European Witch Trials: Their Foundations in Popular and Learned Culture, 1300–1500* (Berkeley, Calif., 1976); Christina Larner, *Enemies of God: The Witch-hunt in Scotland* (Baltimore, 1981), esp. chaps. 11–13; Hildred Geertz, "An Anthropology of Religion and Magic, I" and Keith Thomas, "An Anthropology of Religion and Magic, II," *Journal of Interdisciplinary History* 6 (Summer 1975): 71–89 and 91–109; E. P. Thompson, "Anthropology and the Discipline of Historical Context," *Midland History* 1 (Spring 1972): 41–55. On the colonies, see also Jon Butler, "Magic, Astrology, and the Early American Religious Heritage, 1600–1760," *American Historical Review* 84 (April 1979): 317–46; David D. Hall, "Witchcraft and the Limits of Interpretation," *New England Quarterly* 58 (June 1985), esp. 275–79.

Historians frequently make a distinction between popular and learned (or elite) beliefs, or between magic (or folklore) and religion. Because these terms are value-laden (on this point, see Geertz, "An Anthropology of Religion and Magic, I"), and because specific beliefs and concerns can be identified with but were not limited to particular groups in England, I make a distinction instead between traditional and Puritan beliefs. I use the word "traditional" because most of the beliefs in this category were long-established and were (primarily) handed down orally from generation to generation. I use the word "Puritan" for other beliefs because, in New England, they were both written down and articulated (primarily) by ministers and other literate Puritans in the 17th c. and because they became the central tenets of Puritan witchcraft doctrine. To say that certain ideas were "Puritan" is *not* to argue, however, that they were all originally or exclusively so; at the very least, many of them were held by other Protestant—and Catholic—clergymen in Europe, and many of them preceded the development of Puritanism.

11. See, for instance, Cotton Mather's suspicion that a witch was responsible for his own son's death, in *Diary of Cotton Mather, 1681–1708, Collections of the Massachusetts Historical Society*, 7th ser., 7 (1911), 163–64, and his description of a similar suspicion on the part of two other parents, in Mather, *Wonders of the Invisible World*, 153.

12. See, for instance, Hugh Crosia's witchcraft confession in Connecticut Archives, Crimes and Misdemeanors, 1st ser. (1662–1789) (manuscript volume, Archives, History and Genealogy Unit, Connecticut State Library, Hartford, Conn.), 1 (pt. 1): doc. 185 (hereafter cited as Crimes and Misdemeanors); Norbert B. Lacy, "The

Records of the Court of Assistants of Connecticut, 1665–1701" (M.A. thesis, Yale University, 1937), 193 (hereafter cited as "Conn. Assistants Records").

13. "Church Trial of Mistress Ann Hibbens," in *Root of Bitterness: Documents of the Social History of American Women,* ed. Nancy F. Cott (New York, 1972), 47–58. For more on these characteristics, see below, chap. 4, esp. 150–52.

14. Hutchinson, *History of Massachusetts Bay* 1:187–88.

15. Ibid. 1:187.

16. Since the following overview of New England witchcraft beliefs is drawn from thousands of primary documents, individual sources will be cited here only when direct quotations are used. Later in this chapter and in subsequent chapters, I provide further documentation of the ways in which these beliefs were expressed in trial testimony and in literary accounts of witchcraft.

17. *Witchcraft Papers* 1:94.

18. Ibid. 1:193; 2:560.

19. Ibid. 1:103.

20. Ibid., 103, 190.

21. John Winthrop, *Winthrop's Journal: "History of New England,"* *1630–1649,* 2 vols., ed. James Kendall Hosmer (New York, 1908), 1:267 (hereafter cited as Winthrop, *Journal*).

22. John Hale, *A Modest Enquiry into the Nature of Witchcraft* (Boston, 1702), 18.

23. *Witchcraft Papers* 1:100.

24. Wyllys Papers Supplement, 33.

25. The trial of Winifred Holman, Middlesex Superior Court Folio Collection, Middlesex County Courthouse, East Cambridge, Mass., folio 25.*

26. Samuel G. Drake, *Annals of Witchcraft in New England* (New York, 1869), 259, 283; *Witchcraft Papers* 1:217.

27. *Mass. Records* 3:126.

---

*As this book goes to press, the Middlesex Superior Court Folio Collection, as well as many other Massachusetts manuscript court records, are in the process of being relocated to the Massachusetts Archives at Columbia Point, 220 Morrissey Blvd., Boston, MA. Because decisions about which records will be moved have not been finalized, readers interested in locating any of the Massachusetts manuscript court records cited in these notes should check first with Columbia Point archivists. Some of these records are also being reassembled and renumbered.

28. *Witchcraft Papers* 2:444; Crimes and Misdemeanors 2, doc. 398. In the 17th c., the word "nightmare" meant a female spirit or hag who rode people and animals during their sleep, creating a sensation of suffocation and enormous weight. *Oxford English Dictionary*, s.v. "nightmare."

29. C. Mather, *Wonders of the Invisible World*, 35.

30. Cotton Mather, "Memorable Providences, Relating to Witch-crafts and Possessions," in *Narratives of the Witchcraft Cases, 1648–1706*, ed. Charles Lincoln Burr (New York, 1914), 106 (hereafter cited as C. Mather, "Memorable Providences").

31. *Witchcraft Papers* 1:228; 2:397. The Venus glass and an egg procedure is unclear. Possibly the egg was broken onto the mirror and the glass "read" (as a crystal ball might be "read") for what it said about a person's future.

32. C. Mather, *Wonders of the Invisible World*, 96.

33. Winthrop, *Journal* 2:344; *Witchcraft Papers* 2:343.

34. *Witchcraft Papers* 2:529.

35. C. Mather, *Wonders of the Invisible World*, 195.

36. *Witchcraft Papers* 2:504.

37. Ibid., 388.

38. Wyllys Papers Supplement, 1.

39. Hale, *Modest Enquiry*, 24; Cotton Mather, "A Brand Plucked Out of the Burning," in Burr, *Narratives*, 264; C. Mather, "Memorable Providences," 102.

40. C. Mather, "Memorable Providences," 101; Increase Mather, *An Essay for the Recording of Illustrious Providences* (Boston, 1684), 140 (hereafter cited by its better-known title, *Remarkable Providences*); Deodat Lawson, "A Brief and True Narrative of Some Remarkable Passages Relating to Sundry Persons Afflicted by Witchcraft, at Salem Village," in Burr, *Narratives*, 153.

41. C. Mather, "Memorable Providences," 101.

42. I. Mather, *Remarkable Providences*, 136.

43. Robert Calef, "More Wonders of the Invisible World," in Burr, *Narratives*, 311.

44. C. Mather, *Diary*, 161.

45. *Witchcraft Papers* 2:683.

46. Ibid. 1:107.

47. Ibid., 108.

48. Wyllys Papers Supplement, 1.

49. *Witchcraft Papers* 2:618–19.

50. Ibid. 1:212.

51. Informal, as distinguished from formal, accusations were those that never reached the level of an official complaint. They include, for example, accusations hurled at an adversary in the middle of an argument (which may or may not have resulted in a slander suit), secondhand reports of openly expressed suspicions, and, like those against Hutchinson and Hawkins, accusations and suspicions mentioned in literary sources.

52. Most of the documents pertaining to Anne Hutchinson and the Antinomian controversy are compiled in *The Antinomian Controversy, 1636–1638: A Documentary History*, ed. David D. Hall (Middletown, Conn., 1968). Excerpts from Hutchinson's civil trial, entitled "The Examination of Mrs. Ann Hutchinson at the Court of Newtown," are also included in Cott, *Root of Bitterness*, 34–46. For readers unfamiliar with this controversy, a good starting point is Edmund S. Morgan's brief discussion in *The Puritan Dilemma: The Story of John Winthrop* (Boston, 1958), 134–54. The most detailed secondary account is Emery Battis's *Saints and Sectaries: Anne Hutchinson and the Antinomian Controversy in the Massachusetts Bay Colony* (Chapel Hill, N.C., 1962); unfortunately, it is marred by its treatment of Hutchinson's role in these events as evidence of psychopathology. Contrasting views can be found in Lyle Koehler, "The Case of the American Jezebels: Anne Hutchinson and Female Agitation during the Years of Antinomian Turmoil, 1636–1640," *William and Mary Quarterly*, 3d ser., 31 (January 1974): 55–78; Ben Barker-Benfield, "Anne Hutchinson and the Puritan Attitude toward Women," *Feminist Studies* 1 (Fall 1972): 65–96.

53. Winthrop, *Journal* 1:268.

54. *Mass. Records* 1:224.

55. See, for example, *Johnson's Wonder-Working Providence, 1628–1651*, ed. J. Franklin Jameson (New York, 1910), 132–33.

56. *Mass. Records* 1:224.

57. Ibid., 329.

58. Winthrop, *Journal* 1:266–69.

59. Boston minister John Cotton, on the other hand, interpreted this birth as "a providence of God . . . intend[ed] only [for] the instruction of the parents, and such other to whom it was known. . . ." See Winthrop, *Journal* 1:267–68. For English beliefs on this subject,

see Thomas, *Religion and the Decline of Magic*, 89–94, 106–8.

60. Winthrop, *Journal* 1:268. See also John Winthrop, *A Short Story of the Rise, reign and ruine of the Antinomians, Familists and Libertines*, in Hall, *Antinomian Controversy*, 280–82.

61. Sally Smith Booth, *The Witches of Early America* (New York, 1975), 101.

62. Thomas Weld, "Preface" to Winthrop, *A Short Story*, 214.

63. Winthrop, *Journal* 2:7–8.

64. "Examination of Mrs. Ann Hutchinson," 34. For more on the importance of Hutchinson's gender to her opponents, compare John Winthrop's attitude toward her with his attitude toward Massachusetts Bay's other main heretic, Roger Williams, in Winthrop, *Journal* 1:57, 61–62, 93, 112–13, 116–17, 119, 142, 149, 157, 162–63, 168, 179, 184–87, 190, 193, 195–97, 218–19, 221, 240–41, 243–55, 260–69, 272–74, 277, 286–87, 297, 309; *Journal* 2:7–8, 53–54, 96, 137–38, 197–98, 228–29, 350. See also Koehler, "American Jezebels" and Barker-Benfield, "Anne Hutchinson."

65. This is not to say that Hutchinson and her followers maintained their influence, only that the official actions taken against them (and against other outspoken females at this time) were probably more effective in silencing them than were witchcraft accusations. On this point, see Koehler, "American Jezebels," 69–78, and below, 190–94, 197–98.

66. Winthrop, *Journal* 2:323.

67. Matthew Grant, "Diary, 1637–1654" (Archives, History and Genealogy Unit, Connecticut State Library, Hartford, Conn.), verso of front cover.

68. Ibid., 145–47; Demos, *Entertaining Satan*, 301, 346, and esp. 505, n. 29.

69. During this period, both New Haven and Plymouth were separate colonies. New Haven was incorporated into Connecticut in 1665 and Plymouth into Massachusetts in 1691.

70. Hale, *Modest Enquiry*, 17.

71. Winthrop, *Journal* 2:344.

72. Hale, *Modest Enquiry*, 17.

73. *The Public Records of the Colony of Connecticut*, 15 vols., ed. J. H. Trumbull and Charles J. Hoadly (Hartford, 1850–90), 1:143, 171 (hereafter cited as *Conn. Records*); *Records of the Particular Court of Connecticut, 1639–1663, Collections of the Connecticut Historical Society*, 22

(1928), 43, 56 (hereafter cited as *Particular Court Records*); C. Mather, "Memorable Providences," 135–36; Hale, *Modest Enquiry*, 19–20.

74. C. Mather, "Memorable Providences," 135–36.

75. *Mass. Records* 4 (pt. 1):47–48.

76. Hale, *Modest Enquiry*, 19. See also *Mass. Records* 3:229; Drake, *Annals of Witchcraft*, 64–72, 222, 227–46, 248, 250–51, 253–54; Jameson, *Johnson's Wonder-Working Providence*, 237; *Colonial Justice in Western Massachusetts (1639–1702): The Pynchon Court Record: An Original Judge's Diary of the Administration of Justice in the Springfield Courts in the Massachusetts Bay Colony*, ed. Joseph H. Smith (Cambridge, Mass., 1961), 20–25 (hereafter cited as *Pynchon Court Records*); Stephen Innes, *Labor in a New Land: Economy and Society in Seventeenth-Century Springfield* (Princeton, N.J., 1983), 136–41.

77. *Mass. Records* 3:273; 4 (pt. 1): 96; Drake, *Annals of Witchcraft*, 64–72, 219–58; *Pynchon Court Records*, 20–25. See also Innes, *Labor in a New Land*, 136–41.

78. *Records of the Colony or Jurisdiction of New Haven, from May, 1653, to the Union*, ed. Charles J. Hoadly (Hartford, Conn., 1858), 29 (hereafter cited as *New Haven Colony Records* 2).

79. Documents for the Godman witchcraft case are found in *New Haven Colony Records* 2:29–36, 151–52; *Ancient Town Records: New Haven Town Records*, ed. Franklin Bowditch Dexter (New Haven, 1917–62), 1:249–52, 256–57, 264 (hereafter cited as *New Haven Town Records*). Quotation is from *New Haven Colony Records* 2:152.

80. Hutchinson, *History of Massachusetts Bay* 1:188.

81. Depositions from Eunice Cole's 1656 trial are found in Massachusetts Archives (manuscript volume, Statehouse, Boston, Mass.), 135:2–3. After 1682, Hampton was part of New Hampshire.

82. George Bishop, *New England Judged, by the Spirit of the Lord* (London, 1703), 12; John Whiting, *Truth and Innocency Defended Against Falsehood and Envy* (London, 1702), 12–13.

83. The Trial of Winifred Holman, folio 25.

84. Cole's trial took place within months of Hibbens's. For discussion of Cole's trial and its outcome, see below, 53.

85. Most of the documents relating to the Hartford outbreak are in the Samuel Wyllys Papers: Depositions on Cases of Witchcraft, Assault, Theft, Drunkenness, and other Crimes, Tried in Connecticut, 1663–1728 (manuscript volume, Archives, History and Genealogy Unit, Connecticut State Library, Hartford, Conn.), docs. 1–5

(hereafter cited as Wyllys Papers); Wyllys Papers Supplement, 2–4, 44–45, 55–60. Other source materials include I. Mather, *Remarkable Providences*, 135–39; John Whiting's 4 December 1682 letter to Increase Mather, published in *The Mather Papers, Collections of the Massachusetts Historical Society*, 4th ser., 8 (1868), 466–69 (hereafter cited as Whiting, "Letter"); a 13 October 1662 letter from New Netherland governor Peter Stuyvesant to the Hartford magistrates, found in the Robert C. Winthrop Collection of Connecticut Manuscripts, 1631–1794 (Archives, History and Genealogy Unit, Connecticut State Library, Hartford, Conn.), 1, doc. 1a (hereafter cited as Stuyvesant, "Letter"); *Particular Court Records*, 247, 251, 258–61, 265. The best secondary account is R[ichard] G. Tomlinson, *Witchcraft Trials of Connecticut* (Hartford, 1978), 27–40 (a copy of this work is available in Connecticut Historical Society, Hartford, Conn.). See also Demos, *Entertaining Satan*, 340–41, 349–55, 369, 382–83, and passim; Taylor, *Witchcraft Delusion*, 80–85, 96–100, 151–53.

86. I. Mather, *Remarkable Providences*, 135–36; Whiting, "Letter," 466–67.

87. I. Mather, *Remarkable Providences*, 137–39.

88. Stuyvesant, "Letter."

89. *Particular Court Records*, 259–60; Wyllys Papers, docs. 1–2; Wyllys Papers Supplement, 56–60; Records of the Colony of Connecticut, Connecticut Colonial Probate Records, County Court, 56, 1663–1677 (Archives, History, and Genealogy Unit, Connecticut State Library, Hartford, Conn.), 35–36, 52 (hereafter cited as Connecticut Colonial Probate Records); *Conn. Records* 2:530–31. See also Tomlinson, *Witchcraft Trials*, 32, 34–39.

90. On the internal Hartford conflicts during this period (and related difficulties in surrounding towns), see Demos, *Entertaining Satan*, chap. 11; Sylvester Judd, *History of Hadley* (Springfield, Mass., 1905), 3–17; Tomlinson, *Witchcraft Trials*, 27. On the history of Salem's internal conflicts during the 17th c. and their relationship to the 1692 witchcraft outbreak, see Boyer and Nissenbaum, *Salem Possessed*.

91. Thomas, *Religion and the Decline of Magic*, 444; Holmes, "Popular Culture? Witches, Magistrates, and Divines," 100–2.

92. Elizabeth Godman was another woman who historians have sometimes assumed was poor. Records concerning the contents and disposition of her estate after her death, however, suggest otherwise. See *New Haven Town Records* 1:264, 462–67, 478–79; 2:38; *New Haven Colony Records* 2:306, 497–98; and below, 297–98 n. 6. For more

information on the relative treatment accorded accused witches from different economic groups, see below, 77–80.

93. Hutchinson, *History of Massachusetts Bay* 1:187–88.

94. Although the Salem outbreak has been described as an event during which the number of both men and well-off women among accused witches was surprisingly large, given previous patterns of accusations, the number of well-off women among the Hartford accused seems to have been proportionately as large and the number of men was proportionately larger. Besides Andrew Sanford, the two other men among the accused were John Blackleach and James Wakeley. The two women from wealthy families were Elizabeth Blackleach and Judith Varlet.

95. This quotation is from a jury's verdict in the Pennsylvania trial of Margaret Mattson, reprinted in Burr, *Narratives,* 87.

96. "Conn. Assistants Records," 12–14, 18–19, 23; *Conn. Records* 2:132. The Harrison case is discussed in greater detail below, 84–89 and in Demos, *Entertaining Satan,* esp. 290–91, 355–65.

97. Wyllys Papers Supplement, 53.

98. Cited in Judd, *History of Hadley,* 231.

99. C. Mather, "Memorable Providences," 133.

100. At least 16 of the witches first accused during this period (15 women and 1 man) were accused a second time, and a few a third time. Five of these women were convicted during the Salem outbreak.

101. Wallace Notestein, *A History of Witchcraft in England from 1558 to 1718* (New York, 1909), 284–85.

102. See below, 244–46.

103. See, for example, the response of Beverly minister John Hale to accusations against Dorcas Hoar in the 1670s and the response of minister Samuel Phillips of Rowley to accusations against Elizabeth How in 1682, in *Witchcraft Papers* 2:397–99, 442.

104. Samuel Willard, "A Brief Account of a Strange and Unusual Providence of God Befallen to Elizabeth Knapp of Groton," in *Remarkable Providences, 1600–1760,* ed. John Demos (New York, 1972), 358–71. Quotations are from 358–59.

105. See, for example, Jane James's 1667 defamation suit against her Marblehead neighbor Richard Rowland, in *Records and Files of the Quarterly Courts of Essex County, Massachusetts,* 9 vols. (Salem, 1912–75), 3:413 (hereafter cited as *Essex Court Records*) and testimony pre-

sented against Eunice Cole of Hampton in 1672–73, in Massachusetts Archives, 135:3 (testimony submitted in 1656 and resubmitted in 1672–73) and 15 (2).

106. Willard, "A Brief Account," 367.

107. C. Mather, "Memorable Providences," 134.

108. *Essex Court Records* 4:129, 133.

109. *Documents and Records Relating to the Province of New Hampshire,* Provincial, Town, and State Paper Series, 1, ed. Nathaniel Bouton (Concord, N.H., 1867), 415–19.

110. I. Mather, *Remarkable Providences,* esp. the preface and chaps. 5, 6, 7, 8, 11. The quotation is from the preface (unpaged). For another interpretation of Mather's essay, see Ann Kibbey, "Mutations of the Supernatural: Witchcraft, Remarkable Providences, and the Power of Puritan Men," *American Quarterly* 34 (1982):125–48.

111. C. Mather, "Memorable Providences," 100–3.

112. Ibid., 104–6.

113. Ibid., 99–143.

114. Before her death in 1967, novelist and biographer Esther Forbes was working on a book on New England witchcraft that presumably would have tied the 17th-c. witchcraft accusations, and particularly the Salem outbreak, to the refugee problem created for Boston, Salem, and other northern New England towns by Indian attacks along the northeastern frontier in the 1670s, 1680s, and early 1690s. Her notes and some rough drafts of sections of the first chapter can be found in the Esther Forbes Papers, American Antiquarian Society, Worcester, Mass. I am grateful to David D. Hall for telling me about this valuable collection.

115. Marion L. Starkey, *The Devil in Massachusetts* (New York, 1949), 11–12.

116. The principal documents of the Salem outbreak are found in *Witchcraft Papers* and Burr, *Narratives.* For the best and most comprehensive narrative of the Salem outbreak, see Starkey, *The Devil in Massachusetts.* Boyer and Nissenbaum's *Salem Possessed* offers the most convincing explanation for why this outbreak began in Salem Village. Other important contributions to the Salem discussion include John Demos, "Underlying Themes in the Witchcraft of Seventeenth-Century New England," *American Historical Review* 75 (June 1970): 1311–26; Kai T. Erikson, *Wayward Puritans: A Study in the Sociology of Deviance* (New York, 1966); Chadwick Hansen, *Witchcraft at Salem* (New York, 1969); Weisman, *Witchcraft, Magic, and Religion;*

Kibbey, "Mutations of the Supernatural;" Christine Leigh Heyrman, *Commerce and Culture: The Maritime Communities of Colonial Massachusetts, 1690–1750* (New York, 1984), chap. 3; David Thomas Konig, *Law and Society in Puritan Massachusetts: Essex County, 1629–1692* (Chapel Hill, N.C., 1979), esp. 169–85; Koehler, *A Search for Power,* 383–417; Linnda R. Caporael, "Ergotism: The Satan Loosed in Salem?" *Science,* 2 April 1976, 21–26.

117. *Witchcraft Papers* 1:228; Hale, *Modest Enquiry,* 23, 133.

118. The examinations of these three women are in *Witchcraft Papers* 2:356–59, 609–11; 3:746–55.

119. For Martha Corey's examination, see *Witchcraft Papers* 1:248–55.

120. For documents relating to Dorcas Good, Rebecca Nurse, and Elizabeth Proctor, see *Witchcraft Papers* 2:351–53, 583–608, 657–76. The witchcraft reputation of Nurse's mother, Johanna Towne, is mentioned in *Witchcraft Papers* 2:601. For testimony presented against Elizabeth Proctor's grandmother, Ann Burt, see *Essex Court Records* 4:207–9.

121. For the 1692 court records of these several persons, see *Witchcraft Papers* 1:77, 83–109, 151–78, 221–23, 239–46, 269, 287–304; 2:389–404, 549–79, 655–56, 677–99. For the pre-1692 cases of Martin, Bishop, and Hoar, see *Essex Court Records* 4:129, 133; 7:329–30; *Witchcraft Papers* 2:397–99. The quotation is from *Witchcraft Papers* 1:177.

122. Thomas Brattle, "Letter," in Burr, *Narratives,* 183.

123. See, for example, petitions submitted to the court on behalf of Rebecca Nurse and John and Elizabeth Proctor, in *Witchcraft Papers* 2:592–93, 681–83.

124. Although relatively few of the Salem witches had been formally accused prior to 1692, that most of the accusations lodged by the possessed were supported by neighbors of the accused suggests that the possessed were simply expressing local suspicions. In most cases, then, the possessed were "originators" of the accusations only in the sense that they formalized them. For another, more comprehensive statement of this argument, see Boyer and Nissenbaum, *Salem Possessed.* See below, 245–46 for possible exceptions to this pattern.

125. During the Salem outbreak, the executions of confessing women were delayed so that they could provide information about other witches. This was a temporary expedient, not a permanent change in policy; but because the Salem trials ended before these

hangings could take place, it had the effect of a policy change.

126. It would be equally accurate to say that the majority of the possessed were under 20 or that the majority were over 16.

127. See, for instance, Brattle, "Letter," esp. 177–87; Calef, "More Wonders of the Invisible World," esp. 369–74.

128. Hale, *Modest Enquiry,* 38.

129. William Phips, "Letters of Governor Phips to the Home Government, 1692–1693," in Burr, *Narratives,* 197.

130. Ibid., 201 n.; Calef, "More Wonders of the Invisible World," 360, 369; Brattle, "Letter," 177–78.

131. Increase Mather, *Cases of Conscience Concerning Evil Spirits Personating Men* (1693; facsimile of the 1862 London edition, Ann Arbor, Mich., 1974), esp. 259–60, 279–81. Somewhat inconsistently, Mather also said at one point that the possessed were "sick bewitched Persons"; at another that their seizures may have derived from "Nature, and the Power of Imagination" (see 268–69, 286). For a more comprehensive understanding of the change in Mather's attitude toward possession and the possessed during the Salem outbreak, compare *Cases of Conscience* to his earlier *Remarkable Providences,* esp. chaps. 5, 6, 7, 11. For other views on the context and significance of *Cases of Conscience,* see Boyer and Nissenbaum, *Salem Possessed,* 10–20; Hansen, *Witchcraft at Salem,* esp. chaps. 9–10; Weisman, *Witchcraft, Magic, and Religion,* esp. chap. 10.

132. One of Mather's central arguments was that the Devil could impersonate innocent people, an issue that had been much debated during the Salem events. See *Cases of Conscience,* 225 and passim.

133. See Phips, "Letters," 199. Mather himself never admitted in *Cases of Conscience* that innocent people had been executed; in fact, he claimed that that had not happened (see 255). He may have believed this or he may simply have been reluctant to acknowledge that so many of the ministers and magistrates could have been wrong.

134. Increase Mather's son, Cotton, did try to reaffirm existing Puritan witchcraft beliefs in the half dozen years after the Salem outbreak but met with little support and considerable ridicule. He dealt with the problem of the possessed by simultaneously validating their possession and ignoring their accusations of specific women. See his *Wonders of the Invisible World;* "A Brand Plucked Out of the Burning"; "Another Brand Pluckt Out of the Burning, or, More Wonders of the Invisible World," in Burr, *Narratives,* 307–23; *Magnalia Christi Americana,* 2 vols. (Hartford, 1853), 2:446–79.

135. Calef, "More Wonders of the Invisible World," 382.

136. Most of the documents on the Fairfield outbreak are in the Wyllys Papers, docs. 18–42, and the Wyllys Papers Supplement, 5–36, 54. The best secondary account is in Tomlinson, *Witchcraft Trials*, 52–64. See also Ronald Marcus, " 'Elizabeth Clawson . . . Thou Deservest to Dye': An Account of the Trial in 1692 of a Woman from Stamford, Connecticut, Who Was Accused of Being a Witch" (Stamford, Conn., 1976) (a copy of this pamphlet is in the Connecticut Historical Society, Hartford, Conn.); Taylor, *Witchcraft Delusion*, 62–78, 101–19, 154–55.

137. Calef, "More Wonders of the Invisible World," 385; "Conn. Assistants Records," 262–65; Suffolk Court Files (manuscript volume, Suffolk County Courthouse, Boston, Mass.), 24: 1972; C. Bancroft Gillespie and George Munson Curtis, *A Century of Meriden* (Meriden, Conn., 1906), 254–59.

138. See, for instance, C. Mather, *Wonders of the Invisible World;* Hale, *Modest Enquiry.* For discussion of this process, see Starkey, *The Devil in Massachusetts,* 278–92.

139. Crimes and Misdemeanors 2: docs. 398–401.

CHAPTER TWO
The Demographic Basis of Witchcraft

1. This number for accused witches is higher than that provided by other scholars of New England witchcraft. John Demos, for instance, finds 234 "cases"; Lyle Koehler lists 315 accused persons. (See Demos, *Entertaining Satan,* 11; Koehler, *A Search for Power,* 474–91; and above, chap. 1, n. 3.)

There are several reasons for my larger figure. First, I have included several persons named as witches in the early 18th c., whereas other lists usually end in 1697, with the last witches who were actually prosecuted. My argument for including these persons among the accused is that at least until 1725, when widow Sarah Keene complained to local Maine authorities that John Spinney had called her a witch, accused persons still took accusations seriously enough to initiate official proceedings against their accusers. (For reconstruction of this case, see Neal W. Allen, Jr., "A Maine Witch," *Old-Time New England* 61 (Winter 1971), 75–81. I am grateful to Professor Allen for telling me about Sarah Keene.) See also Sarah Spencer's response to the accusation made against her in 1724 (see above, 45) and Abigail Faulkner's feelings about her witchcraft reputation in 1703 (see below, 220–21). Second, I have found accusations (those against Elinor Hollingworth in 1679 and Lydia Dustin, Sarah Dustin, and Mary Colson in 1681, for instance) that have not been included on any previous lists. (For documentation of these four cases, see *Essex Court Records* 7:238; Middlesex Superior Court Folio Collection, folio 168a.) Finally, and most importantly, previous lists of witches have sometimes excluded persons (like Sarah Hale, Margaret Thatcher, and Mary Phips, for example, all of whom were accused during the Salem outbreak) who were not prosecuted (see above, 41). My own figures include all accusations located, whether or not accusers or accused formalized them by complaining to the authorities. It should also be noted that if I had counted individual witchcraft *cases*, rather than accused persons, the total would increase to 391, since many witches, especially female witches, were accused more than once.

2. Demos, "Underlying Themes in the Witchcraft of Seventeenth-Century New England," 1315. See also Demos, *Entertaining Satan*, 60–62.

3. Note that my numbers for accused witches in outbreak and in non-outbreak years add up to more than the total number of accused witches in New England given in the paragraph above. This discrepancy is accounted for by the 13 women who were accused both prior to and during outbreaks. In order to compare the treatment accorded witches in outbreak and non-outbreak years, these 13 women are counted twice whenever this comparison is made.

4. *Particular Court Records,* 93.

5. See Demos, *Entertaining Satan,* 348–49, for the most successful effort to reconstruct the background and social position of John (and Joan) Carrington. I would also like to thank Phyllis Harris and Russell A. Williams, both of whom are married to Carrington descendants, for their kind assistance in my own efforts to recreate the histories of John and Joan Carrington.

6. The experiences of two of the three women who were punished are detailed below. For Eunice Cole, see below, 52–57; for Katherine Harrison, see 84–89. Elizabeth Seager, who fled from Connecticut to Rhode Island, is discussed above, 26.

7. See Boyer and Nissenbaum, *Salem Possessed,* 54–56 and 195–98 for the best reconstructions of the backgrounds of George Burroughs and John Willard. The testimony presented against these two men can be found in *Witchcraft Papers* 1:151–78; 3:819–52.

8. The records of these last Salem cases are in *Witchcraft Papers* 3:903–44. The quotation is on 938. See also C. Mather, *Wonders of the Invisible World,* 216.

9. Wyllys Papers Supplement, 1.

10. See, for instance, John Hale's discussion of efforts to bring Margaret Jones and Alice Lake to confession, in *Modest Enquiry,* 17–18. Even when confessions were described as voluntary, the evidence indicates efforts on the part of religious and secular authorities (and sometimes neighbors) to elicit this response from accused women. See, for instance, John Whiting's description of Rebecca Greensmith's confession in Whiting, "Letter," 468.

11. C. Mather, "Memorable Providences," 135–36; *Particular Court Records,* 56.

12. I. Mather, *Remarkable Providences,* 137–39; *Particular Court Records,* 258; Wyllys Papers Supplement, 44–45.

13. C. Mather, "Memorable Providences," 103–6.

14. Confessed witch Mary Parsons of Springfield can be seen as an exception to this pre-1692 pattern. She was tried in 1651 for both witchcraft and infanticide, but was convicted and executed for infanticide (see *Mass. Records* 3:229; Hale, *Modest Enquiry,* 19). However, because infanticide was a crime associated with witchcraft in early New England (see below, 141), it is difficult to distinguish between the two crimes in this case. Another possible exception was 16-year-old Elizabeth Knapp, who confessed and retracted her confession several times during her possession experience in 1672–73 (see below, 236–41). Seventeenth-century sources do not treat her as a confessed witch but as a possessed person. As we shall see, young women, like men of any age, were considered unlikely witches in early New England.

15. *Essex Court Records* 1:265.

16. Ibid. 5:426–27.

17. Crimes and Misdemeanors 1 (pt. 1): docs. 185–86.

18. One 16-year-old, the son of a minister, acknowledged communicating with the Devil and was not rebuked for lying; however, like Elizabeth Knapp, he was seen not as an admitted witch but as a possessed person who was confessing to sins that brought the Devil to him. See C. Mather, "Memorable Providences," 136–41.

19. *Essex Court Records* 1:88, and see also 129, 143, 238, 313; Essex County Quarterly Court File Papers, Works Progress Administration Transcripts, 75 vols. (Essex Institute, Salem, Mass.), 1: doc. 93 (here-

after cited as Essex Court File Papers); Records of the Quarterly Court, Ipswich, 1645–1663 (manuscript volume, Essex Institute, Salem, Mass.), doc. 12; Norfolk Court Records, 1648–1678 (manuscript volume, Essex Institute, Salem, Mass.), docs. 30, 50.

20. These depositions are in Massachusetts Archives 135:2–3. Additional testimony presented against Eunice Cole at this time can be found in Suffolk Court Files 2:256a; Trials for Witchcraft in New-England (unpaged), dated 5 September 1656 (manuscript volume, Houghton Library, Harvard University, Cambridge, Mass.).

21. "The humble petition of Unice Coles, wife of William Coles of Hampton, Now prisoner in Boston," undated doc., Massachusetts Archives 10:261.

We cannot be *sure* that Cole was convicted of witchcraft at this time, because the surviving evidence is open to conflicting interpretations. John Demos, for instance, argues that "there is reason to conclude" that she was not. He bases his argument on the fact that she was not executed ("Witchcraft was a capital crime in Massachusetts Bay, and a judgment of guilt invariably brought the death sentence") and on references in local records that suggest that she was in Hampton in 1658 and possibly in 1659. (See *Entertaining Satan*, 322; 494–95, nn. 48–49.)

I find the evidence for a guilty verdict more persuasive. First, as I argue in chapter 1, after Ann Hibbens's execution earlier in 1656, New England magistrates were more cautious than before in their treatment of witches. At least three of the seven persons who were clearly convicted of witchcraft in the three decades following Hibbens's death were not executed. Cole may well have been another, especially considering the brief time period between Hibbens's hanging and Cole's trial. Equally important, an indeterminate prison sentence such as the one Cole said she received, though rare for anyone in early New England, would have been a highly unlikely punishment for a less serious crime. Other documents confirm, moreover, that Cole was actually in prison for an extended, if intermittent, period. In addition, when setting conditions for Cole's possible release several years later, the magistrates threatened to carry out "hir former sentenc" if she did not abide by their terms, and her reappearance in jail at a later time suggests that they followed through with this threat.

Although Eunice Cole was clearly in Hampton at least briefly in late 1660 and again in late 1662, I am not persuaded that she was out of prison before late 1659. Demos has uncovered a previously unknown reference to a payment to the Hampton constable "for

Expense about G. Coule" for 1658 that he finds establishes her presence in Hampton at that time. But other evidence indicates that this expense was for her husband (Goodman, rather than Goodwife, Cole). In a 1659 petition, William Cole said that the town of Hampton had provided him with relief, and later records show that the town did take some responsibility for his maintenance in the years before his death in 1662. (See below, text and notes, for William Cole's subsequent history and supporting documentation for this interpretation.)

22. "The humble petition of Unice Coles." Possibly because the General Court responded to one of Cole's petitions in October 1662, other historians have attributed this undated document to that year. (See, for instance, Demos, *Entertaining Satan*, 323; 495 n. 5; Joseph Dow, *The History of the Town of Hampton, New Hampshire* (Salem, Mass., 1893), 1:68 (hereafter cited as Dow, *History of Hampton*.) However, in this petition, Cole mentioned that she was given her indeterminate prison sentence by the Massachusetts Court of Assistants "the last first month," which by the colonial calendar would have been the previous March. Since there is no evidence that Cole was tried again by the Court of Assistants early in 1662 (or late in 1661), I find it more likely that this petition was written earlier. I suspect that in the wake of the controversy over Ann Hibbens's execution, the magistrates put off their decision about her sentence in her 1656 trial until March 1657, and that Cole sent her petition to the General Court within the following year.

It has not been possible to confirm the date of this document by the age Eunice Cole attributed to her husband. The only available independent estimate of William Cole's age has him 88 early in 1659; see John Demos, "Old Age in Early New England," in *The American Family in Social-Historical Perspective*, 2d ed., ed. Michael Gordon (New York, 1978), 247. Although this evidence ostensibly supports my argument that the document was probably written earlier than other writers have said, given the casualness with which early New Englanders kept track of their ages we can assume possible error in records of adult ages of several years in either direction. Eunice Cole's own age, incidentally, is nowhere recorded.

23. Dow, *History of Hampton*, 1:68. This petition has been lost since Dow wrote his history of the town. The first and last quotations in this paragraph are Dow's paraphrasing of William Cole's plea.

24. Town Book of Hampton, 2:343 (manuscript volume, Town Offices, Hampton, N.H.). See also *Essex Court Records* 3:3, for additional evidence concerning the community's economic assistance to

William Cole in the years before his death in 1662. As early as October 1656, a month after his wife's witchcraft trial, William Cole had deeded a parcel of land to his neighbor, Thomas Webster, in exchange for "the carrying of six loades of wood every winter untill . . . tenn pounds bee payd." See Norfolk Deeds (manuscript volume, Registry of Deeds, Essex County Courthouse, Salem, Mass.), 1:97–98.

25. Although this deed has not survived, it was brought into the Hampton court on 10 October 1671, where one of the original witnesses, Thomas Bradbury, testified that the signature was William Cole's. See *Essex Court Records* 4:428. These court records do not tell us why or for whom this deed was at issue 15 years after it was filed, but it is worth noting that in 1671, Eunice Cole had recently returned to Hampton, with few if any resources, and the town had required all of its inhabitants to contribute to her support (see text, below). Also significant, at roughly the same time that he was testifying about the Cole deed, the witness Thomas Bradbury was also a witness in a protracted inheritance battle involving another accused witch, Susanna Martin—and in the Martin case, the evidence strongly suggests that he was lying. (See below, 89–95.)

26. Dow, *History of Hampton* 1:68.

27. See *Essex Court Records* 2:375; Norfolk Court File Papers, 1650–1680 (Essex Institute, Salem, Mass.), docs. 16, 18.

28. Since the exact dates of both William Cole's death and Eunice Cole's petition were not recorded, it is not clear which came first. If I am correct in my assumption that Eunice Cole's first petition for her release was submitted in 1657 or early 1658, then the contents of her 1662 plea are unknown.

29. This will and some of the subsequent legal actions regarding it are recorded in *Probate Records of the Province of New Hampshire,* Provincial, Town, and State Papers Series, 31, ed. Albert Stillman Batchellor (Concord, N.H., 1907), 53–55 (hereafter cited as *New Hampshire Probate Records*). The original will, along with an inventory of the estate, are in Essex County Probates (Registry of Probates, Essex County Courthouse, Salem, Mass.), doc. 6001. See also *Essex Court Records* 3:3, 61, 100; Norfolk Court Records, 1648–1678, docs. 56, 60, 65.

30. *Mass. Records* 4 (pt. 2): 70. See also *Essex Court Records* 3:3, 61, 100; Drake, *Annals of Witchcraft,* 100.

31. See Massachusetts Archives 135:16; Suffolk Court Files 13:1228. These two documents, part of the record of Eunice Cole's 1673 witchcraft trial (see below, text), refer to November 1662, when

the suspicions were first expressed. See also *Essex Court Records* 3:4 for documentation of a 14 October 1662 payment to Henry Green, "out of old Cole's estate for watching one day and one night with Eunice Coul." Since this payment was made only a week after the General Court set the conditions for Cole's release, it is possible that the county court paid Green for a "watching" of her while she was still in the Boston jail. (See *Mass. Records* 3:126 for an example of a court-ordered observation of accused witch Margaret Jones in 1648.) If so, it may have been that when Cole's former Hampton neighbors heard about her petition to the General Court for her release, they responded not only by counter-petitioning to keep her in jail, but also by arranging for a "watching" to bolster their position—to prove that the Devil or one of her familiars still came to her.

It is not clear when or why Cole was returned to jail. If she was tried again for witchcraft in late 1662 or in 1663, there is no record of it. More likely, she could not meet the condition that she leave the colony for good, and the General Court simply lived up to its promise to put her back in prison if she did not.

32. *Essex Court Records* 3:61, 64, 100; *New Hampshire Probate Records,* 54–55; Norfolk Court Records, 1648–1678, docs. 56, 60, 65. The "one-half" paid to the selectmen for Eunice Cole's "use" was only £8, despite a 1663 inventory that established that William Cole's estate, after debts, amounted to £41.0.5. Possibly it was so small because some of it had been used to pay William Salter for at least part of the cost of her prison maintenance. (See below, text, and *Essex Court Records* 3:100.)

33. Dow, *History of Hampton* 1:67–68; *Mass. Records* 4 (pt. 2):106. The remaining £8 in the Cole estate was paid to Salter after his dramatic move, but it was insufficient to meet his past expenses for Eunice Cole's maintenance, let alone his current ones, which ran about £8 per year. See Drake, *Annals of Witchcraft,* 100–1.

34. *Mass. Records* 4 (pt. 2):149.

35. Dow, *History of Hampton* 1:79–80. See also Massachusetts Archives 135:13; Drake, *Annals of Witchcraft,* 101–2.

36. For the testimony presented against Cole at this time, see Massachusetts Archives 135:4–17 (quotations are from 9 and 13); Suffolk Court Files 13:1228.

37. *Records of the Court of Assistants of the Colony of Massachusetts Bay, 1630–1692,* ed. John Noble and John F. Cronin (Boston, 1901–28), 3:254 (hereafter cited as *Mass. Assistants Records*).

38. *New Hampshire Court Records, 1640–1692,* Provincial, Town, and State Papers Series, 40, ed. Otis G. Hammond (New Hampshire, 1943), 368.

39. Samuel A. Drake, *A Book of New England Legends and Folklore in Prose and Poetry* (Boston, 1901), 328–31. See also Demos, *Entertaining Satan,* 338; 501, n. 130.

40. *Essex Court Records* 1:142. Additional references to John Godfrey's offenses are scattered throughout the local and colony court records. See, for example, Ibid. 1:168, 179; 2:175, 297; 3:240; 4:130–31, 185–87. For a more thorough investigation of Godfrey's life and witchcraft history, see Demos, *Entertaining Satan,* 36–56. My own account is heavily indebted to Demos's reconstruction.

41. John Godfrey was one of only two New England men tried for witchcraft prior to the Salem outbreak who was not related to a female witch.

42. For reference to Godfrey as a usuror, see *Essex Court Records* 4:78–79.

43. Trials for Witchcraft in New-England (unpaged), dated 27 June 1659.

44. *Essex Court Records* 2:159–60.

45. Suffolk Court Files 2:322. Additional witchcraft testimony presented against John Godfrey in 1659 is reprinted in *Essex Court Records* 2:157–60.

46. *Essex Court Records* 2:157.

47. Ibid. 2:166.

48. Demos, *Entertaining Satan,* 42.

49. *Essex Court Records* 3:6–7, 27–28, 39–40, 55, 74, 120–22, 166–67, 214, 222.

50. Ibid. 3:74, 120. Singletary had also testified against Godfrey in Godfrey's 1659 witchcraft trial. See Suffolk Court Files 2:322.

51. *Essex Court Records* 3:120–22. See also Suffolk Court Files 4:543.

52. Testimony submitted during Godfrey's 1665–66 trial is in *Mass. Assistants Records* 3:158–61; Suffolk Court Files 7:725. John Demos argues that Godfrey was probably tried in 1663 as well as in 1665–66. (See *Entertaining Satan,* 44 and 421, n. 30.) He bases his conclusion on evidence that Jonathan Singletary's statement in his defense against Godfrey's defamation suit was subsequently filed in Boston (where a trial would have been held) and on Singletary's alleged remark: "Is this witch on this syde Boston Galloes yet." Given Single-

tary's animosity toward Godfrey and his assumption that Godfrey was a witch, he might well have made this remark about the gallows whether or not a trial had ensued. The filing of Singletary's testimony is more persuasive. However, it could just as easily have been filed during Godfrey's 1665 trial, given that other former complaints were brought in at this time. On the other side of the argument— besides the lack of any mention of a trial in the records—the local court found for Godfrey in his defamation suit against Singletary, both initially in 1663, and in 1664, when it was appealed. With Godfrey so recently cleared by either the General Court or the Court of Assistants (1659), when at least two dozen people had petitioned for their complaints against him to be heard, it seems unlikely that the local court would again find in Godfrey's favor in the slander suit *and* request that the higher court prosecute him.

53. *Mass. Assistants Records* 3:151–52.

54. See *Essex Court Records* 4:152–55; *Mass. Assistants Records,* 3:152–58. The quotation is from *Mass. Assistants Records* 3:152.

55. See Demos, *Entertaining Satan,* 48–49.

56. *Essex Court Records* 7:355–59; Essex Court File Papers 32: docs. 130–33. See also Demos, *Entertaining Satan,* 133–37, 148–49; Joshua Coffin, *A Sketch of the History of Newbury, Newburyport, and West Newbury, from 1635 to 1845* (Boston, 1845), 122–26.

57. *New Haven Colony Records* 2:152.

58. Hammond, *New Hampshire Court Records,* 368.

59. See, for instance, *Essex Court Records* 4:133, for the £100 bond required of Susanna Martin in 1669. The largest bond that I have located in a male witchcraft case is the £20 demanded of Caleb Powell in 1679. Some women, including Elizabeth Godman, were not given the option of a bond after the county court heard the complaints against them, but were simply committed to prison until their cases came up in the higher court. See *New Haven Town Records* 1:252.

60. See, for instance, Hammond, *New Hampshire Court Records,* 127, 137, 148–49, 252, 413–14, 455–60, 464; *Province Records and Court Papers, from 1680 to 1692, Collections of the New Hampshire Historical Society,* 8, ed. Nathaniel Bouton (Concord, N.H., 1866), 99–100. While Jones's husband, Alexander, was still alive, he represented her interests (and his own) in court.

61. Bouton, *Province Records and Court Papers,* 99.

62. For more on the political and economic context of the Jones-Walton dispute, see Richard Chamberlain, "Lithobolia," in Burr,

Narratives, 53–77, esp. Burr's introduction and notes.

63. Hammond, *New Hampshire Court Records,* 38.

64. Ibid., 122, 129; Bouton, *Documents and Records Relating to New Hampshire,* 217–19.

65. Hammond, *New Hampshire Court Records,* 258; Bouton, *Documents and Records Relating to New Hampshire,* 219; "Witchcraft in New Hampshire in 1656," *New England Historical and Genealogical Register* 43 (1889):181–83.

66. Bouton, *Province Records and Court Papers,* 100; Chamberlain, "Lithobolia," 60–61, n. 3.

67. *New Haven Colony Records* 2:88–89.

68. Wyllys Papers Supplement, 5, 16–18, 54; Wyllys Papers, docs. 32, 41–42.

69. The other man was James Wakeley of Wethersfield, Conn., who was first accused during the Hartford outbreak. See Wyllys Papers Supplement, 45–46. Wakeley does not seem to have been prosecuted, but apparently out of fear for his safety, he twice fled to Rhode Island, the second time for good. The best reconstruction of Wakeley's history is in Demos, *Entertaining Satan,* 353–55.

70. *Particular Court Records,* 261; Wyllys Papers Supplement, 44.

71. Bouton, *Documents and Records Relating to New Hampshire,* 219.

72. Like ourselves, early Americans varied considerably in their experience of, and their thoughts about, old age and aging. In 17th-c. New England, where demographic evidence indicates that life expectancy was unusually high for the time, and persons over 60 made up roughly 10 percent of the adult population, age 60 was widely regarded as the point at which old age began. For discussion of this issue, and what old age meant in this society, see Demos, "Old Age in Early New England," 220–56. See also, below, 215–17 for suggestions that New Englanders responded differently to old age in women and old age in men.

73. Documents for these cases are found in *Witchcraft Papers* 1:255; 2:351–53, 662; 3:727–28, 994, 1019–20; *Particular Court Records,* 261; Wyllys Papers Supplement, 44; Hammond, *New Hampshire Court Records,* 368; Bouton, *Documents and Records Relating to New Hampshire,* 416–17.

74. Conclusions about the ages of witches must be tentative because so many of the accused cannot be identified by age. Katherine Harrison of Wethersfield, for example, formally accused of witchcraft for

the first time in 1668, seems to have been about 40 at this time, but she could have been several years older or younger. Because precise information is lacking, she, like so many others, cannot be counted.

75. Documents relating to Sarah Good's trial are in *Witchcraft Papers* 2:355–78, 612–13; 3:746–47, 994, 1019–20.

76. The Dustin and Colson records are in: Ibid. 1:151, 237–38, 273–77, 319; 2:370–71, 487, 539–41, 550; 3:838–39, 935–37. For earlier accusations lodged against Lydia Dustin and her two daughters, see Middlesex Superior Court Folio Collection, 168a.

77. See Demos, *Entertaining Satan*, esp. 64–70, and 153–210.

78. The Elizabeth Kendall case is mentioned in Hale, *Modest Enquiry*, 18–19.

79. See Wyllys Papers, docs. 23, 25, 32, 34–35, 37–41; Wyllys Papers Supplement, 5–6, 9, 35–36; Tomlinson, *Witchcraft Trials*, 59–64.

80. *Mass. Assistants Records* 1:159, 189–90. Most of the testimony presented against Elizabeth Morse has been reprinted in Drake, *Annals of Witchcraft*, 258–96. Additional documents can be found in Coffin, *History of Newbury*, 122–34. For a comprehensive discussion of this case see Demos, *Entertaining Satan*, 132–52.

81. Cotton Mather, *Ornaments for the Daughters of Zion. Or the Character and Happiness of a Vertuous Woman* . . . (Cambridge, Mass., 1692), 103–4.

82. Whiting, "Letter," 468; C. Mather, "Memorable Providences," 100.

83. See, for example, Richard Rowland's accusation of Jane James of Marblehead in 1667 and Richod Holman's accusation of Elizabeth Hooper of Salem in 1678. *Essex Court Records* 3:413; 6:387.

84. This ratio is an estimate based on Linda Bissell, "Family, Friends, and Neighbors: Social Interaction in Seventeenth-Century Windsor, Connecticut" (Ph.D. diss., Brandeis University, 1973); John Demos, *A Little Commonwealth;* John Faragher, "Old Women and Old Men in Seventeenth-Century Wethersfield, Connecticut," *Women's Studies* 4 (1976): 11–31; Susan L. Norton, "Population Growth in Colonial America: A Study of Ipswich, Massachusetts," *Population Studies* 25 (November 1971): 433–52.

Of these, only Bissell provides an age structure for the population; from this I derived a ratio of 1:4.7 for women 60 and over to women 40–59. For Plymouth, Ipswich, and Wethersfield, I converted mortality tables into approximate age structures by calculating the numbers of every 100 20-year-old females surviving in the population at age 40, at age 49, at age 59, and so on. This technique collapses a longitudinal view into a cross-sectional analysis and, barring any significant atypicality in the sample, should yield a roughly accurate picture of age distribution. The possibility of a degree of error that would make the figures unusable is diminished by basing the construction of the mortality tables, in all three cases, on 17th-c. populations over time. These calculations yielded the following ratios: for Plymouth, 1:2.6; for Ipswich, 1:3.1; for Wethersfield, 1:2.6.

Although the Bissell figure would certainly provide the most dramatic demonstration of the argument being made in these pages, it is so at odds with life expectancies generally derived for the 17th c. that I have virtually excluded it from consideration. (See, for example, John Demos, "Old Age in Early New England," esp. 227–28.) I have arrived at my estimated ratio of 1:2.5 by rounding the other three figures downward. Since the community of these three that was most like the towns touched by witchcraft accusations—Ipswich—has the highest of these ratios, the selection of 1:2.5 should ensure a substantial bias against the argument. (See above, 145, for description of the kind of towns in which witchcraft accusations were most likely to occur.)

85. This overall age pattern seems to hold for men as well as women (see table A). Although the pre-Salem data are too sparse to discuss separately from the Salem data, we do have enough information on 34 of the 75 men accused of witchcraft in the 17th c. to show that accusations of men under 40 were rarely taken seriously, that more middle-aged than old men were accused, but that *once accused,* men who were 60 or older appear to have been more vulnerable than middle-aged men to trial, conviction, and execution. Since most of the data pertain to the Salem outbreak, when men were most at risk, these figures are only useful for discussing that event. Of the two

TABLE A. Age Groups, Male Witches, New England, 1620–1725

Action	Men under 40	Men 40–59	Men over 60	Total
Accused	18	12	4	34
Tried	3	3	2	8
Convicted	0	3	2	5
Executed	0	3	2	5

men who were tried, convicted, and executed prior to Salem, one, 49-year-old John Carrington, is included in these figures. The other, Nathaniel Greensmith, is not, because no record of his age exists. His wife, Rebecca Greensmith, however, was the woman minister John Whiting described as "considerably aged"; but other documents show that she gave birth to her last child in 1646 and therefore could not have been much older than 62 or 63 when she was accused of witchcraft. Nathaniel Greensmith may or may not have been about the same age.

86. Since my figures (and hence my conclusions) about the ages of witches differ from those presented by John Demos in *Entertaining Satan* (see esp. 64–70), a word about this difference is in order. Counting both male and female witches, Demos finds that more than half of the accused were middle-aged (67 percent outside of the Salem outbreak, 44 percent during this outbreak), while I find only a third of all the accused fit into this category (36 percent outside of the Salem events, 31 percent during them). I cannot account for all of this discrepancy, but perhaps for most of it.

Our numbers for old persons among the accused are actually quite similar (the small difference here can be attributed, I suspect, primarily to Demos's counting persons age 60 among the middle-aged, while I include them among the old). The more significant discrepancy in the overall percentages lies in my finding many more people *under 40* (by my calculations, a little over half of the accused; by Demos's, less than a third). This difference seems to have to do with the total number of accused witches each of us has located and with Demos's willingness to estimate ages in many cases and my reluctance to do so. In large part thanks to the work done by Demos (and others), my overall figure for accused witches is higher (344 as compared to 234), but because I have done less age estimating, our total age data figures are almost identical (200 as compared with 199, although the persons these numbers represent are not necessarily the same). My hesitation about age estimates has to do with the necessity of making many of them on the basis of recorded ages of spouses. Since I have found many witches who were either considerably older or considerably younger than their spouses (and suspect that that may have been a factor in the accusation itself), I have used estimates only when other evidence, such as the ages of children, supports placement in a particular age range. Because of this reluctance to estimate, my figures no doubt overstate the proportion of persons *under* 40 among the accused and understate the proportions of both middle-aged and older persons, since the existing age records are biased towards younger people. It is in part to correct for this bias in the records that I have also counted the number of people tried, convicted, and executed in each age group, since persons under 40 were rarely prosecuted.

More significant, of course, are the different meanings Demos and I assign to these figures, which influences what other issues we want taken into consideration. In arguing, as I do, that women over 40 were the main targets of witchcraft fears and that women appear to have become even more vulnerable as they aged, I place considerable weight on the age at accusation and on the numbers of middle-aged and old women in the larger population at risk to be accused. I also find the treatment accorded accused witches, both by the authorities and the rest of the community, to be especially relevant. Demos, on the other hand, in arguing that the primary targets of witch fears were middle-aged women (and that the psychology of accusers is particularly relevant here), emphasizes not only the age of a woman at the time of accusation, but her age at the time accusers said their suspicions were first aroused.

87. See Calef, "More Wonders of the Invisible World," 385.

88. Among male witches, the overall marital status picture is somewhat different. As with the age category, the pre-Salem numbers are too small to summarize separately. Still, 49 of the 75 men accused of witchcraft in early New England can be identified by marital status (see Table B). Not unexpectedly, given that most female witches were married and that husbands of witches were the most suspect group of males, married men predominated among those males accused, tried, convicted, and executed. Also not surprisingly, most of the males in the single category were young sons of (female)

TABLE B. Marital Status of Male Witches, New England, 1620–1725

Action	Single	Married	Widowed	Divorced/ Deserted	Total
Accused	15	33	1	0	49
Tried	3	11	0	0	14
Convicted	0	7	0	0	7
Executed	0	7	0	0	7

witches. Where the male pattern sharply diverges from the female one, however, is in the widowed category: unlike widows, widowers were not a suspect group in their communities.

89. Sarah Dustin was 39 when she was accused of witchcraft in 1692. The records concerning her arrest and trial are in *Witchcraft Papers* 1:277; 3:936–37.

90. For documents relating to the Godman case, see *New Haven Colony Records* 2:29–36, 151–52; *New Haven Town Records* 1:249–52, 256–57, 264.

91. Interestingly, this group of women may have had a male counterpart among accused witches. Soldiers, seamen, and other men in transient occupations show up among accused men often enough to encourage questions about them. Unfortunately, the lack of marital status (and other) information on them makes it impossible to know whether, like John Godfrey, they were older, single men, or men who had spouses in other parts of the colonies or in England. As with their female counterparts (excepting itinerant Quaker preachers), accusations against them were rarely taken seriously by the authorities.

92. Data on widows and spinsters in 17th-c. New England are sparse—both because these groups tend to be underrecorded in the documents and because few historians have been interested in studying women apart from families in the colonial period. Thus, the ratio presented is an estimate, patched together from pieces of information in a variety of studies, and arbitrarily doubled to bias the calculations against the argument.

Daniel Scott Smith has estimated that permanent spinsters represented roughly 5 percent of adult females in 17th-c. New England (see "Inheritance and the Position and Orientation of Colonial Women," paper presented at the Second Berkshire Conference on the History of Women, Radcliffe College, 27 October 1974). This percentage is generally supported by two other findings. First, it is entirely congruent with Kenneth Lockridge's finding that spinsters and children accounted for 20 percent of the population of Dedham, Massachusetts, in 1700: if only one-fourth of that number were spinsters, the data would conform to Smith's estimate (see Lockridge's "The Population of Dedham, Massachusetts, 1636–1736," *Economic History Review*, 2d ser., 19 [1966]:325). Also, Philip Greven has discovered that 7.4 percent of the third-generation females of Andover never married. These women reached adulthood in the early 18th c., at a time of rising marriage ages for women, and may represent an unprecedented surge in spinsterhood in the Andover population; indirectly, their numbers give weight to a 5 percent figure of the 17th c. (See Greven, *Four Generations: Population, Land, and Family in Colonial Andover, Massachusetts* [Ithaca, N.Y., 1970], 121.) All of these calculations are for permanent spinsters in the adult female population as a whole. When we narrow this to the adult female population over 30, the proportion would, if anything, increase—since married women experienced their highest mortality rates during their childbearing years.

Estimates of the percentage of widows in the adult female population can be calculated by converting mortality tables into age structures and figuring female survivors for each decade (see n. 84 above). For Ipswich, Plymouth, and Wethersfield, respectively, this yields estimates of 6.9 percent, 2 percent, and 17 percent. I have biased these figures upward by not correcting for remarriage. Clearly, widowhood was a fluctuating social phenomenon in the 17th c. The average of these figures, 8.6 percent, seems a fair estimate; indeed, that it is uncorrected for remarriage and is higher than the Ipswich figure ensures a bias against the argument.

These two estimates, then, yield a combined figure of 13.6 percent for the female population over 30. The estimate I have used (20 percent) is half again as high and assumes as many deserted and divorced women as spinsters or widows.

93. Here, too, my figures (and my conclusions) differ somewhat from those of John Demos (see *Entertaining Satan*, 72–75, and "Underlying Themes in the Witchcraft of Seventeenth-Century New England," 1315). Including male and female witches, Demos finds almost 80 percent of the non-Salem accused and 57 percent of the Salem group were married. My percentages for married witches, male and female, are 74 percent for the non-Salem cases and 53 percent for the Salem cases. Again, the difference can be attributed primarily to the larger number of accused witches that I have located and the larger number of young, single persons among them. Also important, I have found several widows who were not on Demos's list of accused witches, three of whom were accused after the Salem outbreak. We both conclude that women without husbands were more vulnerable than married women after accusations were lodged, but I place greater emphasis on marital status as a factor in the accusation itself.

94. *Witchcraft Papers* 3:720.

95. See Wyllys Papers, docs. 6–17; Wyllys Papers Supplement,

46–53; Hubbard, *General History of New England,* 574; *Essex Court Records* 7:329–30; C. Mather, *Wonders of the Invisible World,* 129–38.

96. Susanna Martin, for instance, had been accused, and possibly tried and acquitted, in 1669, when her husband was alive, but was convicted and executed after she became a widow. See below, 89–95.

97. John Cotton, *A Meet Help, or a Wedding Sermon, Preached at New-Castle in New England, June 19th, 1694* . . . (Boston, 1699), 12, 23.

Chapter Three
The Economic Basis of Witchcraft

1. Macfarlane, *Witchcraft in Tudor and Stuart England,* 149–51. See also Thomas, *Religion and the Decline of Magic,* 457, 520–21, 560–68.

2. See Trials for Witchcraft in New England (unpaged), dated 5 September 1656.

3. On Ann Dolliver, see "Letter from Rev. John Higginson to his son Nathaniel Higginson, August 31, 1698," *Essex Institute Historical Collections* 43 (1907), 182–86; "From Rev. John Higginson of Salem, to his son Nathaniel," letter dated 20 June 1699, *Collections of the Massachusetts Historical Society,* 3d ser., 7 (1838), 198–200; *Witchcraft Papers* 1:271–72; John J. Babson, *History of the Town of Gloucester, Cape Ann, Including the Town of Rockport* (Gloucester, Mass., 1860), 80–81; Sidney Perley, *The History of Salem, Massachusetts,* 3 vols. (Salem, Mass., 1924–28), 1:157–58.

4. Relying on very general indicators (a married woman who worked as a servant, a widow whose husband had left an estate of £39, and so forth), I was able to make rough estimates about the economic position of 150 accused women. Twenty-nine of these women seem to have been poor. Until we have a more detailed picture of women's lives in the 17th c., however, and better ways of conceptualizing women's class experience, we cannot know the extent to which poor women were overrepresented among the accused.

5. For Abigail Somes, see *Witchcraft Papers* 3:733–37; Babson, *History of Gloucester,* 160, 211; Heyrman, *Commerce and Culture,* 105 n, 116–17. For Tituba, see *Witchcraft Papers* 3:745–57. Documents relating to Ruth Wilford are in *Witchcraft Papers* 2:459; 3:961;

The Probate Records of Essex County, Massachusetts, 1635–1681, 3 vols. (Salem, Mass., 1916–20), 3:93–95 (hereafter cited as *Essex Probate Records*). For Sarah Good, see below, 110–12.

6. My conclusion about the economic position of the accused is supported by John Demos's early work on New England witchcraft, which focused on the Salem outbreak. His more recent and more detailed study, however, which deals almost exclusively with the non-Salem cases, argues that prior to 1692, most of the accused came from the low ranks of New England society. (See "Underlying Themes," 1316–17; *Entertaining Satan,* 84–86, 285–92). I agree that during the Salem outbreak (and, I would add, during the Hartford and Fairfield outbreaks as well), prosperous and high-ranking persons were accused more often than they had been at other times, but I find Demos's interpretation of the non-Salem cases problematic. The discrepancy in our arguments here probably has to do both with our different emphases—Demos's on the rank (or status) of the accused, mine on their (or their families') economic position—and with the lack of precise measures of either rank or economic position for the colonial period, especially for women.

The difficulty of categorizing women is perhaps best illustrated by looking at accused witch Elizabeth Godman of New Haven. Although Demos does not mention her social and economic status in *Entertaining Satan,* in his earlier article he described her, much as other historians have, as "poor and perhaps a beggar." (See "Underlying Themes," 1316.) She was a widow or spinster with no household of her own, and a witness who testified against her in her 1655 witchcraft trial said that she had come to his house to beg beer. On the other hand, Godman is called "Mrs." and "Mistress" in the records (as was her only sister, who lived in England) and her possessions included books and a silk gown—indications in the colonial period of both material prosperity and status. Her estate at her death in 1660, moreover, amounted to almost £200 (a sizeable estate at the time, although most of it was in the hands of New Haven's deputy governor, Stephen Goodyear, in whose household she had lived for several years). Her neighbors' remarks about her and the control of her estate by Goodyear can legitimately be seen as indications of both low status and poverty. But Godman can also be seen as a woman from a well-off if not wealthy English family who, because she was a woman alone in New England, had an anomalous status in her neighbors' eyes and was not allowed access to her own economic resources. For records concerning Godman, see *New Haven Town*

Records 1:249–52, 256–57, 264, 462–67, 478; 2:38; *New Haven Colony Records* 2:29–36, 151–52, 306, 497–98.

If Demos has included Godman and other women who shared her ambiguous position in his "low rank" category, that would explain some of the difference in our interpretation. It is also possible that both his "low" and "low middle" ranks include other women—women whose fathers or husbands had estates at their deaths valued at roughly £100 to £200—many but not all of whom I see as "middling." For my own way of conceptualizing New England's economic structure, see text and n. 7, below.

7. Most families in 17th-c. New England had estates worth less than £200. However, since only a very small proportion of convicted witches who were married seem to have come from families with estates worth *more* than £200, it seems reasonable to conclude that married women from families with less than £200 estates were over-represented among the accused. Nearly all of the convictions of married women from families with estates worth more than £200 occurred during the Salem outbreak.

In an attempt to solve the problem of inadequate records concerning the economic position of accused women, I have created three categories within which to place them: from families with estates valued at more than £500, from families with estates valued at between £200 and £500, and from families with estates worth less than £200. In the minds of many New Englanders, possession of a £200 estate distinguished a family "of quality" from other colonists and therefore seems a reasonable dividing line between the majority of colonists and their "betters." The £500 estate dividing line between the "prosperous" and the "wealthy" is more arbitrary, but it seems to fit with general colonial conceptions. Given that most people lived in families with under £200 estates, the designation "middling" overlaps the under £200 estate and the £200 to £500 estate categories.

However the economic pyramid of colonial society is drawn, in most cases placement of individuals within it is impressionistic and subject to error. Often we can locate the value of a family's estate only at the time of death of its eldest male property owner, and by that time the estate may have been substantially reduced by the transfer of property to adult children.

8. Most of the women mentioned here are discussed at greater length elsewhere in this chapter. For Ann Hibbens, Katherine Harrison, Elizabeth Blackleach, and Margaret Thatcher, see below, 84–89, 106, 150–52. Documentation of the accusations against Hannah

Griswold and Margaret Gifford can be found in "Conn. Assistants Records," 6–7; *Essex Court Records* 7:405; 8:23.

9. This discussion of the inheritance system of 17th-c. New England is drawn from the following sources: *The Book of the General Lawes and Libertyes Concerning the Inhabitants of the Massachusetts,* ed. Thomas G. Barnes (facsimile from the 1648 edition, San Marino, Calif., 1975); *The Colonial Laws of Massachusetts. Reprinted from the Edition of 1672, with the Supplements through 1686,* ed. William H. Whitmore (Boston, 1887); John D. Cushing, comp., *The Laws and Liberties of Massachusetts, 1641–91: A Facsimile Edition,* 3 vols. (Wilmington, Del., 1976); *Massachusetts Province Laws, 1692–1699,* ed. John D. Cushing (Wilmington, Del., 1978); *The Earliest Laws of the New Haven and Connecticut Colonies, 1639–1673,* ed. John D. Cushing (Wilmington, Del., 1977); *New Hampshire Probate Records; Essex Probate Records; A Digest of the Early Connecticut Probate Records,* 1, ed. Charles W. Manwaring (Hartford, 1904) (hereafter cited as *Conn. Probate Records*); Marylynn Salmon, *Women and the Law of Property in Early America* (Chapel Hill, 1986); George L. Haskins, "The Beginnings of Partible Inheritance in the American Colonies," in *Essays in the History of American Law,* ed. David H. Flaherty (Chapel Hill, 1969); Edmund S. Morgan, *The Puritan Family: Religion and Domestic Relations in Seventeenth-Century New England* (1944); reprint New York, 1966). See below, chapter 6 for more on actual inheritance practices.

10. On this point, see Morgan, *The Puritan Family,* 81–82. That there may have been varying practices here is suggested by John J. Waters, who argues that in the 18th c. at least, young men and women were expected to bring equal portions to the marriage. See "Family, Inheritance, and Migration in Colonial New England: The Evidence from Guilford, Connecticut," *William and Mary Quarterly,* 3d ser., 39 (1982): 78–79.

11. Barnes, *The Book of the General Lawes,* 17–18. In Massachusetts, the 1647 statute concerning dower also stipulated that the widow was "to have an interest in" one-third of her deceased husband's money, goods, and other personal property. In the 1660 and 1672 editions of Massachusetts' laws, this provision was deleted. In 1692, "An Act for the Settlement and Distribution of the Estates of Intestates" was passed which gave the widow a portion of the personal estate "for ever." Although historians have generally assumed that the one-third of the personal estate was for the widow's own disposing, it is not clear to what extent this was actually the case in Massachusetts over the course of the 17th c. See Barnes, *The Book of the*

General Lawes, 17–18; Cushing, *The Laws and Liberties,* 1:96, 2:268; Cushing, *Massachusetts Province Laws,* 20–21; *Essex Probate Records* 1, 2, 3, passim. See also Salmon, *Women and the Law of Property,* 147–49, for a discussion of related changes in England and Connecticut over the course of the century. In Connecticut, widows had lost whatever rights they had had to a share of their husbands' personal property by 1673. According to Salmon, in most American colonies, "dower in real property only was the rule by the beginning of the eighteenth century."

12. Since only a small proportion of men left wills during the colonial period, intestacy law played a significant role in determining inheritance practices. See Salmon, *Women and the Law of Property,* 141.

13. Barnes, *The Book of the General Lawes,* 53.

14. Young women officially came of age in New England when they reached 18; young men when they reached 21.

15. William Blackstone, *Commentaries on the Laws of England,* 4 vols. (Oxford, 1765–69), 1:433.

16. Once widowed, a woman who inherited land from her father (or who had bought land with her husband in both of their names) could make a will of her own, as could a single woman who came into possession of land. Although these were significant property rights for women, in New England few women were in a position to claim them. On this point, and other complexities of colonial women's relation to property, see Marylynn Salmon's excellent study, *Women and the Law of Property,* 144–45 and passim.

17. See below, 108–9. Although men who wrote wills and the magistrates who handled intestate cases usually stipulated that young children receive their portions "at age or time of marriage" (see, for instance, *Essex Probate Records* 1:377), the evidence suggests that in 17th-c. New England, daughters of fathers who died relatively young (and possibly most sons) did not normally come into their inheritances until they married. If daughters had received their shares when they came of age, we would expect to find probate records for single women who died before they had the opportunity to marry. Though there are many existing intestate records and wills for single men who died in early adulthood, I have located only one record involving a young, single woman.

18. Wethersfield Land Records (manuscript volume, Town Clerk's Office, Town Hall, Wethersfield, Conn.), 1:19, 38.

19. Given the ages of her children, Katherine Harrison had to have been between her late twenties and her mid-fifties when she

was first accused of witchcraft in 1668. See below, text. I suspect that she was in her forties.

20. See Wethersfield Land Records 2:149; Katherine Harrison to John Winthrop, Jr., undated letter (probably early 1667), and Katherine Harrison's Testimony, undated document (probably October 1669), in the Winthrop Papers, Massachusetts Historical Society, Boston, Mass.; Gilbert Collection, Wethersfield Historical Society Archives, Wethersfield, Conn.

21. Witnesses against Katherine Harrison in her 1669 witchcraft trial testified that Josiah Gilbert said that she "called him cousin, but he knew no such matter." See Wyllys Papers, doc. 15. John and Jonathan Gilbert, however, did not deny her claim of kinship; indeed, Jonathan Gilbert's public actions suggest a close relationship with her. See below, text and notes. See also Homer Brainerd, Harold Gilbert, and Clarence Torrey, *The Gilbert Family* (New Haven, Conn., 1953), 10–11, 64, and Demos, *Entertaining Satan*, 356–58, 513–14, n. 94, for other attempts to sort out the uncertainties of Harrison's family background.

22. Sherman W. Adams and Henry R. Stiles, *The History of Ancient Wethersfield*, 2 vols. (New York, 1904), 1: 682. Some of the court depositions submitted against Harrison date from 1668, but they were probably gathered by the local Hartford court. It is not until 11 May 1669 that we have evidence of her appearance before the higher court in connection with witchcraft. See "Conn. Assistants Records," 12.

23. "Conn. Assistants Records," 13.

24. Petition for the Investigation of Katherine Harrison, Recently Released after Imprisonment, Signed by John Chester and Thirty-eight Other Citizens of Wethersfield (Manuscript Collections, Connecticut Historical Society, Hartford, Conn.). (Emphasis mine.) See also Order about Katherine Harrison's Land, in the Winthrop Papers; Connecticut Colonial Probate Records, 56:79–81; *Conn. Records* 2:118.

25. "Conn. Assistants Records," 13–14, 18–19.

26. "The Answers of Some Ministers to the Questions Propounded to Them by the Honored Magistrates," dated 20 October 1669, Wyllys Papers Supplement, 18.

27. "Conn. Assistants Records," 23. See also *Conn. Records* 2:132.

28. Wyllys Papers Supplement, 11.

29. Depositions submitted against Harrison in 1668 and 1669 are in the Wyllys Papers, docs. 6–17; Wyllys Papers Supplement, 46–63.

Some of this testimony is reprinted in Taylor, *The Witchcraft Delusion*, 49–56. For Harrison's response to these accusations, see Katherine Harrison's Testimony, Winthrop Papers.

30. Manwaring, *Conn. Probate Records* 1:206.

31. "A Complaint of Severall Greevances of the Widdow Harrison's," Wyllys Papers Supplement, 53. A transcription of this document is in Taylor, *The Witchcraft Delusion*, 59–61.

32. "The Declaration of Katherine Harrison in her Appeal to this Court of Assistants," dated September 1668, Crimes and Misdemeanors 1 (pt. 1):34.

33. Connecticut Colonial Probate Records 56:80.

34. Ibid., 78–79. For the Griswolds as accusers, see Katherine Harrison's Testimony.

35. Connecticut Colonial Probate Records 56:80.

36. "The Declaration of Katherine Harrison," 34.

37. Manwaring, *Connecticut Probate Records*, 206.

38. Katherine Harrison to John Winthrop, Jr., "Letter."

39. Wethersfield Land Records 2:149.

40. Petition for the Investigation of Katherine Harrison.

41. See "The Cases of Hall and Harrison," in Burr, *Narratives*, 48–49.

42. Ibid., 48–52.

43. See Drake, *Annals of Witchcraft*, 133–34, for indications that witchcraft accusations against Katherine Harrison resurfaced in 1672 and 1673.

44. Connecticut Colonial Probate Records 56:118; Wethersfield Land Records 2:249.

45. Wethersfield Land Records 2:210.

46. See Gilbert Collection.

47. Joseph Merrill, *History of Amesbury, Including the First Seventeen Years of Salisbury, to the Separation of 1654; and Merrimac, From Its Incorporation in 1876* (Haverhill, Mass., 1880), 11–13, 28; *Vital Records of Salisbury, Massachusetts, to the End of the Year 1849* (Topsfield, Mass., 1915), 151, 415; Babson, *History of Gloucester*, 107–8.

48. *Mass. Records* 2:241.

49. For George Martin's objection to his wife's seating assignment in church, see Merrill, *History of Amesbury*, 89–90.

50. Merrill, *History of Amesbury*, 41, 44, 46, 50, 53, 80, 111–12; Norfolk Deeds 1:3, 6, 8, 13, 20–21, 50, 81, 109; 2 (pt. 1):1, 18, 34, 90, 106–7, 146, 179, 217, 307, 334; 3 (pt. 1):54, 112–13; 3 (pt. 2):264, 347–48.

51. *Essex Probate Records* 2:125–27. The original of this will, along with the inventory of Richard North's estate, is in Essex County Probates, doc. 19587.

52. James Savage, *A Genealogical Dictionary of the First Settlers of New England* (Boston, 1860), 1:138; 4:483; Babson, *History of Gloucester*, 107–8.

53. *Essex Court Records* 4:129, 133; Norfolk Court Records, 1648–1678, doc. 105.

54. *Essex Court Records* 4:184, 187, 239.

55. *Essex Probate Records* 2:223–24. The original of Ursula North's will, and the estate inventory, is in Essex County Probates, doc. 19588.

56. *Essex Court Records* 4:347–48. Since most of the Norfolk County court records for 1670–1672 are missing, the nature of this suit and the decision of the court has to be inferred from subsequent records. See esp. *Essex Court Records* 5:235–36; Massachusetts Archives 16:9–10.

57. Massachusetts Archives 16:9–10; 39:436–38.

58. *Mass. Records* 4 (pt. 2):540.

59. *Essex Court Records* 5:148.

60. *Mass. Records* 4 (pt. 2):555.

61. *Essex Court Records* 5:235–36.

62. *Mass. Assistants Records* 1:5–6.

63. *Essex Court Records* 5:297.

64. *Mass. Records* 5:6.

65. Ibid., 26–27.

66. Savage, *Genealogical Dictionary* 2:566; Essex County Probates, doc. 17890. When he died, George Martin left an estate valued at £75, most of which he left to Susanna "during her Widowhood."

67. Records of Susanna Martin's 1692 trial are in *Witchcraft Papers* 2:549–79. Besides the persons listed as summoned before the court and half a dozen possessed persons, several other Amesbury and Salisbury neighbors testified against her.

68. C. Mather, *Wonders of the Invisible World*, 148.

69. *Witchcraft Papers* 2:551.

70. Ibid., 572.

71. Ibid., 558–59.

72. Ibid., 561–62.

73. On Mary Bradbury, see *Witchcraft Papers* 1:115–29; Brattle, "Letter," 185; Starkey, *The Devil in Massachusetts*, 209–11.

74. *Witchcraft Papers* 2:641–42.

75. See Babson, *History of Gloucester*, 104, 126; *Vital Records of Gloucester, Massachusetts, to the End of the Year 1849*, 3 vols. (Salem, Mass., 1917–1924), 2:286, 420; *Vital Records of Salem, Massachusetts, to the End of the Year 1849*, 6 vols. (Salem, Mass., 1916–1925), 1:432; Marshall W. S. Swan, "The Bedevilment of Cape Ann (1692)," *Essex Institute Historical Collections* 117 (1981), 167–69.

76. Thomas Penney's will is in Essex County Probates, doc. 21248. It is reprinted in J. W. Penney, *A Genealogical Record of the Descendants of Thomas Penney of New Gloucester, Maine* (Portland, Me., 1897), 23.

77. See Essex County Probates, doc. 21248. Although the value of his estate is unknown, Thomas Penney had left Josiah Kent only £2 in his will. The court's response to Kent's appeal went unrecorded.

78. *Essex Court Records* 1:250.

79. Ibid. 3:270.

80. Ibid. 4:16; 8:405; *Essex Probate Records* 2:116; Ipswich Deeds (manuscript volume, Registry of Deeds, Essex County Courthouse, Salem, Mass.), 1:166; 3:143–45; 4:114, 397.

81. Ibid. 1:304. The law forbidding "excess in Apparel" was passed in 1651. See Whitmore, *Colonial Laws of Massachusetts*, 5.

82. *Essex Court Records* 4:50.

83. Ibid. 5:38; Essex Court File Papers 18: doc. 91.

84. *Essex Court Records* 4:56–57; Essex Court File Papers 13: docs. 100–101.

85. *Essex Court Records* 4:57, 67.

86. The original deed is in Ipswich Deeds 3:143–44. See also *Essex Court Records* 8:301–2, 406.

87. *Essex Court Records* 8:301–2, 406.

88. Ipswich Deeds 4:439–40.

89. *Essex Court Records* 8:373, 375–76, 405–10.

90. Ibid. 5:311, 405; 6:438; 8:99; 9:335–36.

91. *Witchcraft Papers* 3:881–82.

92. *Vital Records of Andover, Massachusetts, to the End of the Year 1849,* 2 vols. (Topsfield, Mass., 1912), 1:36–37.

93. Essex County Probates, 370. See also Greven, *Four Generations,* 67, 75–76, for a discussion of the terms of these inheritances.

94. See Essex Deeds 7:53; Essex County Probates, docs. 370, 371, 439, 13647, 13687; Greven, *Four Generations,* 67, 75–76, 84 n, 88–91, 164 n. Although it is not possible to ascertain the exact value of all four of these men's estates, even at their deaths, the surviving records support this conclusion, if we take into consideration that the Allen sons were much younger than the Holt sons and that Samuel Holt and Andrew Allen, as eldest sons, received double portions of their respective fathers' estates.

95. *Vital Records of Billerica, Massachusetts, to the Year 1850* (Boston, Mass., 1908), 324; Henry A. Hazen, *History of Billerica, Massachusetts, with a Genealogical Register* (Boston, Mass., 1883), pt. 2:149–50.

96. *Vital Records of Andover* 2:375–76, 466; Essex County Probates, docs. 370, 371, 439.

97. *Vital Records of Billerica,* 35; *Vital Records of Andover* 1:92–93; Essex Court File Papers 13: doc. 28; Sarah Loring Bailey, *Historical Sketches of Andover, Massachusetts* (Boston, Mass., 1880), 201–3; *Witchcraft Papers* 1:189–90, 192–93.

98. *Vital Records of Andover* 2:375–76, 466; Essex County Probates, docs. 370, 371, 439.

99. *Witchcraft Papers* 1:183–96, esp. 185; 2:522–23.

100. C. Mather, *Wonders of the Invisible World,* 159.

101. *Witchcraft Papers* 1:197–203; 2:511–12, 520–30, 598–99; 3:765–74, 871–72, 881–82, 983–84, 1018–20.

102. Ibid. 2:689–90.

103. It is difficult to know which of the two groups is easier to locate: women without brothers or sons or women with brothers or sons. To know whether an accused witch belongs in the former category, we often need to establish the fertility and mortality patterns for only a single generation, either her own or her parents'. To know whether an accused witch belongs in the latter category, we need to establish the patterns for both generations. This would suggest that the available figures are more likely to overstate the proportions of accused witches without brothers or sons. However, the dying out of male lines in families of witches without male heirs makes these women

harder to locate in the first place, since genealogical records usually follow male rather than female lineage. The problem of even establishing these women's fertility and mortality patterns would suggest that the available figures are more likely to understate the proportions of women without brothers or sons to inherit. I suspect that these problems cancel one another out and that were we able to gather all the necessary information, the percentages provided in table 11 for 60 percent of the accused roughly approximate the percentages for all witches.

104. See text above, 24, 27–29.

105. Ann Hibbens's will is reprinted in *New England Historical and Genealogical Register* 6 (1852), 287–88.

106. See *Witchcraft Papers* 3:880–81; Babson, *History of Gloucester,* 174; John J. Babson, *Notes and Additions to the History of Gloucester* (Gloucester, Mass., 1876), pt. 1:83–84; Essex County Probates, doc. 28612; Essex Deeds 10:62; 91:15.

107. *Salem-Village Witchcraft: A Documentary Record of Local Conflict in Colonial New England,* eds. Paul Boyer and Stephen Nissenbaum (Belmont, Calif., 1972), 155–67, esp. 156–57; *Essex Court Records* 7:237, 319, 329; Essex Deeds 5:55; 6:57–59; 10:112. For records of Bridget Bishop's 1692 trial, see *Witchcraft Papers* 1:83–109. See also Essex County Probates, doc. 20009, for the deposition of Thomas Oliver's estate after Bridget (Oliver) Bishop's execution in 1692.

108. *Essex Probate Records* 2:254–55; Ethel Farmington Smith, *Adam Hawkes of Saugus, Mass., 1605–1672* (Baltimore, 1980), 22–27. The original articles of agreement are in Essex County Probates, doc. 12899.

109. See *Witchcraft Papers* 2:387–88; 499–505, 509–12; 3:781–92, 919–20.

110. See Richard B. Morris, *Studies in the History of Early American Law* (New York, 1930), 159–60.

111. *Witchcraft Papers* 3:1006, 1010–19, 1024–25.

112. Savage, *Genealogical Dictionary* 4:66.

113. *New England Historical and Genealogical Register* 10 (1856), 177–80.

114. Savage, *Genealogical Dictionary* 4:273–74; *Mass. Records* 5:245.

115. See text, above, 63.

116. *Essex Probate Records* 3:191–93; Perley, *History of Salem* 1:306.

117. *Essex Probate Records* 3:191; Perley, *History of Salem* 3:80–81.

118. *Essex Court Records* 7:238.

119. *Vital Records of Salem* 5:337; Perley, *History of Salem* 2:355; *New England Historical and Genealogical Register* 3 (1849), 129; Essex County Probates, doc. 13569.

120. Starkey, *The Devil in Massachusetts*, 185.

121. *Witchcraft Papers* 3:988–91. On Mary and Philip English, see also *Witchcraft Papers* 1:105, 151, 313–21; 2:429, 474, 482, 693; 3:805–6, 972–73, 1043–45; Starkey, *The Devil in Massachusetts*, 146–47, 184–86, 276–77, 289–90.

122. For Martha and Giles Corey and Alice Parker, see *Witchcraft Papers* 1:239–66; 2:623–28, 632–33; 3:985–86, 1018–19; Essex County Probates, doc. 6391; Lawson, "A Brief and True Narrative," 154–57; Calef, "More Wonders of the Invisible World," 343–44, 366–67; *Vital Records of Salem* 2:138–39; Perley, *History of Salem* 2:193; 3:56, 288–93; *Essex Court Records* 6:190–91.

The Alice Parker who was executed in 1692 may or may not have been Giles Corey's daughter. Both a Mary Parker of Andover and an Alice Parker, wife of John Parker, of Salem, were hanged as witches that year. Giles (and his former wife Mary) had a daughter who was married to John Parker of Salem, but her name was usually given as Mary. Names like Mary and Alice were sometimes used interchangeably in early New England, and I suspect that the Alice Parker who was executed was in fact Giles Corey's daughter.

123. *Essex Probate Records* 2:119. The following account of Rachel Clinton's experience is heavily indebted to John Demos's chapter on her in *Entertaining Satan* (see 19–35). I am grateful to the author for sharing this chapter with me before his book was published.

124. *Essex Probate Records* 1:144–45.

125. Ibid., 144.

126. Ibid. 2:115–16. The original of Martha Haffield's will, and the inventory of her estate, is in Essex County Probates, doc. 12051.

127. *Essex Court Records* 3:321, 352; Records of the Quarterly Court, Ipswich, 1664–1674 (manuscript volume, Essex Institute, Salem, Mass.), doc. 94.

128. *Essex Court Records* 3:371–73; Essex Court File Papers, 12, docs. 22–25.

129. Essex Court File Papers, 12:24. See also *Essex Court Records* 3:371–73.

130. *Essex Court Records* 4:14, 269; Records of the Quarterly Court, Salem, 1667–1679 (manuscript volume, Essex Institute, Salem, Mass.), doc. 34.

131. *Essex Probate Records* 2:119–20. See Demos, *Entertaining Satan*, 22–30, for a full discussion of this litigation.

132. Essex Court File Papers, 13:29; *Essex Court Records* 3:458.

133. *Essex Court Records* 4:269, 425; 5:37, 312; 6:137, 344; 7:100; 8:17. The quotation is from 8:17. See also Ipswich Deeds, 4, 378; Records of the Quarterly Court, Salem, 1667–1679, doc. 34; Records of the Quarterly Court, Ipswich, 1664–1674, doc. 132; Records of the Quarterly Court, Ipswich, 1666–1682, doc. 279; Essex Court File Papers, 18: doc. 91; 21: doc. 53.

134. On Rachel Clinton, see *Essex Court Records* 3:402; 6:374–75. On Lawrence Clinton, see Ibid. 4:269; 5:267; 6:206, 278, 338; 7:181; Records of the Quarterly Court, Salem, 1667–1679, doc. 34; Records of the Quarterly Court, Ipswich, 1666–1682, docs. 283, 293, 297; Essex Court File Papers, 20: docs. 144, 148; 25: doc. 125; (Mrs.) E.J. Clinton, "The Clinton Family of Connecticut," *New England Historical and Genealogical Register* 69 (1915), 50.

135. *Essex Court Records* 6:344.

136. Massachusetts Archives, 9:104.

137. "Records of the Town of Ipswich from 1674 to 1696," manuscript copy, by Nathaniel Farley, 1894 (Town Clerk's Office, Ipswich, Mass.), 208, 220–22, 224, 229, 252, 273.

138. Depositions filed against Rachel Clinton in 1687 are in Suffolk Files, 2660; "Witchcraft 1687," in the manuscript collections of Cornell University Library, Ithaca, N.Y. For Clinton's 1692 trial, see *Witchcraft Papers* 1:215–19; 3:881.

139. *Essex Probate Records* 2:283–85; Boyer and Nissenbaum, *Salem-Village Witchcraft*, 139–41. The witnesses' original statements are in Essex County Probates, doc. 25861.

140. *Vital Records of Wenham, Massachusetts, to the End of the Year 1849* (Salem, Mass., 1904), 166; *Essex Court Records* 8:163–64; Essex Deeds, 15:298.

141. *Essex Court Records* 8:432–33; 9:6, 111; Boyer and Nissenbaum, *Salem-Village Witchcraft*, 141–42; Essex County Probates, doc. 25862.

142. See, for instance, Essex Deeds, 15:298.

143. Boyer and Nissenbaum, *Salem-Village Witchcraft*, 142–47; *Essex Court Records* 9:579–80; Essex Deeds, 8:147.

144. *Witchcraft Papers* 1:106, 255; 2:351–78, 612–13, 662; 3:746–47, 944, 1019–20.

145. Manwaring, *Conn. Probate Records* 1:7–8.

146. Ibid., 8.

147. *Particular Court Records,* 119.

148. Ibid., 258; I. Mather, "Remarkable Providences," 18–21.

149. Manwaring, *Conn. Probate Records* 1:121–22.

150. Norfolk Deeds, 1:116, 154; Dow, *History of Hampton* 1:85; 2:612–13, 928, 985–86; *New Hampshire Province Records,* 417.

151. *Essex Probate Records* 1:314–16; 2:160; *Essex Court Records* 1:199, 204, 229; 2:213; 3:292, 342, 413; 4:165, 221–22, 255; Essex Court File Papers, 12:86–87.

152. *Essex Probate Records* 2:238–39; *Witchcraft Papers* 3:727–28; Gage, *History of Rowley,* 170–75.

153. Although some of these women may have had sons when they were accused, the records do not indicate any. John Carrington had a son, John, as well as a daughter, Mary, but both children seem to have been the offspring of his former marriage. On the Carrington genealogy, see Demos, *Entertaining Satan,* 349, 506 n. 40.

CHAPTER FOUR
Handmaidens of the Devil

1. The most negative description of New England witches in the recent literature is found in Chadwick Hansen, *Witchcraft at Salem,* esp. 34–37, 58–61, 93–109, 119–20. Hansen's account also argues most forcefully that some of the accused practiced *maleficium.* He is not consistent, however. At one point he says that witch Bridget Bishop "was in all probability a practicing witch"; later he says that "there is, unfortunately, no way of knowing whether [she] was actually using charms or spells" on three of her neighbors. Still later, he asserts uneqivocally that she "practiced black magic, and with demonstrable success." (See 94, 101, 120.) Hansen also uses his sources selectively, accepting accusers' statements when, like Bridget Bishop, the accused were outspoken or defiant women, but ignoring them when, like Rebecca Nurse, the women's usual demeanor was meek and humble. (For Nurse, see 79–82.)

Richard Weisman and John Demos are much more sympathetic to the accused and to the pressures placed upon them, and much more sensitive to the fact that descriptions of them come primarily from people who were in conflict with them. Nevertheless, they

ietimes accept accusers' views uncritically and leave us with the
ression that as a group, witches were an ill-tempered and contentious lot. See *Witchcraft, Magic, and Religion,* 85–91; *Entertaining Satan,*
esp. 86–94. (Weisman, like Hansen, argues that some witches practiced black magic, explaining this behavior as a "mode of accommo-
dation" to their precarious economic circumstances; see 85.)

Studies of the Salem outbreak are more likely to examine accusers' statements about witches in a more critical light and portray the
accused in less stereotypical ways. See, for instance, Boyer and Nissenbaum, *Salem Possessed,* 190–216, and passim. I suspect that the
presence of more men, children, and "respectable" (i.e. well-off)
women among the accused in 1692, and more young females among
the accusers, accounts for much of this difference in the Salem literature. For more on the "character" of the accused, see my review of
Demos's book and Christina Larner's *Enemies of God: The Witch-hunt
in Scotland,* entitled "On Witchcraft and Witch-hunting," *Yale Review*
72 (July 1983), 612–19.

2. Think, for instance, of Myra Gulch, also known as the Wicked
Witch of the West, in the movie version of L. Frank Baum's *The Wizard of Oz.* Appearing every spring on our television screens for as
long as most of us can remember, the Myra Gulch figure has done
more than any single witch to shape the popular stereotype in this
country. In her earthly form, she resembles the most negative recent
depictions of New England witches. Angry, aggressive, contentious,
and vindictive, she is given to unreasonable provocation of the decent
folk who live around her, even innocent children, and shows callous
indifference to the most basic human values. In her supernatural
form, she is murderous.

Interestingly, she also resembles in one particular the witches with
whom I am more familiar, in that she is an "inheriting" woman. If
my memory is correct, Dorothy's Aunt Em makes a point of telling
her (and us): "Just because you own half the property in town, Myra
Gulch, doesn't mean that. . . ."

3. For one of the most benign examples, see Demos's chapter on
Rachel Clinton in *Entertaining Satan,* 19–35. Until the last two para-
graphs, Demos gives us one of the most beautifully written and sen-
sitively rendered portraits of a witch in the literature, showing clearly
both the callousness with which family members and neighbors treated
her and her own ongoing struggle to claim her rights and maintain
her dignity. At the end, though, he suggests that there may have
been "some veiled complicity" on her part in the way she was treated,

"such as one finds in habitual victims." (See 35.)

4. *Witchcraft Papers* 1:231.

5. Ibid. 2:457.

6. Ibid. 3:722.

7. Ibid. 2:343.

8. Trial of Winifred Holman, folio 25.

9. For a somewhat different but important perspective on the role of magistrates in witchcraft trials, see Weisman, *Witchcraft, Magic, and Religion*, esp. chaps. 7–11.

10. See Mary Maples Dunn, "Saints and Sisters: Congregational and Quaker Women in the Early Colonial Period," *American Quarterly* 30 (Winter 1978): 587–90; Richard Gildrie, *Salem, Massachusetts, 1626–1683: A Covenant Community* (Charlottesville, Va., 1975), 77–83; Koehler, "The Case of the American Jezebels," 69–71.

11. For more on this point, see below, 190–94, 197–98.

12. See Dunn, "Saints and Sisters," esp. 595–601; Jeanette Carter Gadt, "Women and Protestant Culture: The Quaker Dissent from Puritanism" (Ph.D. diss., University of California, Los Angeles, 1974), esp. chaps. 2–3.

13. See "A Report of the Trial of Mrs. Anne Hutchinson before the Church in Boston," in Hall, *Antinomian Controversy*, 382–83.

14. Sources for the treatment of Fisher and Austin include Bishop, *New England Judged*, 3–13, 41–42; Whiting, *Truth and Innocency Defended*, 12–14; Humphrey Norton, *New England's Ensign: It Being the Account of Cruelty, the Professors' Pride, and the Articles of Faith* (London, 1659), 5–11. My discussion of this and other early Puritan responses to Quakers is also drawn from Gadt, "Women and Protestant Culture," 119–37; Erikson, *Wayward Puritans*, 107–36; Heyrman, *Commerce and Culture*, 96–110.

15. H. Norton, *New England's Ensign*, 5.

16. *Mass. Records* 4 (pt. 1): 277.

17. Ibid., 277–78.

18. Booth, *Witches of Early America*, 106–7; Bishop, *New England Judged*, 220, 461.

19. Cited in Booth, *Witches of Early America*, 106.

20. Ibid., 107.

21. Cotton Mather, *Magnalia Christi Americana* 2:522–30. See also Mather's *Late Memorable Providences Relating to Witchcrafts and Posses-*

sions (London, 1691), 137. Note that passages cited here are not included in the abridged (and more accessible) version of this work in Burr, *Narratives,* cited elsewhere in these notes; citations are to the abridged edition unless otherwise specified.

22. John Norton, *The Heart of New England Rent at the Blasphemies of the Present Generation* (Cambridge, Mass., 1659), 6. See also Heyrman, *Commerce and Culture,* 108–11, for discussion of additional Quaker witches and other Puritan writings that associated Quakerism with witchcraft. In *Religion and the Decline of Magic,* 486–87, Keith Thomas mentions that Quakers were also accused of witchcraft in 17th-c. England.

23. On witchcraft-as-heresy in the European Christian tradition, see Jeffrey Burton Russell, *Witchcraft in the Middle Ages* (Ithaca, N.Y., 1972).

24. See *Commerce and Culture,* 96–147, for Christine Heyrman's argument that Quakerism continued to be strongly associated with witchcraft during the Salem outbreak. In 1692, Quakers were not themselves named as witches. But Heyrman has found that accusations were lodged against some people "who had ties of blood, marriage, affection, or friendship to the Quakers." (See 51.) Although only one of the persons Heyrman mentions (Abigail Somes) was accused of a church-related offense, Heyrman's evidence suggests that popular concern with heresy may have been stronger than the content of accusations would lead us to believe.

25. *New Haven Colony Records* 2:29.

26. Ibid., 30–31.

27. Ibid., 32, 35–36, 151–52.

28. See below, 297–98, n. 6.

29. *Witchcraft Papers* 2:394, 400.

30. *New Haven Colony Records* 2:77–89. The quotation is from 87.

31. *Witchcraft Papers* 2:375.

32. C. Mather, "Memorable Providences," 135–36.

33. *Witchcraft Papers* 3:781.

34. See, for example, ibid. 2:522; 3:775, 791.

35. Samuel Willard, *A Compleat Body of Divinity in Two Hundred and Fifty Expository Lectures* . . . (Boston, 1726), 183.

36. *Essex Court Records* 7:42–55; *Connecticut Records* 1:143.

37. Hale, *Modest Enquiry,* 17.

38. *New Haven Colony Records* 2:82.

39. C. Mather, "Memorable Providences," 136.

40. *Witchcraft Papers* 2:394.

41. Ibid., 357, 369.

42. Ibid., 600.

43. Winthrop, *Journal* 2:344–45.

44. See, for instance, Richard Walker's testimony against Sarah Bibber, in *Witchcraft Papers* 1:80.

45. C. Mather, *Wonders of the Invisible World*, 216–17.

46. *Witchcraft Papers* 3:709.

47. On scolding and the meaning of the word "scold" in England, see Thomas, *Religion and the Decline of Magic*, 244, 528–30, 533.

48. *The Works of John Robinson*, 3 vols., ed. Robert Ashton (Boston, 1851), 1:172–74, 225–28; Willard, *A Compleat Body of Divinity*, 181–82.

49. See *Witchcraft Papers* 2:449–50.

50. On this point, see also Demos, "Underlying Themes," 1312. I should point out that because of the work done by Keith Thomas on English witchcraft and by anthropologists studying witchcraft in non-Western cultures, I began my research with the assumption that some of the accused must have practiced *maleficium*. Like Demos, however, I did not find that the evidence would support this assumption. My conclusions about the presence of magic in early New England resemble those of historian Jon Butler, who argues that "a wide range of occult ideas and practices . . . were evident in the colonies between 1650 and 1720 . . ." but "the character of early migration to America made the arrival of the full range of English occult practices unlikely and their survival difficult." See "Magic, Astrology, and the Early American Religious Heritage, 1600–1760," 323–25, and passim.

51. *New Haven Colony Records* 2:30.

52. Though primarily a 19th- rather than a 20th-c. explanation, the idea that accusers acted maliciously lives on in the popular imagination through literary works, particularly through Arthur Miller's portrayal of accuser Abigail Williams in *The Crucible*. (Miller himself was ambivalent about the character he created. Originally he included a scene in the play that presented her motives in a more complex fashion, but he deleted it "because it seemed to deflect the tempo of the play." In the Bantam edition of *The Crucible*, Miller includes the original scene as an appendix.)

53. Much of my understanding of this issue is based on anthropological studies of African and Afro-American religions, See, for instance, Zora Neale Hurston, *Mules and Men: Negro Folktales and Voodoo Practices in the South* (1935; reprint, New York, 1970), esp. 239–54, 287–303; Walter Cannon, "Voodoo Death," *American Anthropologist* 154 (1942): 169–81; Alfred Métraux, *Voodoo in Haiti*, trans. Hugo Charteris (1959; reprint, New York, 1970), esp. 266–92.

54. The following account is drawn from depositions submitted during Elizabeth How's 1692 trial. See *Witchcraft Papers* 2:433–55. Quotations are from 439.

55. Willard, *A Compleat Body of Divinity*, 183.

56. See chap. 7 for a comprehensive discussion of possession and the possessed.

57. See, for instance, Starkey, *The Devil in Massachusetts*, 10–11; G. Rattray Taylor, *Sex in History: The Story of Society's Changing Attitudes to Sex Throughout the Ages* (New York, 1970), 38–41, 114–15.

58. Jameson, *Johnson's Wonder-Working Providence*, 28, 127.

59. See Winthrop, "A Short Story," 205, 310; and "A Report of the Trial of Mrs. Anne Hutchinson," 362–63.

60. "A Report of the Trial of Mrs. Anne Hutchinson," 372.

61. See, for instance, *Essex Court Records* 1:265; 5:426–27.

62. *Witchcraft Papers* 2:562–63.

63. Connecticut Colonial Probate Records 56:5, 35–36, 52.

64. Ibid.; *Essex Court Records* 4:129.

65. See, for example, *Witchcraft Papers* 1:111–12.

66. *New Haven Colony Records* 2:30, 34.

67. C. Mather, *Wonders of the Invisible World*, 33.

68. *Records of the Colony and Plantation of New Haven, from 1638 to 1649*, ed. Charles J. Hoadly (Hartford, Conn., 1857), 88–89, 105 (hereafter cited as *New Haven Colony Records*, 1).

69. *Particular Court Records*, 223, 225.

70. Ibid., 238, 240, 243.

71. *Conn. Records* 4:76–77, 79; Wyllys Papers, docs. 23, 25, 32, 34–35, 37–41; Wyllys Papers Supplement, 5–6, 9, 30–36.

72. *Conn. Records* 1:373.

73. Tomlinson, *Witchcraft Trials*, 60–63.

74. Ibid., 63–64.

75. *Essex Court Records* 1:198–99; *Witchcraft Papers* 2:413, 415.

76. C. Mather, "Memorable Providences," 136; I. Mather, *Remarkable Providences*, 138.

77. *Witchcraft Papers* 1:281–82.

78. Hale, *Modest Enquiry*, 18.

79. Winthrop, *Journal* 1:268; Bouton, *Documents and Records Relating to New Hampshire*, 416–19.

80. Cited in Julie A. Matthaei, *An Economic History of Women in America: Women's Work, the Sexual Division of Labor, and the Development of Capitalism* (New York, 1982), 48. See also Alice Clark, *Working Life of Women in the Seventeenth Century* (London, 1919), 254–59.

81. See *Essex Court Records* 4:207–9; Drake, *Annals of Witchcraft*, 281–82; Wyllys Papers Supplement, 49; "Conn. Assistants Records," 23.

82. *Witchcraft Papers* 2:672–73.

83. For Ann Pudeator, see *Essex Court Records* 8:59–60.

84. See Clark, *Working Life of Women*, 242–89; Thomas, *Religion and the Decline of Magic*, 191–92, 496–97, 536–38, 548; Ehrenreich and English, *Witches, Midwives, and Nurses*, 4–18.

85. *Essex Court Records* 4:207; 7:405.

86. Wyllys Papers Supplement, 4; Tomlinson, *Witchcraft Trials*, 27–30.

87. See *Witchcraft Papers* 3:771–74; Hazen, *History of Billerica*, pt. 2:149–50.

88. C. Mather, *Wonders of the Invisible World*, 14–16.

89. Winthrop, "A Short Story," 202, 262–63, 282. See also Barker-Benfield, "Anne Hutchinson," 81–82.

90. J. Norton, *The Heart of New England Rent*, 50, 55–56. See also Gadt, "Women and Protestant Culture," 119–67.

91. See Clark, *Working Life of Women*, esp. 93–149, 221–35. Clark points out, for instance, that brewing, "at one time chiefly if not entirely in the hands of women," was almost exclusively a male occupation in England by the late 1630s.

92. Quite possibly, the frequency of accusations in commercially based towns has more to do with their population size than their economic development. Additional research needs to be done on the geographical distribution of accusations before we can explore this problem further.

93. The citation is from C. Mather, *Ornaments for the Daughters of Zion*, 101.

94. *Essex Court Records* 7:136.

95. Ibid., 395. The records of Mary Hale's trial are in *Mass. Assistants Records* 1:188–89; Suffolk Court Files, 23:1958, 1972.

96. *Witchcraft Papers* 1:122–23.

97. Wyllys Papers, docs. 6–17; Wyllys Papers Supplement, 46–53.

98. *Essex Court Records* 2:390; 3:43–44, 75, 104–5, 222, 256, 260–63, 296, 330–33, 338, 344, 352–53, 383, 386, 420–21. The quotation is from 420.

99. *Witchcraft Papers* 2:437–455.

100. "Examination of Mrs. Ann Hutchinson," 45.

101. *New Haven Colony Records* 2:78.

102. See, for instance, *Witchcraft Papers* 3:876–78.

103. Ibid. 1:211–12; 3:793.

104. Chamberlain, "Lithobolia," 60–61.

105. Willard, *A Compleat Body of Divinity*, 181.

106. C. Mather, *Wonders of the Invisible World*, 191–95.

107. *Witchcraft Papers* 2:357.

108. *Essex Court Records* 8:272–74.

109. We only know, from gossip, that Hibbens was charged with "knowing" that she was the subject of gossip. The story that circulated was that she "unhappily guessed that two of her persecutors whom she saw talking in the street were talking of her." See Hutchinson, *History of Massachusetts Bay* 1:188.

110. See "Church Trial of Mistress Ann Hibbens," 47–49; Morgan, *The Puritan Dilemma*, 67; Darrett B. Rutman, *Winthrop's Boston: A Portrait of a Puritan Town, 1630–1649* (New York, 1965), 52.

111. "Church Trial of Mistress Ann Hibbens," 49.

112. Ibid., 48, 54–58.

113. William Hubbard, *General History of New England*, 574.

114. Hutchinson, *History of Massachusetts Bay* 1:187.

115. Ibid., 188.

CHAPTER FIVE
Handmaidens of the Lord

1. See Mary Douglas, *Implicit Meanings: Essays in Anthropology* (London, 1975), esp. ix–xxi, 3–8. Quotations are from 3–4.

2. Heinrich Institoris and Jakob Sprenger, *Malleus Maleficarum,* ed. and trans. Montague Summers (London, 1948), 41–66; Fray Martin de Castanega, *Tratado de las Superstitiones y Hechicherias* (1529; reprint, Madrid, 1946), chap. 5. I would like to thank Kathryn Kish Sklar for bringing the *Tratado* to my attention and William Christian, Jr., for sharing with me his translation of the early pages of chapter 5, entitled "Why more women than men are ministers of the Devil." Since I have not been able to locate a copy of the *Tratado,* my analysis and all quotations come from Christian's translation. In developing his argument, de Castanega may have stressed themes of which I am not aware.

3. Though men who wrote about women-as-witches said quite openly that women were innately more evil than men, other ideas about women were expressed at this time, of course (even by the three authors discussed here). For analyses of the complexities and contradictions of late medieval and early modern attitudes toward women, see Monter, "The Pedestal and the Stake," 119–36; Joan Kelly, "Early Feminist Theory and the 'Querelle des Femmes,' 1400–1789," in *Women, History and Theory: The Essays of Joan Kelly,* ed. Kelly (Chicago, 1984), 65–109.

4. *Malleus,* 44; *Tratato,* 1.

5. *Malleus,* 47–48, 51–65; *Tratato,* 1.

6. *Malleus,* 41, 66.

7. Ibid., 45–46; *Tratato,* 1.

8. *Malleus,* 46; *Tratato,* 1.

9. *Malleus,* 43; *Tratato,* 1.

10. *Malleus,* 43–45. Because historians have not yet explored the extent to which inheritance concerns were part of the explicit (or implicit) content of European witchcraft, it is hard to know whether this single reference in the *Malleus* is anomalous, or whether it reflects wider cultural tensions. In my reading of the European witchcraft literature, I have discovered a few (actual and fictional) witchcraft cases in which accusers (from the 2d c. to the 17th c.) have linked witchcraft with women's desire to inherit. (See, for instance, Russell, *Witchcraft in the Middle Ages,* 189–92; Apuleius, "The Story of Thelyphron," in *Witchcraft and Sorcery: Selected Readings,* ed. Max Marwick (Middlesex, Eng., 1970), 76–82.) The historian Conrad Russell has also come across one or two cases for the Tudor and Stuart periods in England (personal communication). But without extensive research in the European sources, we cannot know how widespread this asso-

ciation was or how significant a role it played in witchcraft accusations and trials.

11. My sources for this controversy include Kelly, "Early Feminist
Theory and the 'Querelle des Femmes';" Louis B. Wright, *Middle-
Class Culture in Elizabethan England* (Chapel Hill, N.C., 1935), 201–
27, 465–507; Margaret George, "From 'Goodwife' to 'Mistress': The
Transformation of the Female in Bourgeois Culture," *Science and Society*
37 (Summer 1973): 152–77; Gadt, "Women and Protestant Culture," esp. 46–60; *The Whole Duty of a Woman: Female Writers in Seventeenth-Century England*, ed. Angeline Goreau (New York, 1984), esp.
1–20, 67–159.

12. Cited in George, "From 'Goodwife' to 'Mistress'," 160.

13. See Wright, *Middle-Class Culture*, 465–69, 478–79, 492–93.

14. Ibid., 467. See also Clark, *Working Life of Women*, passim;
George, "From 'Goodwife' to 'Mistress'," passim.

15. The following argument about the role of the Puritan ministry in the emergence of a Protestant ideology of womanhood in the
16th c. and (especially) 17th c. began as an early American literature
seminar paper entitled "Puritanism and the Daughters of Zion" (New
York University, 1971). I wish to thank Kenneth Silverman and Car-
olyn Forrey for their comments on this work at that time, and Professor Silverman for suggesting that it "could easily be expanded to
a dissertation." Though I might quibble with the "easily," the present
chapter would not have moved even as quickly as it did to its present
form without the insights of Margaret George, in "From 'Goodwife'
to 'Mistress'," and Jeanette Carter Gadt, in "Women and Protestant
Culture" (esp. chap. 1). My intellectual debts to both of these scholars
are extensive. Also critical influences on this chapter, besides Mary
Douglas's *Implicit Meanings*, are Morgan, *The Puritan Family*; Michael
Walzer, *The Revolution of the Saints: A Study in the Origins of Radical
Politics* (Cambridge, Mass., 1965); Larzer Ziff, *Puritanism in America:
New Culture in a New World* (New York, 1973); Natalie Zemon Davis,
Society and Culture in Early Modern France (Stanford, 1975); Clifford
Geertz, *The Interpretation of Cultures: Selected Essays* (New York, 1973).
For a more recent (and fascinating) analysis of many of the same
issues that I deal with here, albeit from a distinctly literary perspec-
tive, see Christine Froula, "When Eve Reads Milton: Undoing the
Canonical Economy," *Critical Inquiry* 10 (December 1983): 321–47.

One caveat is in order. For the most part in this chapter, I am
talking about the development of an ideology of womanhood, not
about actual women's experiences in England or New England. I

[handwritten annotation: against very influential later me cult of domesticity arguments]

would argue that this ideology had a decided influence on women's lives, most especially on the lives of middle-class Protestant women, but that is not my focus here. For studies of white women's experience and the social relations of the sexes in 17th-c. New England, see (besides most of the rest of the present study) Laurel Thatcher Ulrich, *Good Wives: Image and Reality in the Lives of Women in Northern New England, 1650–1750* (New York, 1982); Koehler, *A Search for Power;* and the other family and women's history studies cited below in notes to chap. 6. For 17th-c. England, important works to begin with are Clark, *Working Life of Women;* Carole Shammas, "The Domestic Environment in Early Modern England and America," *Journal of Social History* 19 (1980–81): 3–24; Lawrence Stone, *The Family, Sex and Marriage in England, 1500–1800* (New York, 1977).

16. Robert Cleaver, *A Godly Form of Householde Governement* (London, 1598), 156–57; John Cotton, *A Meet Help*, 8, 14, 21; Robinson, *Works* 1: 236; Willard, *A Compleat Body of Divinity*, 125. I have avoided using works published after 1700 because of perceptible shifts in Puritan beliefs in the early 18th c. (some of these changes are discussed in Lonna M. Malmsheimer, "Daughters of Zion: New England Roots of American Feminism," *The New England Quarterly* 50 (September 1977): 484–504). Willard is the exception here. Although *A Compleat Body of Divinity* was not published until 1726, Willard wrote most of the sections cited in this chapter before 1700 and this work is a compendium of 17th-c. Puritan thought. On this last point, see Sydney E. Ahlstrom, *A Religious History of the American People* (New Haven, 1972), 280.

17. Historians disagree about the extent to which Puritans differed from other Protestant ministers in their literary treatment of women. For a discussion of these divergent views, see Gadt, "Women and Protestant Culture," 38–39. My own reading of the sources supports Gadt's argument that whereas most Protestant writers emphasized the family and the value of women's place within it, Puritans showed the most intense concern with these issues.

18. By the early 19th c., for instance, white, middle-class women were generally portrayed in both the ministerial and popular literature as "passionless," while men in this literature had become the lustful sex. See Nancy F. Cott, "Passionlessness: An Interpretation of Victorian Sexual Ideology, 1790–1850," in *A Heritage of Her Own*, ed. Nancy F. Cott and Elizabeth H. Pleck (New York, 1979), 162–81. See also Cott, *The Bonds of Womanhood: "Woman's Sphere" in New England, 1780–1835* (New Haven, 1977), chap. 4, for evidence of a similar

shift in beliefs about women's spiritual "natures." See below, 256–57.

19. This paragraph, and the following two, are based on Walzer, *The Revolution of the Saints,* and Ziff, *Puritanism in America.*

20. Ziff, *Puritanism in America,* 14.

21. Robinson, *Works* 1:246.

22. William Gouge, *Of Domesticall Duties* (London, 1622), 17–18.

23. Morgan, *The Puritan Family,* 20, and passim.

24. Ibid., 9–28.

25. William Perkins, "A Treatise of the Vocations or Callings of Men," in *The Work of William Perkins,* 443–76. The quotations are from 446, 457. For more on particular callings, see Morgan, *The Puritan Family,* 66–78; Charles H. George and Katherine George, *The Protestant Mind of the English Reformation, 1570–1640* (Princeton, 1961), 126–43.

26. Gadt, "Women in Protestant Culture," 40–60; George, "From 'Goodwife' to 'Mistress'," 163–70.

27. Gouge, *Of Domesticall Duties,* 26; Thomas Gataker, *Marriage Duties Briefly Couched Together* (London, 1620), 26–30.

28. See below, 256–57.

29. Cotton, *A Meet Help,* 20; Cleaver, *A Godly Form of Householde Governement,* 148, 152. In the 17th c., the word "oeconomic" was practically synonymous with the word "domestic."

30. Lawrence Stone, *The Crisis of the Aristocracy, 1558–1641,* abr. ed. (New York, 1967), 21; Philippe Ariès, *Centuries of Childhood: A Social History of Family Life,* trans. Robert Baldick (New York, 1962), 365–415.

31. Willard, *A Compleat Body of Divinity,* 610–12.

32. Cotton, *A Meet Help,* 21; Willard, *A Compleat Body of Divinity,* 125.

33. From the perspective of the psychoanalyst Theodor Reik, this biological reversal is the essential content of the Judeo-Christian origin myth. See *The Creation of Woman: A Psychoanalytic Inquiry into the Myth of Eve* (New York, 1960), 131. See also Reik, 113–32, and Froula, "When Eve Reads Milton," 326–36, for the argument that this reversal reflects male envy of female procreative power.

34. Sixteenth- and seventeenth-century Puritans, like their Protestant counterparts, can also be seen as ignoring the female principle in their larger belief system. Although Cotton Mather (in *Ornaments for the Daughters of Zion,* 3–4) noted that "a Woman had the Glory of

bringing into the World the second Adam. . . . [and thus] we may safely account the Female Sex herein more than a little Dignifyed," for the most part Puritans denied the powerful and compassionate figure of Mary affirmed by Catholics, just as they did the Catholic female saints. This is not to say that Puritans ignored female imagery. They described the relationship between the church and Christ in terms of a relationship between a bride and bridegroom, and espe-. cially in the early 18th c., they celebrated selected female biblical figures and deceased Puritan women who had led unusually "vertuous" lives. For different assessments of the significance of the bride-of-Christ imagery in early New England, see Morgan, *The Puritan Family*, 61, 161–68; Barker-Benfield, "Anne Hutchinson and the Puritan Attitude toward Women," 72–74; Margaret W. Masson, "The Typology of the Female as a Model for the Regenerate: Puritan Preaching, 1690–1730," *Signs: Journal of Women in Culture and Society* 2 (Winter 1976): 304–15. For the celebration of biblical figures and virtuous women, see Laurel Thatcher Ulrich, "Vertuous Women Found: New England Ministerial Literature, 1668–1735," in Cott and Pleck, *A Heritage of Her Own*, 58–80, and *Good Wives*, passim. On the larger question of the differential effects of Catholicism and Protestantism on women's lives, see Natalie Zemon Davis's influential article on 16th-c. France, entitled "City Women and Religious Change," in *Society and Culture in Early Modern France*, 65–95.

35. Robinson, *Works* 1:237.

36. Ibid., 241.

37. Barnes, *Book of the General Lawes*, 6; Keith Thomas, "The Double Standard," *Journal of the History of Ideas* 20 (1959): 199–204, 212.

38. Thomas discusses both of these concerns in some detail in "The Double Standard," 209–16.

39. See George and George, *The Protestant Mind*, 273.

40. Thomas, "The Double Standard," 212; *The Book of the General Lawes*, 6. In New England, actual executions for adultery were rare. See Edmund S. Morgan, "The Puritans and Sex," in *The American Family in Social-Historical Perspective*, 369. See below, 194–202 for more on Puritan treatment of sexual offenses. On the way the Puritan definition of adultery affected both women's petitions for divorce and the outcome of divorce proceedings in the 17th and 18th centuries, see Thomas, "The Double Standard," 199–202; Nancy F. Cott, "Divorce and the Changing Status of Women in Eighteenth-Century Massachusetts," in Gordon, *The American Family*, 115–39.

41. Cotton, *A Meet Help*, 21.

42. See, for example, Cleaver, *A Godly Form of Householde Governement*, 168–69; Increase Mather, *The Life and Death of that Reverend Man of God, Mr. Richard Mather* . . . (Cambridge, 1670), 25. For the continuation of this ideal in the 18th c., see Samuel Hopkins, *The Life and Character of the Late Reverend, Learned and Pious Mr. Jonathan Edwards* (Edinburgh, 1799), 112–16.

43. Willard, *A Compleat Body of Divinity*, 610; C. Mather, *Ornaments for the Daughters of Zion*, 82.

44. C. Mather, *Ornaments for the Daughters of Zion*, 9, 80. See also Willard, *A Compleat Body of Divinity*, 610; William Secker, *A Wedding Ring, Fit for the Finger* (Boston, 1690), 14.

45. Cotton, *A Meet Help*, 21.

46. Ibid.; C. Mather, *Ornaments for the Daughters of Zion*, 83–84; Secker, *A Wedding Ring*, 14, 17–18. For more on the growing invisibility of the economic value of women's labor in the colonial period (and into the 19th c.), see Jeanne Boydston, "Home and Work: The Industrialization of Housework in the Northeastern United States from the Colonial Period to the Civil War" (Ph.D. diss., Yale University, 1984). In this study, and in "To Earn Her Daily Bread: Housework and Antebellum Working-Class Subsistence," *Radical History Review* 35 (April 1986): 7–25, Boydston also analyzes the manner in which this developing ideology obscured the realities of women's household work. See also *The Journal of Esther Edwards Burr, 1754–1757*, ed. Carol F. Karlsen and Laurie Crumpacker (New Haven, 1984), for the impact of this changing ideology on a latter-day Puritan woman's experience of her own work.

47. Cotton, *A Meet Help*, 22; Gouge, *Of Domesticall Duties*, 345–48; Cleaver, *A Godly Form of Householde Governement*, 168–69.

48. Robert Bolton, *The Workes*, 4 vols. (London, 1631–1641), 4:245–46. Some men were even reluctant to allow that women had souls at all. See George and George, *The Protestant Mind*, 282. As late as 1711, according to Mary Sumner Benson, New England's Samuel Sewall felt compelled to write a defense of the argument that women could be saved. See *Women in Eighteenth-Century America: A Study of Opinion and Social Usage* (New York, 1935), 120–22.

49. Cotton, *A Meet Help*, 22.

50. See Keith Thomas, "Women and the Civil War Sects," *Past and Present* 13 (April 1958): 42–62; Roger Thompson, *Women in Stuart England and America: A Comparative Study* (London, 1974), 93–94.

51. Willard, *A Compleat Body of Divinity*, 125.

52. See Edmund S. Morgan, "New England Puritanism: Another Approach," *William and Mary Quarterly*, 3d ser., 18 (April 1961): 238–39; Dunn, "Saints and Sisters," 590.

53. For Mather's explanation of Puritan women's religious commitment, see *Ornaments for the Daughters of Zion*, 44–45. For recent discussion of this issue, see Ulrich, "Vertuous Women Found," 67–68 and *Good Wives*, 215–26.

54. Gouge, *Of Domesticall Duties*, Preface.

55. See below, 174–77.

56. See Anthony F. C. Wallace, *Religion: An Anthropological View*, (New York, 1966), 57–58, for a discussion of the way origin myths express, justify, and maintain the ideological formulations and institutional arrangements of a society.

57. Robinson, *Works* 1, 240; Matthew Griffiths, *Bethel: or a Forme for Families* (London, 1633), 232.

58. Willard, *A Compleat Body of Divinity*, 180–81.

59. The following discussion of the Puritan account of the Fall is based primarily on Samuel Willard's version. See ibid., 180–85.

60. Ibid., 180–82.

61. Ibid., 184–85.

62. Ibid.

63. Ibid., 184.

64. Ibid., 125, 157, 180–85, 610.

65. Gouge, *Of Domesticall Duties*, 345–48.

66. Cleaver, *A Godly Form of Householde Governement*, 167; C. Mather, *Ornaments for the Daughters of Zion*, 67; Gouge, *Of Domesticall Duties*, 193, 345–48; Willard, *A Compleat Body of Divinity*, 649.

67. Cotton, *A Meet Help*, 23; Secker, *A Wedding Ring*, 11; Robinson, *Works* 1, 240; Gataker, *Marriage Duties*, 9–10.

68. See, for example, Max Marwick, "Introduction," *Witchcraft and Sorcery*, 11–18; Philip Mayer, "Witches," in Marwick, *Witchcraft and Sorcery*, 45–64.

69. Monica Hunter Wilson, "Witch-Beliefs and Social Structure," in Marwick, *Witchcraft and Sorcery*, 263.

70. Natalie Zemon Davis, "Women on Top," in *Society and Culture in Early Modern France*, 124–51.

CHAPTER SIX
New England's Well-ordered Society

1. Cases where the accuser *can* be identified present problems of their own. We are likely to locate the initial accuser where there was only one, when the larger community did not support the accusation, and no official action was taken against the accused. These cases show how some colonists created their own, often highly personal, witches, and reveal the kinds of daily interactions that led to accusations, but they often obscure the larger social tensions underlying most witchcraft suspicions.

2. These figures resemble in many respects those complied by John Demos (see "Underlying Themes," 1314–16, and *Entertaining Satan,* 154. In Demos's article on Salem, the persons that I describe as non-possessed accusers he identifies as witnesses, but they are the same group). The main differences in our findings concern the proportions of men and women among non-possessed accusers, and in particular the proportions of men and women among middle-aged accusers. For the Salem outbreak, Demos found that 75 percent of the witnesses were males, but that only 57 percent were males in the non-Salem cases. More significantly for our differing interpretations, Demos found proportionately more women among middle-aged accusers in the non-Salem cases than I did. We agree that men greatly outnumbered women among middle-aged accusers during the Salem outbreak: Demos found that only 32 percent of middle-aged accusers were women in that outbreak, while my data show 31 percent. But we disagree about the proportions of women among middle-aged accusers in other witchcraft cases: Demos found that 64 percent of them were women, while I found that only 27 percent were.

The relatively small difference in our findings for Salem is probably attributable to the recent publication of Boyer and Nissenbaum's *The Salem Witchcraft Papers;* much more information on accusers is accessible now than it was when Demos did his original Salem research. Our differences on the non-Salem cases are harder to account for, but they may have to do with the fact that Demos's figures are based on the nine cases he researched most thoroughly, while mine are based on the information I could locate for all non-Salem cases.

3. My conclusions about the economic position of non-possessed accusers are also not the same as those John Demos records for the non-Salem cases. See *Entertaining Satan,* esp. 288–91. Here too, our differences may be largely attributable to the data we worked with,

but it may also have to do with the way we conceptualize economic position in early New England. See above, 297–98, nn. 6 and 7.

4. Given the paucity of historical studies that examine the relative positions of men and women in 17th-c. New England's emerging social structures, the following analysis is necessarily tentative. It is based primarily on my own research on Essex County, Massachusetts, on the work done by Mary Maples Dunn, Lyle Koehler, Laurel Thatcher Ulrich, and others on colonial women's history, and on the many family and town histories available. I am especially grateful here to Jeanne Boydston, who has mined the latter sources (which focus on the relationships between fathers and sons), for the light they shed on both women's experience and the social relations of the sexes.

5. See Perley, *History of Salem,* 1:230; Hubbard, *History of New England,* 204–5; Alice Morse Earle, *Customs and Fashions in Old New England* (1893; reprint, Rutland, Vt., 1973), 37.

6. Earle, *Customs and Fashions,* 37–38; Hubbard, *History of New England,* 205.

7. Herbert Moller, "Sex Composition and Correlated Culture Patterns of Colonial America," *William and Mary Quarterly,* 3d ser., 2 (1945): 114–16.

8. This calculation is found in Jeanne Boydston, "Women Alone: A Review of the Quantitative History of Widows and Spinsters in Colonial New England" (seminar paper, Yale University, 1978), 5.

9. Maris A. Vinovskis, "Mortality Rates and Trends in Massachusetts Before 1860," in *Studies in American Historical Demography,* ed. Vinovskis (New York, 1979), 236–43 (hereafter cited as Vinovskis, *Demography*).

10. John Demos, "Notes on Life in Plymouth Colony," in Vinovskis, *Demography,* 58; Lockridge, "The Population of Dedham," 330.

11. See Greven, *Four Generations,* 33–35, 120–22; Bissell, "Family, Friends, and Neighbors," 45; John Demos, "Families in Colonial Bristol, Rhode Island: An Exercise in Historical Demography," in Vinovskis, *Demography,* 110; Norton, "Population Growth in Colonial America," 444–45; Daniel Scott Smith, "The Demographic History of Colonial New England," in Vinovskis, *Demography,* 38–39.

12. Cited in Earle, *Customs and Fashions,* 38–39.

13. Ibid., 38.

14. Demos, "Notes on Life in Plymouth Colony," 53–54; Greven, "Family Structure in Seventeenth-Century Andover, Massachusetts,"

in Gordon, *The American Family,* 21–23.

15. See Vinovskis, "Mortality Rates," 237, 241.

16. For discussion of the Andover figures, see Vinovskis, "Mortality Rates," 237–39; David E. Stannard, *The Puritan Way of Death: A Study in Religion, Culture, and Social Change* (New York, 1977), 53–55.

17. Greven, Lockridge, and Demos do not supply figures on widowhood for 17th-c. Andover, Dedham, or Plymouth. John Faragher offers some for Wethersfield, in his "Old Women and Old Men in Seventeenth-Century Wethersfield," 18–19, and so does Norton for Ipswich, in "Population Growth in Colonial America," 446–47; neither study, however, distinguishes between earlier and later decades of the century.

18. See Alice Morse Earle, *Colonial Dames and Good Wives* (Boston, 1895), 29–44; Arthur W. Calhoun, *A Social History of the American Family from Colonial Times to the Present,* 3 vols. (Cleveland, 1917–19), 1:69–70.

19. On the relationship between mortality rates and inheritance in Maryland, for instance, see Lois Green Carr and Lorena S. Walsh, "The Planter's Wife: The Experience of White Women in Seventeenth-Century Maryland," in Cott and Pleck, *A Heritage of Her Own,* 25–57.

20. This discussion of the early Salem probate records is based on *Essex Probate Records* 1. Because only 17 of these records have survived for these two decades, the evidence here can only be suggestive.

21. On English inheritance practices, see *Family and Inheritance: Rural Society in Western Europe, 1200–1800,* ed. Jack Goody, Joan Thirsk, and E. P. Thompson (Cambridge, England, 1976); Margaret Spufford, *Contrasting Communities: English Villagers in the Sixteenth and Seventeenth Centuries* (London, 1974). Spufford's discussion of dower variations in different parts of England is especially useful. See 88–90, 112–18, 161–64.

22. Cushing, *The Laws and Liberties,* 3:699.

23. See below, 208–13.

24. Barnes, *Book of the General Lawes,* 17–18; Cushing, *The Laws and Liberties,* 1:96.

25. See above, 172.

26. Koehler, "American Jezebels," 69–70.

27. Dunn, "Saints and Sisters," 587; Isabel Calder, *The New Haven Colony* (New Haven, 1934), 93–94.

28. Gildrie, *Salem, Massachusetts,* 78. On male heretics in other early New England communities, see David S. Lovejoy, *Religious Enthusiasm in the New World: Heresy to Revolution* (Cambridge, Mass., 1985); Philip F. Gura, *A Glimpse of Sion's Glory: Puritan Radicalism in New England,* 1620–1660 (Middletown, Conn., 1984).

29. These Salem cases are discussed in Gildrie, *Salem, Massachusetts,* 78–83; Koehler, "American Jezebels," 70; Winthrop, *Journal* 1:281–82. On Mary Oliver, see also *Essex Court Records* 1:8, 12, 34, 99, 138, 152, 154, 160, 173, 180, 182–83, 185–86; *Mass. Assistants Records* 2:80; *Mass. Records* 1:247; 2:258, 283; 3:140.

30. Winthrop, *Journal* 1:281–82.

31. Ibid., 282.

32. Many of the issues in this debate are discussed in Dunn, "Saints and Sisters," 588–90.

33. See Gerald F. Moran, " 'Sisters' in Christ: Women and the Church in Seventeenth-Century New England," in *Women in American Religion,* ed. Janet Wilson James (Philadelphia, 1980), 53–54.

34. Dunn, "Saints and Sisters," 589–90.

35. *Mass. Records* 1:92.

36. Ibid., 91.

37. *Mass. Assistants Records* 2:30.

38. Ibid., 60.

39. *Mass. Records* 1:225.

40. See Koehler, "American Jezebels," 71 n.

41. Ibid.

42. These figures are compiled from *Essex Court Records* 1. It is often impossible to distinguish cases of male sexual coercion from cases involving mutually consenting parties (see, for instance, the prosecution of Auld [old?] Churchman in 1643 "for having the wife of Hugh Burt locked with him alone in his house," ibid. 1:56); therefore, these figures include all recorded sexual offenses, and they necessarily understate the degree to which a sexual double standard was developing in Essex County.

43. Cited in William K. Holdsworth, "Adultery or Witchcraft? A New Note on an Old Case in Connecticut," *New England Quarterly* 48 (September 1975): 400.

44. Dunn, "Saints and Sisters," 589–90.

45. For a discussion of the post-1660 ministerial literature on women, see Ulrich, "Vertuous Women Found," 58–80. Although we

have little information on the actual gender arrangements within individual congregations after 1660, women still participated actively in at least some church controversies. See, for instance, Boyer and Nissenbaum, *Salem Possessed*, 60–81.

46. C. Mather, *Ornaments for the Daughters of Zion*, 44–45. On the increase in female church membership after 1660, see Moran, " 'Sisters' in Christ," 47–65; Dunn, "Saints and Sisters," 590–95; Morgan, "Puritanism: Another Approach," 236–42.

47. The following analysis of Essex County sexual offenses is based largely on the *Essex Court Records* 1–9. It includes all cases mentioned in these volumes. Since the published records only go up to 1686, I have supplemented them with manuscript records from the Essex Court File Papers, 47–52; Records of the Quarterly Court, Ipswich, 1682–1692; and the Essex County Court of General Sessions: Salem, Ipswich, Newbury, 1696–1719, 3 vols. (Essex Institute, Salem, Mass.). Because they were widely scattered when I did my research, I have not attempted to find all the unpublished records dealing with sexual offenses from 1686 to 1700.

48. This was also the case elsewhere in Massachusetts, in Connecticut, and in other parts of colonial America. See Robert V. Wells, "Illegitimacy and Bridal Pregnancy in Colonial America," in *Bastardy and Its Comparative History*, ed. Peter Laslett, Karla Oosterveen, and Richard M. Smith (London, 1980), esp. 350, 355–56, 358–59; David Flaherty, "Law and the Enforcement of Morals in Early America," *Perspectives in American History* 5 (1971), esp. 224–26, 230–32.

49. Because we cannot eliminate male sexual abuse cases from the figures (see above, n. 42), it is impossible to portray accurately the double standard of sexual treatment in the courts. Nevertheless, table C provides some indication of the courts' bias.

In Massachusetts' ecclesiastical courts during the period 1620 to 1689, 63 percent of the persons disciplined for fornication were women. See Emil Oberholzer, Jr., *Delinquent Saints: Disciplinary Action in the Early Congregational Churches of Massachusetts* (New York, 1956), 254–55. (Oberholtzer does not show if or how the proportions of male and female prosecutions changed over the course of this period.) Given the larger numbers of females in most congregations, however, and given that churches only disciplined their own members, it is not clear whether or not the churches shared the courts' bias.

50. For the class bias of the courts in sexual offense cases in other regions, see Flaherty, "Law and the Enforcement of Morals," 216, 239–40.

TABLE C. **Prosecutions for Sexual Offenses, Essex County, Massachusetts, 1636–1700**

Period	Number of Cases	Women		Men	
1636–1650	56	30	(54%)	26	(46%)
1651–1660	77	37	(48%)	40	(52%)
1661–1670	102	51	(50%)	51	(50%)
1671–1680	237	123	(52%)	114	(48%)
1681–1690*	153	91	(59%)	62	(41%)
1691–1700*	46	28	(61%)	18	(39%)

*The data for these years are incomplete. See n. 47 above.

51. This conclusion is based on court cases, not laws. The heightened concern with illegitimacy was not expressed in Massachusetts laws until the 1660s.

52. *Essex Court Records* 1:323, 361–62, 380.

53. For support for this conclusion, see Flaherty, "Law and the Enforcement of Morals," 214, 229–37.

54. Cushing, *The Laws and Liberties* 1:29, 103.

55. Ibid. 1:178.

56. On disenfranchisement, see Flaherty, "Law and the Enforcement of Morals," 229. For an analysis of a later (and unsuccessful) ministerial attempt to force a marriage in a fornication case, see Kathryn Kish Sklar, "Martha vrs. Elisha and Jonathan Edwards vrs. Joseph Hawley: A Case of Conscience in Northampton in the 1740's" (paper presented at the annual meeting of the American Studies Association, Boston, Mass., October 1977).

57. Cushing, *The Laws and Liberties* 1:205.

58. *Essex Court Records* 1:414. Swinerton, for example, was merely fined for this offense.

59. See, for example, the case of Abigail Carrell and Freeborn Balch, Essex Court File Papers 50: doc. 67; Records of the Quarterly Court, Ipswich, 1682–1692, doc. 83; Essex County Court of General Sessions, 1692–1695, 56.

60. See, for example, the case of Sarah Stickney and John Atkinson, *Essex Court Records* 3:99; 7:316–18; 8:99, 259–63, 288–89, 296, 385–87, 433; 9:17.

61. By 1699, clauses enjoining single men to marry the mothers of their illegitimate children had disappeared from the Massachusetts legal records, as had those clauses calling for disenfranchisement of men convicted of fornication. At the same time, the magistrates had set limits on the fines and whippings allowed as punishments for these men, deleted requirements that they assist in the "bring[ing] up" of the children, and clarified that mothers were to assist them with the financial burdens of raising the children. See Cushing, *The Laws and Liberties 1:205* and Cushing, *Massachusetts Province Laws,* 29–30, for the subtle and not-so-subtle changes in the bastardy law between 1668 and 1699.

62. On the continuation of this process in New Haven Colony in the 18th c., see Cornelia Hughes Dayton, "Women Before the Bar: Gender, Law, and Society in Connecticut, 1710–1790" (Ph.D. diss., Princeton University, 1986), 89–186. For the colonies as a whole, see Flaherty, "Law and the Enforcement of Morals," esp. 213–17, 225–49; Wells, "Illegitimacy and Bridal Pregnancy," esp. 353–61.

63. In New Haven County, at least, women and their parents shouldered most of this burden by the early 18th c. See Dayton, "Women Before the Bar," 178–79. I suspect this was the case earlier, and in other parts of New England as well.

64. See above, 168–69.

65. Daniel Scott Smith, "Population, Family, and Society in Hingham, Massachusetts, 1635–1800" (Ph.D. diss., University of California, 1973), 59–60, 278; Robert A. Gross, *The Minutemen and Their World* (New York, 1976), 197, n. 22. On the variations in New England's sex ratios in the 18th c., see Robert V. Wells, *The Population of the British Colonies in America before 1776: A Survey of Census Data* (Princeton, 1975), 74–75, 85–86, 93–94, 102–4.

66. Norton, "Population Growth in Colonial America," 446; Demos, "Notes on Life in Plymouth Colony," 59.

67. Herbert Moller argues that a declining sex ratio was a function of the age of settlement. See "Sex Composition," 125–31.

68. The evidence here is not consistent. In Salem and Wethersfield, for instance, women's chances of living to old age seem to have increased over time, while in Andover, in the early 18th c., it appears that on the average women were dying at earlier ages than women

had in the 17th c. See James K. Somerville, "A Demographic Profile of the Salem Family, 1660–1770" (paper presented at the Conference on Social History at Stony Brook, N.Y., 25 October 1969), 13–17, 18–19; Faragher, "Old Women and Old Men in Seventeenth-Century Wethersfield," 12–18; Greven, *Four Generations*, 185–97. For a discussion of the problems with some of this evidence, see Vinovskis, "Mortality Rates," 236–43.

69. Here too the indications are sometimes contradictory. In Hingham, for instance, the loss of young men during King Philip's War seems to have been counterbalanced by the role of fighting in effectively closing the frontier, which dramatically reduced outward male migration until the Peace of Utrecht in 1713. Thus, in towns like Hingham, the sex ratio may not have changed as dramatically as it did in other communities. See Smith, "Demographic History," 41.

70. Greven, *Four Generations*, 39–40; Boyer and Nissenbaum, *Salem Possessed*, 89–91. Although Greven stresses the number of young men who stayed in Andover, his data also indicate that many men moved on. In Salem, the proportion of men who left was even higher.

71. Demos, "Notes on Life in Plymouth Colony," 58–59; Greven, *Four Generations*, 33–36, 117–20; Smith, "Demographic History," 39.

72. For a sense of what an average age of 22.8 meant for a female population, see Robert V. Wells, "Quaker Marriage Patterns in a Colonial Perspective," in Cott and Pleck, *A Heritage of Her Own*, 82–83.

73. See below, 208–9.

74. Norton, "Population Growth in Colonial America," 444.

75. In Andover, for instance, the rise in the age at first marriage for women led to the reduction by one child in the average size of families between the first and third generations. See Greven, *Four Generations*, 201. Demos found an increase in the average number of children in families over the course of the 17th c., even with the increase in the age at first marriage for women; if Susan Norton's critique of the Plymouth data is correct, however, that may be the result of the families Demos selected for investigation. See Demos, "Notes on Life in Plymouth Colony," 53; Norton, "Population Growth in Colonial America," 444.

76. Smith, "Population, Family, and Society," 12, 237–39; Greven, *Four Generations*, 121; Demos, "Notes on Life in Plymouth Colony," 59.

77. Norton, "Population Growth in Colonial America," 446–47; Faragher, "Old Women and Old Men in Seventeenth-Century Weth-

ersfield," 18–19; Smith, "Population, Family, and Society," 281–84. See also Boydston, "Women Alone," 15–16.

78. Faragher, "Old Women and Old Men in Seventeenth-Century Wethersfield," 20–28; Smith, "Population, Family, and Society," 283. In her study of late 18th- and early 19th-c. Petersburg, Virginia, Suzanne Lebsock's findings on widow's decisions on remarriage resemble those of Faragher. See *The Free Women of Petersburg: Status and Culture in a Southern Town* (New York, 1984), 26–27.

79. On this point see Boydston, "Women Alone," 15.

80. See Kenneth A. Lockridge, "Land, Population and the Evolution of New England Society, 1630–1790," *Past and Present* 39 (April 1968): 62–80. Lockridge discusses this process in the 18th c., when it had its worst effects, but its characteristic social tensions were already present in some communities in the 17th c.

81. This description is drawn from Boyer and Nissenbaum, *Salem Possessed*, esp. 44, 86–91; Gildrie, *Salem, Massachusetts*, esp. 105–8, 116–22; Donald Warner Koch, "Income Distribution and Political Structure in Seventeenth-Century Salem, Massachusetts," *Essex Institute Historical Collections* 105 (1969): 50–71; William I. Davisson, "Essex County Wealth Trends: Wealth and Economic Growth in 17th Century Massachusetts," *Essex Institute Historical Collections* 103 (1967): 291–342.

82. This discussion of Springfield is based on Innes, *Labor in a New Land*, esp. chaps. 1–5.

83. See Greven, *Four Generations*, chaps. 1–6.

84. The following analysis of Salem's inheritance patterns is based primarily on the published Salem probate records, collected in *Essex County Probates* 1–3. These include 99 wills and 83 intestate records. I have also used 20 wills from the period 1682 to 1689, most of them published in *Essex Court Records* 8–9, and 24 manuscript wills for the years 1691–1700. These latter documents are found in the Registry of Probate, Essex County Courthouse, Salem, Mass.

85. Children whose fathers died young and whose mothers did not remarry were, with their mothers, among the poorest members of the community.

86. Interestingly, while adhering fairly closely to the principle of a double share for the eldest son, women who left wills rarely discriminated between daughters and younger sons. Their estates, however, were few and usually quite small; hence the impact of their

actions was more psychological than material.

87. Smith, "Population, Family, and Society," 121–23. Smith also notes that in Hingham the "relative wealth of the father of the wife" was "an excellent predictor of the direction of intergenerational mobility."

88. See, for example, the case of Salem Quaker Tamsen Buffin in *Essex Probate Records* 2:174–77. In 1669, Robert Buffin died, leaving an oral will in which he bequeathed his whole £270 estate to his wife Tamsen, even though the couple had several children to inherit. As justification for his highly unusual decision, according to the two women who witnessed the will, he said "that what he had as to his estate he would leve to his wife for shee helpt to gett it and the Children were hers." A logical conclusion of even a Puritan view of woman as helpmeet, this reasoning nonetheless struck both the court and Buffin's sons-in-law as unacceptable. Neither acknowledged the legality of the will, the court on the grounds that the Quaker witnesses refused to take oaths, the sons-in-law apparently for more personal reasons. The estate was not initially settled until ten years later, and the litigation continued for many years after that. Though the court never supported Tamsen's claim to the whole estate, she may have died thinking she had the last word. The deed to some of the family's land was in her own name; this property she divided among her four sons-in-law, but "entailed unto their grandchildren belonging to them that have been and now are their wives." Some of these women would not have grandchildren for many years.

89. Boyer and Nissenbaum, *Salem Possessed,* passim.

90. Innes, *Labor in a New Land,* esp. 136–41.

91. Increase Mather, *Two Discourses, Shewing . . . II, The Dignity and Duty of Aged Servants of the Lord . . .* (Boston, 1716), 100–101; Cotton Mather, *Maternal Consolations, An Essay on the Consolations of God . . . on the Death of Mrs. Maria Mather . . .* (Boston, 1714), 9. This paragraph is based on Jeanne Boydston, "Aged Handmaidens of the Lord: Views of Widowhood in Boston, 1679–1728" (seminar paper, Yale University, 1978). Especially useful are her comparisons of the clergy's treatment, in their writings, of old men and old women, passim.

92. See, for example, Thomas Foxcroft, *The Character of Anna, the Prophetess . . . In a Sermon Preached after the Funeral of . . . Dame Bridget Usher . . . Being a Widow of Great Age* (Boston, 1723), 36–37, 56. On the economic realities of widowhood for women at this time, see

Alexander Keyssar, "Widowhood in Early Eighteenth-Century Massachusetts: A Problem in the History of the Family," *Perspectives in American History* 8 (1974): 83–119.

93. This interpretation owes a great deal to Edmund Morgan's insights into the way in which economic and political discontent among elites and among different classes of white men in late 17th-c. Virginia was vented in racial hatred during Bacon's Rebellion. See *American Slavery, American Freedom* (New York, 1975), esp. chaps. 11–13. Bernard Bailyn's "Politics and Social Structure in Virginia," in *Seventeenth-Century America: Essays in Colonial History*, ed. James Morton Smith (Chapel Hill, 1959), 90–115, was also helpful in my thinking on this issue.

94. The following discussion of Francis Faulkner is drawn primarily from Greven, "Family Structure," esp. 32; *Four Generations*, esp. 95–97.

95. Essex County Probates, doc. 9305.

96. See *Witchcraft Papers* 1:327–34; 3:966–68, 970, 972–73, 991–92, 1010–19, 1034–37. Unless otherwise noted, the following discussion of Abigail Faulkner is drawn from these documents.

97. See *Essex Court Records* 3:5; *Vital Records of Andover* 1:117–19; Savage, *Genealogical Dictionary* 1:2; 2:5–6, 148, 557; Essex County Probates, doc. 43.

98. *Witchcraft Papers* 1:267; 2:335–37, 499–505; Bailey, *Historical Sketches of Andover*, 199.

99. *Witchcraft Papers* 1:328.

100. *Witchcraft Papers* 3:967–68.

101. See below, 256–57.

CHAPTER SEVEN
Brands Plucked Out of the Burning

1. See above, 183–85.

2. Little evidence on male possession experience in New England has survived. For the best available documentation, see C. Mather's discussion of John Godwin, Benjamin Godwin, and "a Boy at Tocutt," in his "Memorable Providences," 99–140. See also n. 20 below.

3. See above, 183–84.

4. See Demos, "Underlying Themes," 1315–16, and Weisman, *Witchcraft, Magic, and Religion,* 50–52, 222–23, for other findings on the sex, age, and marital status patterns among the possessed. Demos's figures here are for the Salem outbreak, and he describes the possessed in this article as accusers who "experienced fits of one sort or another." Weisman's figures are for all Massachusetts cases; he describes the possessed as "victims of bewitchment." Although we use different words to describe this group of accusers, and although our numbers and percentages vary somewhat, we agree that most of the possessed were young single females.

5. This view of possessed accusers is suggested by several recent accounts of the Salem outbreak. See, for example, Boyer and Nissenbaum, *Salem Possessed,* 1–9, 23–30, and passim.

6. The attacks on these Maine communities during these years are discussed in William D. Williamson, *The History of the State of Maine,* 2 vols. (Hallowell, Me., 1839), 1:515–53, 604–26; John S. C. Abbott, *The History of Maine* (Augusta, Me., 1892), 174–244; *Province and Court Records of Maine,* 6 vols., ed. Charles Thornton Libby, Robert E. Moody, and Neal W. Allen, Jr. (Portland, Me., 1928–75), 3:xxi–xxix, xlviii–lv. For other important interpretations of the relationships between these attacks and witchcraft fears and accusations, see James E. Kences, "Some Unexplored Relationships of Essex County Witchcraft to the Indian Wars of 1675 and 1689," *Essex Institute Historical Collections* 120 (1984), 179–212; Richard Slotkin, *Regeneration Through Violence: The Mythology of the American Frontier, 1600–1860* (Middletown, Conn., 1973), esp. chap. 5. Evidence for the presence of many of the Salem possessed and their families in these Maine towns prior to the Salem outbreak is located in *Genealogical Dictionary of Maine and New Hampshire,* ed. Sybil Noyes, Charles Thornton Libby, and Walter Goodwin Davis (Portland, Me., 1928–1939) (hereafter cited as Noyes, Libby, and Davis, *Genealogical Dictionary*), and in the numerous town histories and family genealogies housed in the Maine Historical Society, Portland, Maine. The Forbes Papers also provide considerable information on the Maine refugees. (From Esther Forbes's notes and her drafts of the opening pages of a chapter of her never-completed book on New England witchcraft, it appears the Indian wars played a central role in her thinking about the causes of the Salem outbreak.)

7. See below, 244–46.

8. See, for instance, *Documentary History of Maine* (Portland, Me., 1889), 9:36–37.

9. Noyes, Libby, and Davis, *Genealogical Dictionary*, 98–99, 142. For the history of Sarah Churchill's maternal ancestors, the Bonythons, see George Folscm, *History of Saco and Biddeford . . . in Maine* (Saco, Me., 1830), 113–19, as well as numerous references to them in *Maine Province and Court Records* 1–3.

10. Noyes, Libby, and Davis, *Genealogical Dictionary*, 430; Savage, *Genealogical Dictionary* 3:88; William Willis, *The History of Portland, from Its First Settlement, Collections of the Maine Historical Society* 1 (Portland, Me., 1865), 150.

11. *New England Historical and Genealogical Register* 44:168–70; Noyes, Libby, and Davis, *Genealogical Dictionary*, 723.

12. *York Deeds* (Portland, Me., 1894) 10:99.

13. Noyes, Libby, and Davis, *Genealogical Dictionary*, 430.

14. Calef, "More Wonders of the Invisible World," 383–84; *New England Historical and Genealogical Register* 44:168–70; Massachusetts Archives 105:25; Forbes Papers.

15. See above, chap. 6.

16. Cited in Edith Abbott, *Women in Industry* (New York, 1910), 33.

17. See above, 198–202.

18. See above, 194–96, 198–202. Young women's sexual position may have been further complicated by what several historians have described as some colonists' assumption that sexual privileges began not with marriage, but with the promise of marriage. See, for instance, Wells, "Illegitimacy and Bridal Pregnancy," 351. Although the evidence is scanty, Wells also points out that illegitimacy rates seem to have been low in the 17th c., but that they increased over the course of the century (see 354). In "Premarital Pregnancy in America" (esp. 114), Smith and Hindus indicate similar findings for the incidence of premarital pregnancy.

19. Despite a lack of evidence, the idea that the possessed were sexually "promiscuous" is an element in 20th-c. perceptions of these women. This impression stems in part from the popularity of Arthur Miller's *The Crucible*. In his play, which is historically accurate in most other particulars, Miller changed the age of one of the possessed, Abigail Williams, from 11 to 17 and made sexual motives the basis of her accusations against Elizabeth and John Proctor. Some late 17th-c. colonists did suggest that the possessed "went unmistakably bad" after their possession experiences (on this point, see Starkey, *The Devil in Massachusetts*, 248–49, 315). But even the evidence for

the subsequent behavior of the possessed is suspect, since it may be based on the sexual double standard of observers. Except for one adultery case, the later sexual lives of the possessed do not seem to have differed much from those of other colonists.

20. Evidence for this religious pattern is scattered throughout the witchcraft records. See, for instance, I. Mather, *Remarkable Providences*, 135–36, 139, for a description of the piety of Hartford's Ann Cole; C. Mather, "Memorable Providences," 99–100, for discussion of the godly environment in which the Godwin children were raised in Boston; Lawson, "A Brief and True Narrative," 152–55, 160, for mention of the possession of minister Samuel Parris's daughter and niece in Salem. This pattern holds for at least four possessed males.

21. The following interpretation of possession is informed by a vast anthropological and psychological literature on demonic possession, spirit possession, and related cross-cultural phenomena. The studies that have most influenced my thinking include: George Rosen, *Madness in Society: Chapters in the Historical Sociology of Mental Illness* (Chicago, 1968); *Case Studies in Spirit Possession*, ed. Vincent Crapanzano and Vivian Garrison (New York, 1977); Clifford Geertz, *The Interpretation of Cultures: Selected Essays* (New York, 1973); Erika Bourguignon, "Culture and the Varieties of Consciousness," Addison-Wesley Module in Anthropology, 47 (Reading, Mass., 1973); *Possession* (San Francisco, 1976); Grace Gredys Harris, *Casting Out Anger: Religion Among the Taita of Kenya* (New York, 1978); "Possession 'Hysteria' in a Kenya Tribe," *American Anthropologist* 59 (January 1957): 1046–66; Victor Turner, *The Forest of Symbols: Aspects of Ndembu Ritual* (Ithaca, N.Y., 1967); *The Ritual Process: Structure and Anti-Structure* (Ithaca, N.Y., 1969); I. M. Lewis, *Ecstatic Religion: An Anthropological Study of Spirit Possession and Shamanism* (Middlesex, England, 1971); *Magic, Witchcraft, and Curing*, ed. John Middleton (Garden City, N.Y., 1967); *Spirit Mediumship and Society in Africa*, ed. John Beattie and John Middleton (London, 1969); David Holmberg, "Shamanic Soundings: Femaleness in the Tamang Ritual Structure," *Signs* 9 (Autumn 1983): 40–58; *Witchcraft Confessions and Accusations*, ed. Mary Douglas (London, 1970); Josef Breuer and Sigmund Freud, *Studies in Hysteria*, trans. James Strachey (New York, 1957); Thomas S. Szasz, *The Manufacture of Madness: A Comparative Study of the Inquisition and the Mental Health Movement* (New York, 1970); *The Myth of Mental Illness: Foundations of a Theory of Personal Conduct*, rev. ed. (New York, 1974); Ilza Veith, *Hysteria: The History of a Disease* (Chicago, 1965); Michel Foucault, *Madness and Civilization: A History of Insanity*

in the Age of Reason (New York, 1965); Carroll Smith-Rosenberg, "The Hysterical Woman: Sex Roles and Role Conflict in Nineteenth-Century America," *Social Research* 39 (Winter 1972): 652–79; Marc H. Hollander, "Conversion Hysteria: A Post-Freudian Reinterpretation of Nineteenth-Century Psychosocial Data," *Archives of General Psychiatry* 26 (April 1972): 311–14; William C. Lewis, "Hysteria: The Consultant's Dilemma: Twentieth Century Demonology, Pejorative Epithet, or Useful Diagnosis?" *Archives of General Psychiatry* 30 (February 1974): 145–53; *Psychiatry and Its History: Methodological Problems in Research,* ed. George Mora and Jeanne L. Brand (Springfield, Ill., 1970).

22. I am especially indebted here to Veith, *Hysteria,* esp. chaps. 4 and 9, and Geertz. *Interpretation of Cultures,* esp. chap. 4.

23. Willard, "A Brief Account," 358.

24. Ibid., 358–59.

25. C. Mather, "Memorable Providences," 100–101; C. Mather, "A Brand Plucked Out of the Burning," 259–60.

26. For a comprehensive discussion of the various behaviors that were defined as hysteria over the course of Western history, see Veith, *Hysteria.* See esp. chap. 5 for 16th- and 17th-c. beliefs and for the use and meaning of the term "suffocation of the mother."

27. C. Mather, "Another Brand Pluckt Out of the Burning," 313.

28. Veith, *Hysteria,* chap. 4.

29. Cited in George Rosen, "Enthusiasm, 'a dark lanthorn of the spirit,' " *Bulletin of the History of Medicine* 42 (September–October 1968): 394. See also Veith, *Hysteria,* chaps. 6–7.

30. C. Mather, "Another Brand Pluckt Out of the Burning," 312.

31. Ibid.

32. C. Mather, "A Brand Plucked Out of the Burning," 266.

33. Psychopathological interpretations have dominated 20th-c. historians' thinking on New England possession. The most persuasive arguments of this nature are found in Demos, *Entertaining Satan,* 97–131, 209; and Hansen, *Witchcraft at Salem,* esp. chaps. 2–4.

34. See, for example, discussions of either spirit or demonic possession in Crapanzano and Garrison, *Case Studies in Spirit Possession,* esp. Crapanzano's "Introduction," 1–20, and Gananath Obeyesekere, "Psychocultural Exegesis of a Case of Spirit Possession in Sri Lanka," 235–94; George Rosen, *Madness in Society;* "Mental Disorder, Social Deviance and Culture Pattern: Some Methodological Issues

in the Historical Study of Mental Illness," in Mora and Brand, *Psychiatry and Its History*, 172–94; I. M. Lewis, *Ecstatic Religion*, 178–205. Perhaps the strongest evidence against a mental illness explanation of possession is the existence of cultures in which a substantial minority if not a majority of women (and in some cases men) experience possession at some point in their lives. See, for example, Ivan Karp, "Power and Capacity in Rituals of Possession" (paper presented at the Ethnohistory Workshop, University of Pennsylvania, 16 October 1986, forthcoming in *The Creativity of Power*, ed. Ivan Karp and W. Arens, Smithsonian Institution Press, Washington, D.C.); Bourguignon, *Possession*, 15–41. Crapanzano ("Introduction," 1–7) offers a perceptive interpretation of observers' fascination with possession, parts of which may be applicable to New England's clergy.

35. The following discussion of the conflicts manifested in possession is shaped by anthropological arguments that these conflicts are generated less by the trauma of infancy and early childhood experiences within a familial context than by childhood and adulthood traumas caused by the society itself. According to this view, rather than a sign of "mental breakdown," possession can be seen as an attempt to maintain mental stability in a context of immediate—and extreme—cultural pressure. Individual histories play a role, but mainly to illuminate the particular stresses (past and present) that lead one woman rather than another to respond to those pressures through possession. See Crapanzano and Garrison, *Case Studies in Spirit Possession*, passim. For colonial New England, those stresses (especially those of childhood) are for the most part impossible to locate, but some of them are suggested by the presence of so many of the possessed in households of ministers (or of unusually godly parents) and by the violent deaths of so many of their parents and siblings.

36. C. Mather, "A Brand Plucked Out of the Burning," 259–87; C. Mather, "Another Brand Pluckt Out of the Burning," 308–23.

37. Willard, "A Brief Account," 359–60.

38. Ibid., 360–66.

39. Ibid., 366–67.

40. Ibid., 367.

41. Ibid., 367–69.

42. Ibid., 369–70.

43. Ibid., 370–71.

44. Ibid., 371.

45. Knapp's marriage in 1674 is mentioned in Lucius R. Paige, *History of Cambridge, Massachusetts, 1630–1877* (Boston, 1877) 652, and the births of her children in *The Early Records of Groton, Massachusetts, 1662–1707*, ed. Samuel A. Green (Groton, Mass., 1880), 43. See also Demos, *Entertaining Satan*, 114.

46. See, for example, Lawson, "A Brief and True Narrative," 161; C. Mather, *Wonders of the Invisible World*, 125–26.

47. *Witchcraft Papers* 1:168–69.

48. C. Mather, "A Brand Plucked Out of the Burning," 268–71.

49. Hale, *Modest Enquiry*, 132–33.

50. Whiting, "Letter," 467.

51. C. Mather, "Remarkable Providences," 109.

52. See, for example, C. Mather, "A Brand Plucked Out of the Burning," 272; Lawson, "A Brief and True Narrative," 162; C. Mather, "Memorable Providences," 109–10.

53. This view of possession rituals, as Vincent Crapanzano has pointed out, is difficult for those of us in present-day Western societies to understand, because our sensibilities have been shaped by psychoanalytic interpretations. In the Freudian tradition, the accusations lodged by the possessed are projections of internally unacceptable feelings, desires, etc. In the Puritan tradition, the unacceptable feelings, desires, etc. were seen as external; that is, as originating outside the possessed, with the Devil. See Crapanzano and Garrison, *Case Studies in Spirit Possession*, 11–13.

54. *Witchcraft Papers* 1:211–12.

55. Ibid. 2:683–84; 3:793–804.

56. For Tituba, see ibid. 3:757.

57. Ibid. 2:610–11.

58. C. Mather, "Memorable Providences," 99–107.

59. John Proctor and George Jacobs were not the only colonists to begin to see the possessed as witches. As mentioned in the text, at least nine females, some of whom had been possessed decades before, found themselves among the accused at Salem in 1692.

60. See above, 35–42, 213–14.

61. Records of these men's accusations and / or trials are in *Witchcraft Papers* 1:51–55, 151–78, 183; 2:345, 564–66; 3:871–72, 938.

62. Ibid. 1:52–53, 153, 162–64, 166–69, 174; 2:474–86.

63. Willard, "A Brief Account," passim.

64. See esp. C. Mather, "Memorable Providences," 112–14, 119–21.

65. Ibid., 119–20; C. Mather, "A Brand Plucked Out of the Burning," 267–72; Lawson, "A Brief and True Narrative," 154.

66. My understanding of the way possession reinforced New England's social structure is deeply indebted to discussions of status reversal rituals in Turner, *The Ritual Process*, chap. 5, and Davis, "Women on Top," 124–51.

67. See above, 40–43, and below, 253–54.

68. See below, 254–56.

69. Crapanzano and Garrison, *Case Studies in Spirit Possession*, 7–20; Lewis, *Ecstatic Religion*, esp. 100–26; Bourguignon, "Culture and the Varieties of Consciousness," 3–6, 13–18. The quotation is from Crapanzano and Garrison, *Case Studies in Spirit Possession*, 9. My thinking on these issues has also been greatly influenced by Carroll Smith-Rosenberg, "The Hysterical Woman," 652–79; Hollander, "Conversion Hysteria," 311–14.

70. See, for instance, C. Mather, "Another Brand Pluckt Out of the Burning," 316–17.

71. See Bourguignon, "Culture and the Varieties of Consciousness," 11–13, for a discussion of the relationship between possession and hierarchical social structures. Possessed individuals in other cultures tend to be either women, or men who share with women inferior, marginal, or ambiguous social positions in their societies. See Lewis, *Ecstatic Religion*, 100–7; Crapanzano and Garrison, *Case Studies in Spirit Possession*, xi–xii.

EPILOGUE

1. See Demos, *Entertaining Satan*, 387–400.

2. See, for example, Starkey, *The Devil in Massachusetts*, esp. 137–61.

3. E. William Monter, "The Historiography of European Witchcraft: Progress and Prospects," *Journal of Interdisciplinary History* 2 (1972), 440–43; Thomas, *Religion and the Decline of Magic*, 518–83; Demos, *Entertaining Satan*, 392–94; Hansen, *Witchcraft at Salem*, 284.

4. E. William Monter, "French and Italian Witchcraft," *History Today* 30 (November 1980): 34–35; *Witchcraft in France and Switzerland*, 59–60, 138–41; Thomas, *Religion and the Decline of Magic*, 480–92. Mon-

ter notes that the possessed in France were usually young and/or
female, while Thomas argues that in England no gender or age patterns are discernible.

5. This is not to argue that Puritanism caused witchcraft, only
that witchcraft did not take on much significance in colonies where
Puritans were not in control. Traditional witchcraft beliefs existed
and occasional accusations were lodged in all of the colonies, but the
authorities in other places paid the accusations little heed and there
were few witchcraft trials and almost no executions.

6. Boyer and Nissenbaum, *Salem Possessed*, 23–30.

7. See Patricia Tracy, *Jonathan Edwards, Pastor: Religion and Society
in Eighteenth-Century Northampton* (New York, 1979), 86–108.
Northampton, Massachusetts, was settled at the end of the 17th c.;
in the 1730s, it was experiencing many of the land tensions that Salem
and other eastern Massachusetts towns had faced much earlier.

8. See Dayton, "Women Before the Bar," 158–86.

9. For the treatment of men in other communities, see Flaherty,
"Law and the Enforcement of Morals," 101–3.

10. Malmsheimer, "Daughters of Zion," 497–504.

11. Ulrich, *Good Wives*, 103–5; Cott, "Passionlessness," 162–181.
See also Demos, *Entertaining Satan*, 389–92.

12. This analysis owes much to Ulrich's discussion of the role of
the witch figure in Samuel Richardson's *Pamela*, the English novel
which achieved considerable popularity in the colonies in the mid-
18th c. See *Good Wives*, 104–5.

13. See Cott, *Bonds of Womanhood*, for a thorough discussion of
the tenets of domesticity.

14. *Black Women in White America: A Documentary History*, ed. Gerda
Lerner (New York, 1973), 149–215; Deborah Gray White, *Ar'n't I a
Woman?: Female Slaves in the Plantation South* (New York, 1985), 27–
61; Charles E. Rosenberg, "Sexuality, Class and Role in 19th-Cen-
tury America," *American Quarterly* 25 (May 1973), 131–53; Kathy Peiss,
*Cheap Amusements: Working Women and Leisure in Turn-of-the-Century
New York* (Philadelphia, 1986). In the South, black women had taken
on the image of evil as early as the beginning of the 18th c. See
Winthrop Jordan, "Fruits of Passion: The Dynamics of Interracial
Sex," in *Our American Sisters*, ed. Jean E. Friedman and William G.
Shade, 3d ed. (Lexington, Mass., 1982), 154–69.

Index

abortion, sin of, 141
accidents, witchcraft blamed for,
 6
accusations, of witchcraft:
  ages of women, 64–71, 76,
   289n–93n
  burdens of, 61–63, 132–33,
   309n–10n
  causes of, 46, 131–34, 138,
   197–98, 213–14, 217–18,
   222–23
  and deaths of male family
   members, 104–8
  and economic status, 77, 78–
   79, 297n–98n
  end of, 44–45, 221, 253–57
  evidence for, 131–34, 151–52
  and families without male heirs,
   102–5, 108, 115–16, 305n–
   6n
  informal, 14–15, 272n
  and lying, 148–49, 151
  and marital status of women,
   71–76
  more than one time, 276n
  number of, 267n, 280n–81n
  and possession, *see* possession
  and Quakers, 122–25, 197
  relationship between accuser
   and accused, 182–85, 225
  in Salem outbreak, 39, 40, 115,
   245–46, 253–54, 278n
  source of, 184
  and stereotype of New England
   witch, 118–19
  testimony and depositions of
   accusers, 130–34, 138, 183
  vulnerability to, 46–47, 115–
   16, 117–19, 144–47
accusers, 183–84, 222–24
  effect of accusation on, 133–
   34
  non-possessed, 222, 223, 224–
   25
  possessed, 222–26
  relationship with accused, 182–
   83, 225
  see also possession

ABOUT THE AUTHOR

Carol F. Karlsen is professor of history at the University of Michigan.